ARCHERY

Sixth Edition

About the Authors

Dr. Wayne C. McKinney is a retired Professor of Biomedical Sciences interested in the role of exercise as one form of preventive medicine to delay or offset hypokinetic diseases in humans. His longitudinal research is related to the effect of varying levels of energy expenditure during supplemental aerobic exercise on cardiovascular fitness and cardiac risk. His Ph.D. was earned at the University of Southern California. Archery started as a lifetime interest while he was an undergraduate student at California State University at Long Beach. He also participated in intercollegiate baseball and football as an undergraduate. Archery continues to be a strong athletic and academic interest along with the aerobic activity of long distance running. Dr. McKinney has logged over 38,000 training miles plus numerous marathons from Boston to Pike's Peak. He has authored or coauthored articles in scholarly journals as well as the following books published by WCB: *Biophysical Values of Muscular Activity* (Second Edition), *Kinesiology, Anatomic Kinesiology, Introduction to Biomechanic Analysis of Sport,* and *Analysis of Sport Motion: Anatomic and Biomechanic Perspectives.*

Mike W. McKinney is a professional physical educator who has had a strong interest in target archery and bow hunting for most of his life. His undergraduate degree was received at Southwest Missouri State University and his master of science degree was earned at the University of Arizona. He competed in target archery and intercollegiate wrestling as an undergraduate student. He has bow hunted extensively throughout the southwestern portion of the U.S.A. and in Missouri. Elk and javalina are two of his favorite game animals.

JUL. 2 0 1992

ARCHERY
Sixth Edition

Wayne C. McKinney
Professor, Southwest Missouri State

Mike W. McKinney
Professor, University of Arizona

 Wm. C. Brown Publishers

Book Team

Editor *Chris Rogers*
Developmental Editor *Cindy Kuhrasch*
Production Coordinator *Carla D. Arnold*

 Wm. C. Brown Publishers

President *G. Franklin Lewis*
Vice President, Editor-in-Chief *George Wm. Bergquist*
Vice President, Director of Production *Beverly Kolz*
Vice President, National Sales Manager *Bob McLaughlin*
Director of Marketing *Thomas E. Doran*
Marketing Communications Manager *Edward Bartell*
Marketing Manager *Kathy Law Laube*
Production Editorial Manager *Colleen A. Yonda*
Production Editorial Manager *Julie A. Kennedy*
Publishing Services Manager *Karen J. Slaght*
Manager of Visuals and Design *Faye M. Schilling*

Consulting Editor
Physical Education
Aileene Lockhart
Texas Women's University

Sports and Fitness Series
Evaluation Materials Editor
Jane A. Mott
Texas Women's University

Cover image © Garry Gay/The Image Bank

Cover design by Jeanne Regan

Library of Congress Catalog Card Number: 88–63885

ISBN 0–697–10413–3

Printed in the United States of America by Wm. C. Brown Publishers,
2460 Kerper Boulevard, Dubuque, IA 52001

10 9 8 7 6 5 4 3 2 1

Contents

Preface

The major purpose of this book is to provide the reader with a substantive introduction to the multifaceted sport of archery. It is an intriguing and challenging sport, and the many ways in which archery can be enjoyed as an avocational activity throughout a lifetime are presented.

The major emphasis within this book is placed on introducing the reader to target archery. Target archery is the most demanding of all the competitive forms of archery in terms of accuracy and precision shooting. It is highly recommended that a person with a strong interest in areas such as bow hunting or field archery should first acquire considerable knowledge and skill in target archery fundamentals. Those skills will serve the archer as his or her "foundation for success." This is true for target archery and almost any other area of archery one might wish to pursue.

The reader is also introduced to field archery, bow hunting, bow fishing, crossbows, flight shooting, and clout shooting. Opportunities for participation in archery by handicapped individuals are also presented. Archery in its many forms can be a participant sport for anyone motivated to take on the challenge. First, however, the individual must know that the sport and participation opportunities exist. Therein lies another purpose of the book-in-hand. All of the activities provided through participation in archery sports can be used to enhance the quality of the individual's leisure time. *The majority of people who take target archery instruction eventually try one or more of the archery sports.* The National Field Archery Association reports that seven million people in the United States own archery tackle, and there are over two million bow hunters and bow fishers.

A unique feature of this book is the comprehensive and specific physical conditioning program for archers. Anatomic detail is presented to explain the forces and motions needed to properly execute the shooting fundamentals. That is followed by scientifically based fitness guidelines which establish the intensity, frequency, and duration criteria for developing strength, muscular endurance, and cardiovascular endurance. Energy expenditure values for various conditioning activities and archery practice are also described. The serious archer is also shown exercises that apply the scientifically based theory to the practice of conditioning for archery. The emphasis is placed on the specificity of conditioning for archery to enhance skill execution for better scores in target archery, more game while bow hunting or bow fishing, or greater distances while flight shooting. The better conditioned archer has the best chance for success.

Archery as an academic subject correlates nicely with the classic humanities, physics, biomechanics, anatomic kinesiology, and exercise physiology. Archery is an integral part of the literature, art, philosophy, religions, and history of the human race. The reader is introduced to those academic dimensions of archery plus some of the scientific aspects of the sport. The participant who chooses to become intellectually aware of the academic side of archery will greatly enrich his or her use of leisure time.

For readers interested in bow hunting and bow fishing, Appendix A contains the names, addresses, and phone numbers of virtually all the official wildlife agencies in the United States and Canada. This provides a ready reference for all of the latest rules and regulations related to bow hunting and bow fishing anywhere in these two countries.

Appendix B provides the reader with the names and addresses of archery organizations throughout the world. These are the controlling organizations for such things as target archery, field archery, bow hunting, crossbows, and others. This gives the reader easy access to learning more about the programs and opportunities offered by the organization(s) in the aspect of archery where interest is stimulated.

Special acknowledgment is made to Doug Kittredge of Auburn, California. Our informal discussions about archery several years ago at The University of Southern California led indirectly to the writing of the first edition of this book. Appreciation is also extended to Dr. Aileene Lockhart for providing the opportunity to write the book.

Many illustrations in this text are from *Anatomic Kinesiology,* Third Edition, by Gene A. Logan and Wayne C. McKinney. © 1970, 1977, 1982 Wm. C. Brown Company Publishers, Dubuque, Iowa and from *Adapted Physical Education* by Gene A. Logan. © 1972 Wm. C. Brown Company Publishers, Dubuque, Iowa. Reprinted by permission.

Special acknowledgment is made to E. G. Heath of England for granting permission to reproduce several illustrations from *The Gray Goose Wing,* his classic book on the subject of archery published by Osprey Publishing Limited in Berkshire, England.

The assistance of the following people for their contributions to the earlier editions of this book is appreciated: Doug Allen, Allen Archery; the late H. W. Allen out of Billings, Missouri, who had the creative genius to invent the compound bow in 1966; Ken Beck, Black Widow Bow Company, Dave Brilhart, expert bow hunter, Wilbur Corley, expert bow fisherman; J. Robert Davis, expert bow fisherman, Jerry Day, Arizona Game and Fish Department; Jack Frazier, expert bow hunter; G. C. "Butch" Herold, Executive Secretary, NFAA; Loyd Howell, Indian artifact hunter; Dr. L. Dennis Humphrey for taking numerous photographs; Diane Logan for her art work; Arlyne Rhode, *The U.S. Archer;* Larry Rogge, expert bow hunter; Pete Shepley, Precision Shooting Equipment; and Jack, Bob, and the late Norman Wilson, the expert bowyers who made the quality Black Widow Bow for many years. Finally, Kickapoo and Gene A. Logan's expertise as game hunters is admired and appreciated.

The valuable assistance of the following people for their contributions to the sixth edition is appreciated: William Bartlett, PSE; Wilbur Corley, Corley's Bowfishin' Stuff; J. Robert Davis, expert bowfisher; Debbie Finch, Accra 300; "Butch" Herold, NFAA; Mac Johnson, *Missouri Conservationist*; Gerry Koehlke, PSE; Christine P. McCartney, NAA; Arlyne Rhode, *The U.S. Archer;* Bob Rhode, Hoyt/Easton; Pete Shepley, PSE; Paul T. Shore, *Bowfishing Magazine;* and Ron Skirvin, Shure Shot.

Special acknowledgment is made to Shirley A. Randall for her expertise in preparing the manuscript. Finally, recognition and thanks are given to Jenni and Iva McKinney for their understanding of the authors during the writing process plus their help with the manuscript.

The content and objectives of the book are the sole responsibilities of the authors.

Wayne C. McKinney, Ph.D.
Mike W. McKinney, M.S.

Introduction to Archery

1

From the beginning of recorded history archery has been and is an activity with diversified objectives for human beings. The successful use of archery skills by primitive people literally meant survival for them by providing food. Skilled archers through the ages were able to win battles, and that changed the course of history for many nations. In contemporary society, target archery is considered a challenging sport for the competitor who places value on the pursuit of excellence. It is a challenging sport even for the person who perceives himself or herself to be a perfectionist. Archery is also for the individual who enjoys the physical and intellectual challenges of using perfectly matched and tuned archery tackle effectively on a target range or during a bowhunt; it is for the man or woman who enjoys being in the out-of-doors during a bow hunting season, a field archery tournament, or bow fishing for sharks or gar; it is for the person who enjoys the spirit of competition with other people and shooting effectively in unusual weather conditions in target archery tournaments as well as bow hunting and fishing situations. Archery can be enjoyed within a wide spectrum of physical and intellectual pursuits. As a result, it has the potential to help make the participant's leisure more rewarding and meaningful throughout a lifetime.

The current popularity of archery is well documented. It is used as a sport in its various forms by millions of people throughout the world. Beginning in 1972 target archery was officially included as a sport in the Olympic Games. This added considerable impetus for the sport in all competing nations. As one example, a recent Nielsen Survey indicated that 2,634,000 Americans participate in archery. American target archers have had considerable success in international competitions (fig. 1.1).

The major emphasis within this book is placed on introducing the reader to target archery. Target archery is the most demanding of all forms of archery in terms of accuracy and precision shooting. It is highly recommended, therefore, that a person with a strong interest in such archery sports as field archery, bow hunting, and/or bow fishing should first acquire considerable knowledge and skill in target archery fundamentals. Target archery competition can be enjoyed, plus those skills will serve as the "foundation of success" in virtually any other archery

Figure 1.1
Mastery of target archery fundamentals serves as "The Foundation of Success" for target archery and almost any other archery sport you wish to pursue. The shooting line and spectator's stadium at the 1984 Olympic Games. Photo by *The U.S. Archer.*

sport one wishes to pursue. As can be seen in figure 1.2, the challenges in other archery sports also take on huge and exciting dimensions! When bow fishing, how do you shoot and safely land a shark that outweighs you? You will be introduced to several archery sports in Chapters 5, 6, and 7. These sports appeal to both sexes, and competition categories are established for men and women. Archery is an equal opportunity sport!

Bow hunting, especially for deer, is increasing in popularity each year in North America. Many gun hunters are: (1) expanding their hunting seasons by using both the gun and bow seasons for game, (2) switching to bow hunting due to the fact that the hunter is less likely to be shot by a fellow hunter during the hunting season, or (3) changing to bow hunting because it is a purer form of hunting wild game than gun hunting. There are approximately 2,100,400 bow hunters in North America. This growing sport will be discussed in Chapter 6.

Most individuals become involved in archery initially due to an interest either in target archery, bow hunting, field archery, or bow fishing. Once involved in the sport, many people learn that archery is a subject with a rich heritage in history, literature, art, religion, and philosophy. In this book an attempt is made to introduce the reader to some of these areas of interest. The serious student of the humanities can derive intellectual satisfaction by studying about archery as portrayed by authors throughout history. Mythological literature, as one example, abounds with tales about archers and the utilization of archery skills. Art

Figure 1.2
Knowledge of target archery shooting fundamentals also allows the archer to pursue such specialized areas as bow fishing. "Suzie" J. Davis with a 6'11¼", 165-pound, brown shark she landed while bow fishing. (Courtesy J. Robert Davis, RFD. 4, Box 380, Spearin Road, Salisbury, Maryland 21801)

museums throughout the world contain many famous works of art depicting archers in action. The scholarly student of archery may want to pursue the sport beyond the demanding challenge of shooting. The study of this sport from a liberal arts perspective should not be overlooked.

There are numerous scientific dimensions to archery. The physics of the sport has been the subject of academic and intellectual pursuits by professionals and amateurs alike for years. (See the Bibliography.) The changes seen in archery tackle over the past quarter of a century attest to the positive results of these pursuits. Bow designs and arrows are better. Ballistics and trajectories are improving, and this leads to excellent accuracy.

The sciences that study the archer himself or herself are fascinating. The study of anatomic form and function of archery techniques has kept pace with the tackle changes, so archers are improving. Physiologically, the archer is an athlete who needs to condition in order to meet the demands of his or her specialty. Intellectually, the anatomic kinesiology, biomechanics, and exercise physiology related to archery are interesting areas for study. The reader is introduced to some aspects of these academic areas throughout this book. Archery can be a rewarding lifetime activity from combined intellectual-neuromuscular perspectives. A person who pursues the sport in that context has long been known as a *toxopholite* (fig. 1.3).

Figure 1.3
"The Toxophilites." A pen and ink sketch by W. Murray, 1840. (From E. G. Heath, *The Grey Goose Wing*)

Benefits of Archery

Each sport has the potential to provide unique benefits to its participants. The benefits derived from a diverse sport such as archery will not be the same for all participants. The outcomes are dependent upon such factors as the facet of the sport pursued, intensity of participation, and other individual factors or interests.

Those not cognizant of its many uses and physical demands usually think of archery as an "easy sport." (The anatomic and physiologic demands on archers, and related conditioning, are discussed in detail in Chapter 8.) An hour of target archery practice in one's backyard or on the local archery range is not as physiologically demanding as comparable time spent playing singles tennis or running. As an example, an hour of anaerobic target archery practice would expend 269 kilocalories of energy for a 152-pound archer. Running an hour at a 9-minute-per-mile pace for the same archer is an aerobically intense activity that would produce an energy expenditure of 799 kilocalories, i.e., 530 more kilocalories than target archery practice. In contrast, however, the same archer bow hunting for elk or deer in the high mountains of Arizona, Colorado, or California undergoes comparable aerobic workloads and cardiorespiratory demands as observed for running over relatively flat surfaces. The reason lies in the fact that the stalking of large game animals can be sustained for relatively long periods of time in high altitude over rough terrain. Our 152-pound archer may spend five hours during a day, as an example, stalking elk through the Rocky Mountains at altitudes between 7,000 and 10,000 feet. This would be an aerobic energy expenditure in the range of 2000 to 2500 kilocalories! The archer must be prepared for demands of that intensity on the organism. Details on how to do this are presented for you in Chapter 8.

The serious target archer, in addition to target practice, must prepare for competition by specifically developing strength, muscle endurance, and flexibility to excellent levels. That has the potential to enhance accuracy. It is also recommended (see Chapter 8) that the target archer's conditioning include work to develop cardiovascular endurance to at least an average level for his or her age. The serious bow hunter should also add cardiovascular endurance work to the daily conditioning pattern to prepare for the type of physiologic situation described above. If that is done, the archer's daily shooting and conditioning workouts will be just as demanding as comparable time spent in other sports which many people perceive to be more difficult physiologically. The serious, conditioned bow hunter benefits by being totally fit. This enhances his or her chances of taking game and packing it out of the wilderness area for human consumption. The sport can be as easy or difficult as the participant desires.

One major benefit of archery is that the participant can find an area within the sport and adjust it to meet his or her own interests, needs, and physical conditioning. In its many forms, archery can be engaged in by old and young, men and women, the physically handicapped, and superbly conditioned athletes. The versatility of its use as described in this book has the potential to provide numerous benefits for archers with diversified interests. Therein lies one reason why archery has fascinated humans in virtually all cultures throughout history. The one "common bond" that links the sport to all of its forms is a basic understanding of *target archery.* That is the foundation, and it is the reason target archery receives the major emphasis in this introductory book to the sport.

The practice of archery on a regular basis has the potential to counteract or offset a specific problem exhibited by people who work in offices at desks. These people have a natural tendency to protract their shoulders—the shoulder blades or scapulae are pulled away from the spine and held in that position for prolonged periods of time. This abnormally lengthens muscles in the back and shortens muscles in the chest and shoulders. Holding the protracted position of the shoulders for long periods causes physical discomfort. Normal breathing is inhibited, and this has a negative impact on respiratory function. This posture adds to the tired feeling one may have at the end of the day after sitting in an office for eight hours, because energy metabolism is adversely effected.

Shooting a bow for a period of time daily helps counteract the atypical muscular actions caused by prolonged sitting. To draw a bow, the archer must contract back muscles which have been lengthened throughout the day. These muscles are attached to the scapulae or shoulder blades. During the bow drawing process against the resistance of the bow weight, the scapulae are being adducted or moved toward the spinal column. The muscles lengthened during the day are shortened or contracted in this process, while the chest and shoulder muscles shortened while sitting are lengthened during the bow drawing exercise. The greatest benefit of this for the desk worker is to offset the adaptive shortening of the chest and shoulder muscles. That enhances the breathing and respiratory processes. Energy metabolism becomes more efficient, and the person feels better.

Figure 1.4
Archery sports have been family activities for years for Robie Davis, his wife, "Suzie" Davis, and J. Robert Davis. (Courtesy J. Robert Davis, Route 4, Box 380, Spearin Road, Salisbury, Maryland 21801)

There is a myth that the practice of target archery contributes to the development of good posture. There is no scientific evidence to support that type of hypothesis. What it does do for the adult is offset potential static or hypokinetic problems such as the one described above. Archery practice could have some positive effects on proper alignment of the spine, shoulder joints, and shoulder girdles of young children who have not reached anatomic maturation. Target archery practice with the proper workload (bow weight) for a child with musculoskeletal problems in these body segments could be utilized as an interesting rehabilitative exercise. It most certainly has intrinsic motivating qualities not seen in other rehabilitative modalities.

One major criticism of our society made by sociologists and psychologists is the decline of family unity. To paraphrase a familiar theological statement: The family that plays together stays together. With the onset of a wide variety of avocational activities for children as well as *adult-centered activities for children* (examples are Little League Baseball and Pop Warner Football), the family in modern America often finds itself literally and figuratively going in different directions during leisure time. Archery is one sport that can be enjoyed by all members of the family at one time at home, on a field archery range, bow hunting, bow fishing, or on a target archery range. There are psychologic and sociologic benefits inherent within an activity such as archery, which has the potential to develop family unity (fig. 1.4).

Many sport activities learned early in life cannot be used throughout a lifetime. Age is not a limiting factor in any area of archery. It can be enjoyed at any age. Target archery competition, as one example, is found for both sexes in high schools, universities, the Olympic Games, and the Senior Olympics. The latter Games include people from 40 to beyond one hundred years of age. If you played basketball at the age of seventeen and enjoyed the game, there is a strong possibility that you will not continue to utilize your skills on a regular basis in the sport for the next sixty years! One does not see many "middle-aged" people getting together in groups of ten or more to compete on a basketball court on a regular basis. In contrast to that team sport scenario, archery in all of its forms can be enjoyed on a daily basis throughout a lifetime. Furthermore, you do not have to assemble a group of people to practice archery on a daily basis. That is a real plus factor that contributes to the continuity and regularity of practice.

One major biophysical value of exercise when it is used at the proper intensity, frequency, and duration is its contribution in helping the individual cope with distress. Uncontrolled distress over a *prolonged* period of time has been identified as one of the major risk factors contributing to the onset of coronary heart disease. Emotional tension of this type tends to be cumulative in nature in humans, and this becomes devastating over a long period of time to the cardiovascular mechanisms. Using a "short-term stressor" such as exercise on a daily basis helps to counteract some of the negative biochemical, anatomic, and physiologic effects of long-term stress. Exercise at the proper intensity, frequency, and duration levels is one way to help cope with stress.

Psychiatrists and other physicians indicate that it is a good idea to "blow off steam" in a socially acceptable way when the individual finds himself or herself in a stress situation. That "short-term stressor" helps maintain homeostasis in terms of the cardiorespiratory system, and it aids one's mental health as well. Daily target practice plus associated conditioning on an archery range or field archery unit is a great way to expend energy and release emotional tension when you have had a "bad day" or are caught up in a prolonged distress situation at work or home.

Shooting the bow and arrow for an hour or more after a "bad day" has the potential to relax the archer. Indeed, exercise or physical work of any type with good intensity and duration performed on a regular basis will serve as a relaxant for the participant. *The concept of intense exercise or work being a relaxant is so abstract that it is not too well understood by most people.* Exercise is a much better relaxant than the drugs used by many individuals ostensibly for that purpose, i.e., vigorous exercise will work to relax the participant while alcohol, tranquilizers, and other drugs are contraindicated and counterproductive. From the standpoint of health-related fitness, an hour of target archery practice works better as a relaxant for the archer than drinking a six pack of beer!

The difficulty of archery is cited by many as being a part of its mystique and value for the participants. Mastery or the attempt to master archery skill is a major motivating factor for many archers. Archery is not an easy skill in which to achieve excellence, since there are many opportunities for the occurrence of human error. This facet of the sport has the greatest appeal to many individuals who seek perfection in whatever they attempt. Shooting "tight groups" of arrows in the center ring during a FITA Round at distances of ninety meters (98.46 yards) or seventy meters (76.58 yards) is extremely challenging and difficult to do consistently even in perfect weather conditions for target archery. Therein lies a portion of the challenge of archery.

The individual who enjoys social activities will find that archery is a good medium for this purpose. Most cities of any size have archery clubs which provide opportunities for the archer to share interests with fellow archers. Clubs are locally operated by a system of self-government, and funded by modest dues. Rounds are shot periodically for practice. There are intraclub and interclub tournaments. Members also compete in large professional and amateur tournaments conducted within the state, region, and nationally. Clubs in communities are usually organized to accommodate target archers, bow hunters, bow fishers, and field archers. Also, most community-based archery clubs are family oriented. As a result, competitions are scheduled on a regular basis for both sexes and various age groupings.

Archery clubs are also found in many secondary schools, junior colleges, and universities. Intramural athletic competitions are held on a yearly basis. Archery as a varsity intercollegiate sport is alive and well throughout the United States. Competitions are held from league to national levels.

In contrast to club involvement and utilization of archery as a social activity, an archer can practice and compete without contact with other people if he or she so desires. No partner or team is necessary to enjoy archery in any of its forms. It has been said that the greatest form of competition is with one's self. Archery sports allow the archer to compete as an individual even in highly structured competitive tournaments. Individuality is a trait valued by many archers, and archery can be individualized as much or as little as the participant desires.

Appendix A contains the names, addresses, and phone numbers of all the official wildlife agencies in the United States and Canada. These are for the readers who are interested in bow hunting and bow fishing. Current rules, regulations, and information regarding seasons and limits can be obtained by contacting the agency of your choice.

Appendix B lists the names and addresses of archery organizations throughout the world. These are the controlling organizations for target archery, field archery, bow hunting, bow fishing, flight shooting, clout shooting, crossbows, archery for senior citizens, and archery for the handicapped. The reader is encouraged to contact the organization(s) of interest to see what is offered in terms of programs, services, and competitions for the archer.

Review Questions

1. Discuss what you consider to be the unique aspects and benefits of archery as a sport.
2. Find out whether there is an organized target archery club in your community. Visit one of the meetings.
3. Name the ways in which people participate in archery.
4. What are the areas of liberal arts related to archery?
5. What are the scientific dimensions to be found in the study of archery?
6. What archery sport serves as "the foundation" for participation in all other forms of archery?
7. Discuss what seems to be a paradox that intense exercise is a relaxant for the human organism.
8. Archery has influenced the course of human history. Can this be said of other sports—which and why?
9. Why is it recommended for a person who is interested in fishing or hunting with archery tackle to first become skillful at target archery?
10. Are there other sport activities that challenge the intellectual aspects of the participant as much as does archery? If so, give examples.

The Evolution of Archery

2

The history of archery and its significance to mankind, if known completely, would fill an encyclopedia. A few selected historical events are outlined in this chapter to help place archery's history in some perspective for the reader. The bibliography included in this book contains some excellent references on the history of archery.

Archery skill was of vital importance for the survival of mankind for thousands of years. In this respect, archery played a prominent role in the growth and development of individuals, societies, and nations. Archery appears as important as the development of the wheel, fire, and speech. Ancient man certainly learned how to use the bow and arrow effectively. If today's archer had to depend upon archery skill for personal protection and securing food, the skill level would be dramatically accelerated.

Primitive artists drew bow hunters in caves located in Spain and Southern France. Ancient sculptors carved archer warriors in Egypt to honor them for their feats. The bow is known to have been used by primitive tribes throughout the world as a musical instrument. Many theologians believed that David's biblical harp was his bow. The bow can be plucked much like the bass fiddle and the harp.

Archery feats have given rise to many myths throughout history. The mythology of Greece, as one example, includes archery feats by such famed characters as Apollo, Diana, Hercules, and Eros. The English had their Robin Hood, and ancient cultures in the Far East had their heroes who were analogous to Robin Hood.

Archery has been used as an integral aspect of religious ceremonies by numerous sects in the past. The Assyrians concluded a religious ritual by shooting an arrow toward the sun. It is interesting to note that this same type of ritual, the sun vow, was practiced by Indians on the southwest plains of America many centuries later.

The Zen Buddhists place great value on archery. The Zen sect does not recognize any dichotomy between the so-called "mind" and "body." Their philosophy includes the concept that various exercises of the body, including archery, can bring the practitioner into a state of one complete being. There are times when Buddhists hold the bow at full draw for many hours until they feel the union of "mind" and "soul." At that time, *Satori* is reached. The archer is no longer conscious of himself or the target, and the arrow is released. Figure 2.1 shows Eugen Herrigel, the author of *Zen in the Art of Archery,* who was one of the few non-Orientals accepted to study the Way of Archery within the Zen Buddhist philosophy. His book is considered to be a classic in this area. The reader should compare and contrast his stance and nonexistent anchor point with figure 4.18. The draw without an anchor is typical among Zen archers.

Man's ability to use the bow and arrow to advantage has changed the course of history on several occasions. Let us look at a few of these events chronologically.

Upper Paleolithic Period

It is virtually impossible to document historically that time in prehistory when man started using bows and arrows. From artifacts such as arrow points and tools believed to have been used in making tackle, it is generally agreed that man started using crude archery tackle at a time during the Upper Paleolithic period, or ten thousand to twenty thousand years ago.

Drawings in caves, believed to have been inhabited by Cro-Magnon man, depict archers hunting for wild game with fairly sophisticated bows and arrows. It is logical, therefore, to assume that archery tackle must have been in use many centuries prior to the time of Cro-Magnon man. The results of carbon testing techniques applied to stone artifacts tend to support this assumption. Figure 2.2 shows a Mesolithic hunting scene from a rock painting at Los Caballos, Valltorta, Spain. It is significant to note the various types of bows carried by the archers, and the fact that the archers are depicted as being very accurate.

Figure 2.1
A rare photograph of the late Eugen Herrigel, author of *Zen in the Art of Archery.* (From E. G. Heath, *The Grey Goose Wing*)

Figure 2.2
Mesolithic hunting scene from a rock painting at Los Caballos, Valltorta, Spain. (From E. G. Heath, *The Grey Goose Wing*)

No bows of any great age have been found, because wood deteriorates rapidly. The oldest extant bows date back to about 1000 B.C. These were found in the Nile River valley—a very dry climate. Some museums in America have bows made by Indians of the Southwest or arid region of the United States, but these date back no more than two to three hundred years.

Holocene Period

5000 B.C.

The Egyptians were able to free themselves from the Persians during this age. They became superior archers through diligent practice, and this proved to be their most important combat technique in battle. Spears, sling shots, and slings probably were the primary weapons of war prior to the refinement of the bow and arrow and archery skill by the Egyptians during this period in history.

1000 B.C.

The Persians moved to the area north and east of the Black and Caspian Seas to battle the Scythians. Each army had trained archers as foot soldiers, but the mounted archers of the Persians proved to be too much for the Scythians. This utilization of mounted archers added another dimension to the use of archery skills during time of war—a technique that was applied time and again by other military leaders for several centuries.

A.D. 850–950

There are records which indicate that during this hundred-year period, the Vikings helped design a new procedure for the use of the bow and arrow in time of war. It appears that prior to some amphibious assaults, their archers launched great clouts or volleys of arrows into their intended target area. This was an early form of naval bombardment. Naval bombardment of a different and more sophisticated type was used extensively in World War II, the Korean War, and to a limited extent in the Vietnam War.

A.D. 1066

The Norman archers taught the English a long-lasting lesson at the Battle of Hastings (fig. 2.3). The Normans planned and executed a false retreat maneuver designed to draw the English archers out of their hiding places to pursue what seemed to them to be fleeing Normans. When the English made their move into the open, they were attacked by the enemy and slaughtered. In this particular situation, the English were the superior archers and probably would have won the Battle of Hastings if the false retreat by the Normans had not been successful. This lesson was not wasted on the English, because they used the same kind of tactics on the French some three hundred years later at the Battle of Poitiers.

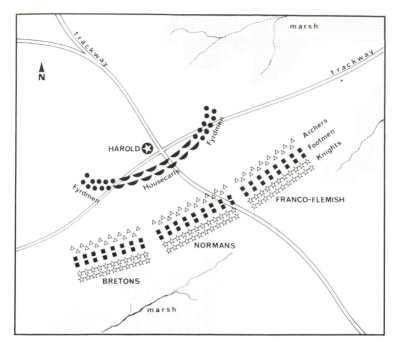

Figure 2.3
The Battle of Hastings showing the positions of the Saxon and Norman armies at 9:00 A.M. on the 14th of October, 1066. (From E. G. Heath, *The Grey Goose Wing*)

A famous work of art, the Bayeux Tapestry, was embroidered by the women friends and relatives of the English archers who fought at the Battle of Hastings (fig. 2.4). This tapestry is a band of linen 20 inches wide and 231 feet long. Various aspects of the Battle of Hastings are portrayed on the tapestry. One segment shows clearly that King Harold was hacked to death by Norman horseman instead of dying as a result of an arrow wound in the eye, as erroneously recorded by some historians. Figure 2.4 shows Norman archers carrying short bows and drawing them to their rib cage in order to obtain maximum range. The type of bow depicted is very inefficient from a physics standpoint, especially when compared to contemporary bows. Actually, the bows shown in the Bayeux Tapestry are believed to be closer to the Saxon pattern than to the longer Norman version. One explanation of this lies in the fact that the women who embroidered this tapestry were not bow experts.

A.D. 1220

Like the Persians, Genghis Khan, placed his soldiers/archers on horseback. This "Golden Horde" had great mobility as well as contempt for human life. These factors enabled Genghis Khan to capture territory from the Pacific Ocean to the Volga River, and from the Caspian Sea to Northern Siberia. The Japanese also used mounted samurai warriors effectively (fig. 2.5). In order to obtain some

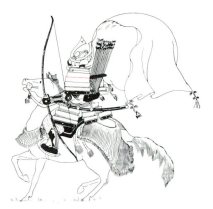

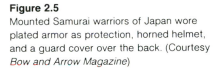

Figure 2.4
A portion of the Bayeux Tapestry. (From E. G. Heath, *The Grey Goose Wing*)

Figure 2.5
Mounted Samurai warriors of Japan wore plated armor as protection, horned helmet, and a guard cover over the back. (Courtesy *Bow and Arrow Magazine*)

insight into the accuracy problems encountered by the mounted archer, it is suggested that the reader try nocking, drawing, and shooting an arrow while mounted on a galloping horse.

A.D. 1252

It was during this period in English history that the long bow became the national weapon of England. This is a surprising fact, because recurve bow designs were well known to the English bowyers. Various types of recurve bows had been used for centuries and are portrayed in various works of art. As one example, there is a series of statues dated 490–80 B.C., from the Temple of Aigina, which depict archers using highly sophisticated recurve bows. Since this design is superior from a physics standpoint, why did the English choose the long bow as their national weapon? One possible explanation lies in the fact that the recurve bow must be made of a composite of materials glued together. England is a damp country, and the crude glue used at that time was not durable. Consequently, a composite bow might well fall apart when put to use by archers. This type of malfunction on the part of the bow would have been intolerable, in fact fatal in the midst of battle. In these circumstances the long bow, although not as efficient as the recurve bow, was more reliable for the English.

A.D. 1340–63

This period marked the start of the rise of English archery superiority. The Hundred Years' War with France was getting under way. The first of the large-scale encounters was the Battle of Crecy in A.D. 1346 (fig. 2.6). Edward III, King of England, had thirteen thousand archers at his disposal plus three thousand

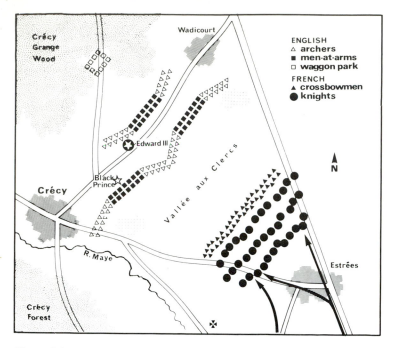

Figure 2.6
The Battle of Crécy, August 26, 1346. (From E. G. Heath, *The Grey Goose Wing*)

knights and men-at-arms who were deployed in three divisions. It is interesting to note that a teenager, the sixteen-year-old Prince of Wales (The Black Prince), was the commander of one of these divisions. The English used their archers in wedge formations. This tactic, together with their superior skill with the bow and arrow, enabled them to slaughter the majority of the French archers. The French force, numbering approximately forty thousand, was soundly beaten. To recognize the efforts of some of his knights in this battle, Edward III established the famous Most Noble Order of the Garter.

It was during this time period that Edward declared that archery had to be practiced by the people, and that all other sports would be illegal. This dictate by the king had a direct effect on the quality of archery skill for the entire population. It is interesting to note that this type of national legislative action would be analogous to President Franklin D. Roosevelt recommending legislation during World War II requiring every American to practice daily with the military rifle. Although the edict of Edward III had some positive ramifications for England, it is most likely that a democratic society would frown on that type of legislation.

The Battle of Poitiers took place in A.D. 1356 (fig. 2.7). The English warriors were now under the command of the Black Prince. In this battle, they were outnumbered more than two to one, but were able to conquer the French. They did this by drawing the French into the open, using false retreat tactics similar to that employed against them by the Normans three hundred years earlier. The

Figure 2.7
The Battle of Poitiers, 1356. (From E. G. Heath, *The Grey Goose Wing*)

Figure 2.8
An archer of 1400 A.D. from a design, originally produced for a rifle shooting trophy, by Benjamin Wyon the medalist. This is now the emblem for the Grand National Archery Society of England. (From E. G. Heath, *The Grey Goose Wing*)

French were literally killed by the thousands. The horses were special targets in this particular battle. When the horses were wounded, the riders were unable to control them, thus adding to the confusion and chaos.

The Grand National Archery Society of England has a rich historical heritage. Its emblem is based on an archer circa A.D. 1400 (fig. 2.8).

A.D. 1414

The Battle of Agincourt was the last great battle won by English archers. The English were outnumbered by the French four to one, but King Henry V was able to conquer the French chiefly because of superior archery ability on the part of the English. Shakespeare wrote of the casualties of this battle in his *King Henry V.* He indicated that twenty-nine English were slain as opposed to ten thousand French archers. The critical day of the battle of Agincourt is shown in figure 2.9.

A.D. 1453

This date marked the end of the Hundred Years' War. The fact that the English archers were superior to the French is historically significant both to those countries and to America as we know it. What if the French had won the Hundred Years' War? There probably would have been an entirely different series of events following the fifteenth century. The sixteenth century was marked by religious and social upheaval in England, which helped bring about the subsequent exploratory migrations to America by various English populations. It is doubtful

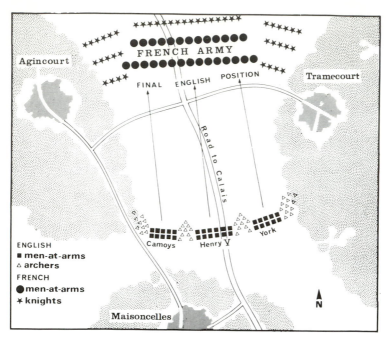

Figure 2.9
The Battle of Agincourt, October 25, 1415. Note how the space narrows between the two forests of Agincourt and Tramecourt, which hampered any forward action by the French. (From E. G. Heath, *The Grey Goose Wing*)

whether the same volume of migration from England would have materialized had the French won that war. America would undoubtedly, have been settled, but the political, social, and religious structures of this country might have been entirely different. The edict of Edward III requiring all Englishmen to practice archery did in fact shape history, especially American history!

A.D. 1455–71

The Wars of the Roses came about as a result of the rebellious feudal power displayed by some English lords who had acquired strength during the preceding century. Professional military archers returning from France were hired by these nobles for the purpose of solidifying their place in the political structure of the nation. Generally, the soldiers did a poor job simply because they lacked both the military leadership and the discipline they had previously known. The last battle during the Wars of the Roses was at Tewkesbury. The significance of archery as a weapon of war was still prominent, but firearms were beginning to be used, and were more of a factor, during this period.

Figure 2.10
Archery of Edward IV (1442–1483). The archers in military costume are using the yew longbow and carry twenty-four arrows. (From E. G. Heath, *The Grey Goose Wing*)

A.D. 1545

Roger Ascham published his book, *The Schole of Shootynge*. This was the first book ever written in the English language about archery tackle and techniques. This classic archery textbook was also published later under the title of *Toxophilus*.

A.D. 1588

The English and Spanish used firearms rather extensively at the invasion of the Spanish Armada. Most historians use this battle to illustrate the decline of archery as a weapon of war, but archers were nevertheless used on a smaller scale in battles for the next two hundred years.

A.D. 1917–73

The compound bow was invented in January 1966 by the late H. Wilbur Allen of Missouri. His main objective for inventing and subsequently manufacturing the compound bow was to make bow hunting more efficient. It is now a very popular bow for hunting purposes, because it is easier to handle at full draw, produces greater arrow velocity than composite bows, and as a result, has better penetration capacity than recurve or long bows. These are important factors for the hunter. It is now legal to use the compound bow for hunting in all fifty states.

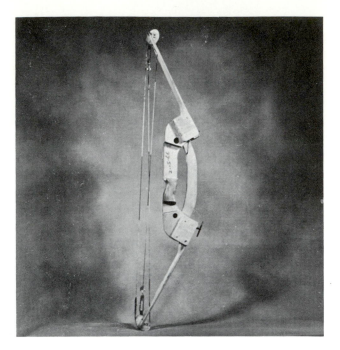

Figure 2.11
The original compound bow invented by H. Wilbur Allen is now in The National Museum of American History at The Smithsonian Institution. (Courtesy Mrs. Elizabeth Allen and the *Missouri Conservationist*)

It is interesting to note that the basic concepts of bow design have undergone more changes since 1966 than in the preceding 5000 years! This technologic breakthrough became possible primarily due to the efforts and ingenuity of H. W. Allen. In recognition of his contributions to archery, the original Allen Compound Bow (fig. 2.11) is now in The National Museum of American History at The Smithsonian Institution in Washington, D.C. In addition, his contribution to archery is recognized by the Wilbur Allen Memorial Wildlife Area located in the Missouri Ozark Mountains. Deer may be hunted with bow only in this wildlife area.

During World War I, World War II, the Korean War, and Vietnam War, bows and arrows were used on a very limited basis. This seems somewhat incongruous in the "atomic age," but it is true. Some military missions call for killing people very quietly. There are not too many ways to do this, especially from a distance. Expert archers have been trained in the military for sniper duties, reconnaissance work, and sabotage. Special arrows are made for demolition work and killing by hemorrhage. Marines train men for this type of activity in their reconnaissance companies, and the Army trains special ranger groups in many of the ancient arts of killing human beings silently. Archery is one of these potential techniques.

Although somewhat outdated in terms of more sophisticated killing techniques, it must be remembered that an arrow is a very effective killing instrument whether it be for a game animal or another human being. An arrow at short range has greater penetrating potential, for example, than a .45 caliber bullet shot from a pistol. Furthermore, a skilled military archer on a reconnaissance mission has a better chance of surviving that mission than a soldier who kills with a noisy pistol. This is one reason archery was used during this period.

It is hoped that archery will never again be utilized for killing human beings in war. During the last quarter of the twentieth century, archery is used extensively as a sport. This is the best single use for bows and arrows!

The Present Time

Archery has evolved to the point that it is a diversified and significant recreational activity for millions of people throughout the world. Target archery has been a part of the Olympic Games as an official gold medal sport since 1972, and that added tremendous impetus to the sport. As we will learn in the next chapters, people keep finding and refining the ways in which archery may be used avocationally.

Review Questions

1. No written documents tell us when archery was first developed but it is believed to have been between ten and twenty thousand years ago. What evidence supports this belief?
2. What explanation has been put forward as a possible reason for the adoption of the long bow by the English rather than the more efficient recurve bow?
3. For what military purposes has archery proved useful as recently as the war in Vietnam?
4. Describe some of the relationships between archery and religion in various cultures throughout history.
5. Why must documentation on bow designs be done through art primarily versus archaeological artifacts?
6. Discuss the ramifications of the political mandate by Edward III which required his subjects to practice archery.
7. Research the writings of William Shakespeare and analyze his portrayals of the use of archery.
8. Why do you suppose the Zen Buddhist archer's stance and anchor point differ from customary practice?
9. Discuss the relationship between skill and strategy as exemplified historically, for example, in the Battle of Hastings and the Battle of Crecy.
10. How is archery related to the Most Noble Order of the Garter, the cherished British honor?

Target Archery Tackle

3

In terms of precision shooting, target archery is the most demanding of all the competitive forms of archery. Furthermore, it serves as the skill foundation for virtually all of the other uses of archery. It is a serious oversight for an archer interested in bow hunting, as an example, not to attain first a good level of competency in target archery shooting skills. The first step in learning target archery is to acquire an understanding of the equipment. *"Tackle" is the term used by archers for their bows, arrows, and related shooting equipment.* There is an axiom in sport that a properly prepared athlete will be as good or poor as his or her equipment. The precision of target archery most certainly demands quality tackle for success.

The beginner should be provided with every opportunity to learn the sport efficiently. This requires that the first set of archery tackle must be matched properly. Matched tackle means that arrows, exactly alike in every detail, should be designed for use with a specific bow suitable for the individual archer. Each archer differs in regard to muscular strength, length of limbs, and aesthetic preferences. Therefore, great care must be taken to acquire archery tackle suitable for the unique anatomic attributes and other differences of each archer. The "matched tackle principle" is just as appropriate for the issuing of archery tackle in class situations as it is for the individuals who purchase their own tackle.

A beginner who is mismatched for archery tackle will experience considerable frustration. For example, it is actually possible to perform all fundamentals correctly with inferior tackle, yet have little success as far as accuracy is concerned. In target archery, it is absolutely essential that the archer obtain a consistent, tight grouping pattern on the target. With cheap or mismatched tackle each arrow shot will have a different flight pattern, resulting in very erratic arrow grouping. Overcoming the human factors that contribute to mistakes or accuracy is enough in and of itself to make archery a challenging sport for beginner and expert alike. The archer should not be burdened by the use of inefficient tackle, which would only add to the unique problems and challenges inherent in learning to become accurate in target archery.

If possible, the beginning archer should receive instruction from a qualified archery instructor prior to doing any shooting. The reason for this lies in the fact that bad habits can be learned by the individual who teaches himself or herself by trial and error. These poor shooting techniques become very difficult to unlearn, and that would have to be accomplished *before* the proper fundamentals could be mastered. As a result, the learning process becomes much more difficult.

Would you try to teach yourself to play the piano, perform brain surgery, or master a computer? Not likely! Mistakes learned make perfection of techniques under the guidance of a good mentor more time consuming. So, in archery as in any other skill area, good instruction must come first if you are interested in becoming a highly skilled archer.

Ideally, the first set of archery tackle, matched for the individual, should be issued by the instructor. The cost of tackle can be prohibitive. Due to this economic factor, most students may desire to learn and try the sport for a period of time with issued tackle to determine whether or not archery appeals to his or her avocational interests.

If archery becomes an interest as a lifetime sport after you have received instruction and gained a functional level of skill, that is the time to purchase your own matched archery tackle. It is highly recommended that the tackle be purchased from a professional archery shop where the salespeople are aware of the complexities of matching the components of the tackle to the requirements of the individual archer. Places such as mail-order houses, sporting goods stores, and general merchandise companies are usually poor places to purchase archery tackle. This is especially true for the beginning archer. Salespeople in such stores as a general rule simply are not cognizant of the many technical and scientific aspects required to match arrows to bows and the total tackle to the unique features of the archer.

It is recommended that the archer who plans to use target archery as an avocational activity purchase the following units of tackle:

1. Twelve fiberglass, aluminum, or graphite arrows matched to the bow purchased and to the draw length of the archer.
2. One working recurve or take-down bow with center shot design, arrow rest, clicker, stabilizer(s), and sight. The bow weight must be matched to the archer and to the spine of the arrows.
3. One leather finger tab or glove.
4. One leather arm guard.
5. One arrow quiver.
6. One bowstringer.
7. One finger or bow sling.

This amount of matched tackle would be enough to enable the beginning archer to learn the sport efficiently and utilize it avocationally for a long period of time.

The overall cost depends upon the quality of tackle purchased. The cost is minimal for archery tackle when you prorate it over the years of use. Bows, as one example, are used by some archers for decades. Arrows are expensive. *Cost should never be reduced by purchasing inexpensive arrows.* Keep them in good shape, and develop your accuracy to the point that you do not damage or lose them too often. Parts of arrows such as the nocks and fletching can be replaced if broken.

The Arrow

Although there are some good, inexpensive Port Orford Cedar arrows on the market, *wooden arrows are not recommended.* They are not reliable, and it is very difficult to match them for use with various bows. It is best not to purchase wooden arrows for any purpose. A serious mistake made by many beginning archers is to be issued a bow for use in a class situation and then purchase arrows for it without considering the mechanical properties of the bow. That diminishes the probability of learning target archery effectively.

Fiberglass arrows are satisfactory for use by learners *IF* they are matched to each other and to the bow which will be used. They are manufactured with precision. Research has led to the development of a light, durable, and hollow fiberglass shaft. It is possible for arrow manufacturers to maintain quality control to the point that there are only microscopic deviations in regard to shaft thickness, shaft diameter, and actual arrow weight. The fiberglass arrow shaft always remains straight. This is a distinct advantage of the fiberglass arrow over the aluminum arrow shaft. The fiberglass, like the wooden arrow, will break if it strikes a target stand or other hard object at an odd angle. The frequency with which this occurs is minimal. Fiberglass arrows can, however, be smashed if stepped on, because the shafts are hollow.

Aluminum arrows are recommended as the most desirable target archery arrows for beginners and experts alike. They are the most accurate to shoot. Aluminum alloys allow manufacturers to construct arrows which are nearly perfect. When shot by a machine during testing from fifty yards, it is not uncommon to see arrows grouped within a diameter of two inches. Aluminum arrows are among the most expensive on the market. If the beginner desires to purchase aluminum arrows initially, it should be kept in mind that there will be times when these arrows will completely miss the target and become lost in the grass. Also, aluminum shafts, unlike fiberglass arrows, will bend when they strike the target stand or other hard objects instead of the target mat. (There are, however, procedures for straightening a bent aluminum shaft.) If the beginner will accept these factors prior to purchasing, aluminum arrows are highly recommended as compared to fiberglass arrows.

It must also be kept in mind that arrow velocities are now greater due to improved bow design. Aluminum alloy arrows are better designed to handle greater force than wooden or fiberglass arrows. They are manufactured in a wide range of sizes and arrow weights to match a greater number of bows, draw weights, arrow lengths, and shaft spine or stiffness needs. These factors are additional reasons for recommending the use of aluminum arrows.

The use of new materials and combinations of "old materials" makes arrow selection more exciting now than ever before. There are now tapered aerodynamic arrows on the market made of aluminum-carbon materials. These kinds of arrows with superior performance physics will enhance accuracy in years to come.

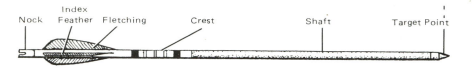

Figure 3.1
Arrow terminology.

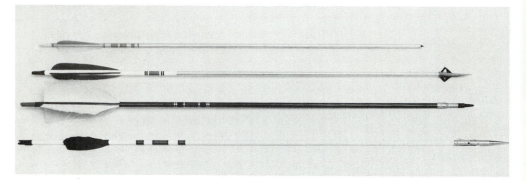

Figure 3.2
Arrow designs. From top to bottom: target arrow, bow hunting arrow with broadhead, field archery arrow with a field point, and bow fishing arrow with string-a-ree point.

The graphite arrows now on the market are also designed with quality and precision. They do not bend, and they are shatter resistant. These shafts are lighter than aluminum with a higher static spine. Those features translate into higher velocities and flatter trajectories for graphite arrows over aluminum or the older fiberglass arrows. Graphite may be the arrow shaft material of the future, so it is recommended that the archer compare and contrast properly matched (for the bow) aluminum and graphite arrows for accuracy, velocity, and trajectory.

The novice who uses a traditional end of matched arrows—six arrows with the same physical weight, degree of shaft stiffness (spine), length, and fletching (feathers)—will shoot more accurately than the beginning archer who shoots unmatched arrows. Terminology for the various parts of the arrow is shown in figure 3.1.

For comparative purposes, figure 3.2 shows some common types of arrows used in the four most popular sport areas of archery. Each arrow was designed for a unique purpose. The reader should visually compare and contrast these four arrows with that in mind. The arrow designs shown in figure 3.2 are for target archery, bow hunting, field archery, and bow fishing.

Spine

The spine of an arrow shaft is the deflection of the shaft, measured in inches, when depressed by a two-pound weight at its center. There are instruments that measure the degree of spine with minute precision. This measurement is important, inasmuch as the degree of spine is a basic factor to consider when obtaining arrows. Spine must be compatible with the archer's bow weight. One reason for matching bow weight and spine is a phenomenon known as the *Archer's Paradox.* Contrary to what the archer thinks is seen as the arrow leaves the bow, an arrow does not fly straight toward the target immediately upon being released. By means of cinematographic analysis, it has been clearly demonstrated that the arrow shaft actually deflects around the bow immediately after release. The reader can readily understand that an arrow shaft too stiff or flexible could cause problems during this phase of its flight pattern. An arrow of sufficient spine, which has been released properly, tends to stabilize itself rapidly and follows a straight flight pattern during its trajectory toward the target. The fact that an arrow first deviates to the left for a right-handed archer when it leaves the bow, but stabilizes itself in flight to travel directly to the intended target, is known as the *Archer's Paradox.*

The newer bow designs that utilize carbon graphites as well as the aluminum alloys plus the graphite now being used for arrow shafts tend to miminize this paradox when contrasted with designs and materials used several years ago. This type of efficiency leads to better accuracy.

What are some of the consequences of having improperly spined arrows for a bow? (It must be kept in mind that several factors other than spine are also involved with accurate arrow flight. These will be discussed later.) Improper spine can cause the following arrow flight patterns: (1) an arrow naturally starts its flight by deviating a few degrees to the left for a right-handed archer. If the spine is too stiff, the shaft of the arrow or the fletching will actually brush the bow. This causes a reduction in arrow velocity. In addition, a flight pattern change occurs in the opposite direction. The archer's shot will be low and to the right of the intended target, or (2) if the spine is too weak and flexible, the arrow may never stabilize and follow its intended trajectory. Instead, it will fly consistently to the left of the target. Improperly spined arrows are a definite causative factor for erratic arrow grouping.

What should be considered when selecting the proper spine for arrows? First, *the bow weight,* i.e., *the pounds of pull exerted on the bowstring by the archer for his or her specific arrow length,* is very important. Second, the arrow length and weight to the grain must be known accurately. Third, the type and weight of the arrow point are also basic considerations. Target points are made very light. This places the quality target arrow's center of gravity close to its actual center. This makes the arrow aerodynamically sound, as compared to its heavier counterparts in bow hunting and field archery as seen in figure 3.2.

By knowing these exact measurements, the proper spine can be selected for the arrows. There are charts for spine and weight specifications as well as shaft selection charts available from manufacturers and in professional archery stores. One should be very careful and follow the guidelines set forth in these charts when matching and purchasing tackle. If you have a question regarding two spine classifications of arrows suitable for a bow, it is best to take the stiffer of the two arrows.

Correct arrow selection in terms of spine can mean the difference between tight groups and multiple misses during a target archery tournament. The stiffer-spined arrow that is light in weight will have a higher velocity. But, the increased spine must be compatible with your bow weight. The increased spine will provide fewer deviations in flight due to human errors at release or to wind conditions on the range. Finally, the technical matching of arrow spine to the proper bow weight that can be handled efficiently by the archer is a major reason why archery tackle should be purchased in an archery pro shop instead of your average sporting goods or department store.

Fletching

The feathers of an arrow are known collectively as fletching. Fletching is as important to an arrow as the tail assembly is to an airplane. The function of the two analogous parts is essentially the same. They both serve to stabilize airborne objects. Fletching stabilizes an arrow by channeling, as much as possible, the wind currents encountered by the arrow during flight. Inflight equilibrium is maintained, in part, by a high velocity rotation of the arrow around the longitudinal axis of the shaft.

The type of fletching one uses is largely a matter of personal preference. However, the trend seems to be moving away from turkey feather fletching to vinyl and plastic vanes. The latter vanes tend to be more durable than real feathers, and they do not become useless during inclement weather. On the other hand, feather fletching in good condition and shot in dry weather is more likely to exhibit better flight characteristics following a poor release. A poor release usually produces fletching contact with the bow. The relatively rigid plastic vanes striking the bow produce a yaw condition or lack of stability during arrow flight. This reduces the arrow's linear velocity and usually results in a low shot. While the same contact would occur between the bow and the feather fletched arrow upon a poor release, the adverse effects on arrow flight would be minimized. The flexible feathers would be less likely to rebound as much from the bow handle. As a result, the arrow flight would not be as adversely affected. The better target archers are using the firmer plastic vanes in competition. They weigh more than turkey feathers, so point weight must be adjusted.

The length of the fletching is very important, because of the fletching's role in stabilizing the flight of the arrow after it bends around the bow upon release. Generally, longer and heavier arrows require longer and sturdier fletching. Shorter and lighter target archery arrows require fletching only 3 to 3½ inches in length. Three vane fletching of either plastic or feathers can be used effectively by target archers. Larger fletching is needed to add flight stability for heavier arrows as used in bow hunting, bow fishing, and field archery.

Figure 3.3 shows fletching variations on hunting, target, field, and bow fishing arrows. The fletch on the top arrow is 5 inches in length, and this is a hunting arrow. The next arrow is a target arrow, and the fletch is 3 inches in length. The larger fletching on the middle arrow is 5½ inches in length, and this type of fletch is designed to increase the drag resistance on a field or bow-hunting arrow. Obviously, these arrows will not fly as far if a target is missed. Therefore, they are

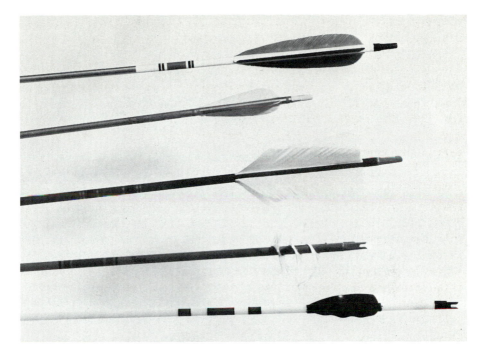

Figure 3.3
Fletching variations. From top to bottom: Hunting, target, flu-flu, spiraled flu-flu, and rubber fishing fletching.

not lost as frequently by field archers or bow hunters. The next arrow shows a spiraled flu-flu fletch; this type of fletching is also designed to increase air resistance so arrows will not travel as far in flight. The bottom arrow is an example of rubber fletching on a bow fishing arrow. Fletching is not very important on bow fishing arrows, because the arrow simply does not have to fly very far to reach its intended target. Some bow fishers remove the fletching completely from their arrows.

Fletching is usually colored in a distinct and traditional manner. On a three-fletched arrow, two vanes will be drab in color and one vane will usually be rather flamboyant. The bright or odd-colored feather is known as the "index feather," and is placed at a ninety-degree angle to the slit in the nock of the arrow. This can be seen in the upper two arrows in figure 3.3.

As a historical note, the three vanes of the fletching were once called "hen feathers" and "cock feather." The two drab colored vanes were known as "hen feathers," and the brightly colored vane was called the "cock feather." That terminology had an ornithological origin, i.e., the feathers of male birds tend to be more colorful than the feathers of the female of the same species. Fletching terminology was changed to indicate arrow placement by using the term "index" for the vane which points outward from the bow when it is nocked in the bowstring. It is recommended that experienced archers try shooting periodically on an experimental basis, with the index feather downward or toward the bow. Flight patterns shot both ways should be evaluated. The best technique of fletching placement should be adopted permanently after a satisfactory evaluation. Most archers prefer that the index feather be placed so it points outward from the bow.

Length

Length of the arrow varies for each individual. Arm length and anchor point are the determining factors. *The anchor point is the placement of the archer's bowstring hand on the chin or face with the bow at full draw.*

The beginner should allow an additional inch for the arrows. It will be found that anchor-point adjustments must be made as skill develops. It is much better to have arrows too long for the bow than too short. It will be found that more accurate arrow lengths can be determined once shooting habits become learned properly.

There are several ways to establish an initial arrow length for yourself with and without the use of a bow. If you have a bow and an over-length arrow, mark the arrow in one-inch increments from the bottom of the arrow nock groove to the arrow point. While you draw the bow to your anchor point and hold, note the inch mark nearest the back of the bow. That should be your arrow length if the anchor point is established. If not, add about an inch as noted to the first arrows purchased.

Another commonly used method of determining arrow length is to have the archer hold both arms out to the sides at shoulder level (abduct both shoulder joints ninety degrees). Obtain the arm spread measurement in inches from the ends of the middle fingers:

Spread Measurement	*Arrow Length*
57–59 inches	22–23 inches
60–62 inches	23–24 inches
63–65 inches	24–25 inches
66–68 inches	25–26 inches
69–71 inches	26–27 inches
72–74 inches	27–28 inches
75–77 inches	28–29 inches
78+ inches	30 inches

Note: To change from inches to centimeters, multiply by 2.54.

A yardstick may be used to determine arrow length if you do not have a bow and marked arrow. Two techniques may be used. First, stand at right angles to a wall. Place your clenched fist against the wall simulating a bow hold. The elbow and wrist are extended, and the head is placed in the shooting position looking toward a target (wall). The distance along the bow arm from the wall to the corner of your mouth is the arrow length. The second technique is to hold, or have a person place, a yardstick on your sternum or breastbone. Hold both arms at shoulder level in front of you and move them to the yardstick. Your correct arrow length will be very close to the measurement your middle fingertips reach on the yardstick.

Figure 3.4
The target archery arrow point should be matched in weight to be aerodynamically compatible with the total arrow configuration.

Points

Arrow points are manufactured in a wide variety of assortments and sizes. Target archery and field archery points are fairly standardized, but you will find a great variety of bow hunting and bow fishing points. The beginning archer should start with light points for target archery (fig. 3.4). The various arrow points used in the other areas of archery will be discussed in Chapters 6 and 7.

Target archery points are designed to be ultralight to facilitate arrow aerodynamics. Proper point weight for each shaft size is just as essential in target archery as it is for the heavier broadhead points used in bow hunting. The nearly symmetrical equilibrium of the target archery arrow is very important for accuracy. The proper point weight and fletching size are the critical components on the arrow. Most of the more sophisticated target archery points on quality aluminum arrows are designed as nickel plated steel points fitted to an aluminum sleeve. This unit is then fitted solidly into the arrow shaft. Target archery points designed and fitted in this manner should not loosen and cause flight problems. They should be checked after being shot as the arrows are cleaned; and arrows need to be cleaned after each end is shot. The added weight of small amounts of dirt causes erratic arrow flight.

The Bow

The bow has fascinated human beings throughout history. They have used it for hunting animals, killing their enemies, making music, drilling holes in the ground, and for sport.

Bows have been built in all sizes and shapes (see Chapters 2 and 9). Some archers in the Far East have used seven-foot bows with straight, uneven limbs; some African tribes use a three-foot bow with straight, even limbs; Englishmen of the eleventh century used a bow five feet long with straight limbs; warriors at the Temple of Aigina used bows with duo-flexed limbs; the Navajo Indians of the southwestern United States used a crude, short bow for hunting purposes; modern target archery champions prefer working recurve bows. Throughout history all the diversified bow designs met their intended objectives in the hands of expert archers. That is an important fact to keep in mind in this age of ultra-efficient archery tackle. The skill and adaptability of the archer to his or her tackle remains the paramount factor for success. Bow selection from a variety of quality bows is one of those "nice problems" that the contemporary archer has which never confronted his or her American Indian counterparts in the eighteenth century.

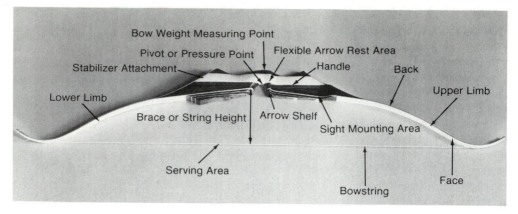

Figure 3.5
Target archery bow terminology. (Courtesy Black Widow Bow Company, H. C. R. #1, Box 357–1, Highlandville, Missouri 65669)

The target archery bow has unique nomenclature which needs to be learned. This bow terminology is presented in figure 3.5. *The reader should also utilize Chapter 10 while reading text material for definitions of terms used in archery.* The bow shown in figure 3.5 is a recurve target archery bow.

Which type of target archery bow should be selected? A well-constructed working recurve bow will be more than adequate. A working recurve bow can be identified by observing the position of the bowstring on the face of the bow. The working recurve bow, as contrasted with the old long bow designs (see fig. 2.5), will have the string lying on the face of the bow for at least two inches at each end of the limbs. This feature greatly enhances the leverage potential of the bow and adds to the subsequent velocity of the arrow. An example of an older model recurve is shown in figure 3.5. This bow was of solid, one piece construction. The limbs were made from laminated fiberglass and hard rock maple, with the handle section of Brazilian rosewood. A beginning archer may think about purchasing an older style, used bow of that type to learn the sport. They are extremely efficient, durable, and functional. In addition, they can be purchased from archery shops that trade and sell tackle at prices much below the current take-down recurve bow. From the standpoints of cost and efficient skill development, the purchase of a used working recurve bow is a good way for some people to get started in target archery. Arrows must match any bow purchased.

It should be noted that compound bows, bows with mechanical parts, and cam bows are not used in the sport of target archery. These bows will be discussed in Chapters 5, 6, and 7, because they are used in bow hunting, bow fishing, and field archery.

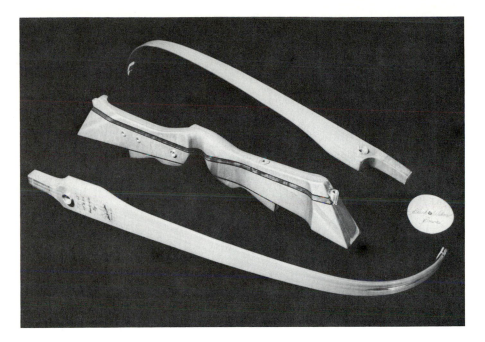

Figure 3.6
A take-down target archery bow showing the lower limb, handle, and upper limb. (Courtesy Black Widow Bow Company, H. C. R. #1, Box 357–1, Highlandville, Missouri 65669)

If the target archer desires a state of the art target bow, the finest tournament archery bows are three-piece, take-down bows. An example is shown in figures 3.6 and 3.7. Figure 3.6 illustrates a take-down target bow disassembled into the lower limb, handle, and upper limb sections. This bow is made of maple; other take-down models on the market have handles made of a magnesium alloy. Carbon graphite is also now being used in target bow construction. The bow in figure 3.6 is reinforced and protected by a transparent glass covering over the laminated maple limb curves. This makes it very efficient in terms of leverage, durability, and arrow velocity. It is also very aesthetic. Draw weights for take-down bows usually range from 30 to 50 pounds. A distinct advantage of a take-down bow over the earlier one-piece recurve models is the fact that the archer can change limb lengths as desired. Limbs may be purchased in lengths ranging from 64 to 70 inches. Take-down bows are assembled quickly and easily.

Figure 3.7 shows the equipped target archery bow. This is the same take-down working recurve bow as shown in figure 3.6. It is equipped with stabilizers. The bow has three stabilizer inserts in the back of the handle riser plus one on the face of the bow. A clicker is mounted on the sight window. A clicker is a shooting aid which insures a consistent draw and helps the target archer concentrate on aiming and release of the arrow. A bowsight is mounted on the bow.

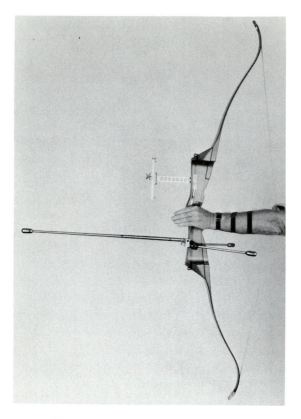

Figure 3.7
A competitive target archery bow equipped with arrow rest, stabilizers, clicker, and bowsight. This is the same bow as shown in figure 3.6. (Courtesy Black Widow Bow Company, H. C. R. #1, Box 357–1, Highlandville, Missouri 65669)

The bow is braced or strung, and the draw is being started in figure 3.7. This is the same type of target archery bow one would expect to see on the shooting lines of international archery tournaments, including the Olympic Games (see fig. 1.1). Each archer would equip his or her bow to meet individual requirements based on such factors as shooting idiosyncracies, target archery rules, and personal preferences. Each competitive target archer is unique.

A quality bow has a section cut away at the midline of its upper limb. This is called center shot design. The cutaway area is used as the sight window. This feature minimizes the components of the Archer's Paradox, because the arrow is able to move past the bow in a relatively close path to the bow string alignment with the face of the bow. Another very important feature of a bow with center shot design is the practical aspect of allowing the archer to see the intended target.

Figure 3.8 shows the center shot design of the same bow shown in figure 3.7. You are looking through the sight window toward the target in figure 3.8. Can you identify the: (1) bow face? (2) upper limb? (3) lower limb? (4) riser? (5) stabilizers? (6) pressure point? (7) arrow shelf? (8) arrow rest? (9) clicker?

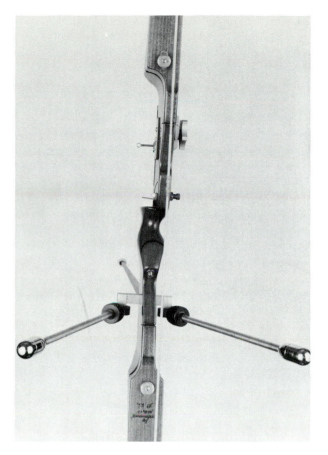

Figure 3.8
Sight window of a target archery bow looking at the bow face through the bowsight. (Courtesy Black Widow Bow Company, H. C. R. #1, Box 357–1, Highlandville, Missouri 65669)

(10) bowstring? (11) bowsight? and (12) bowsight adjustment knob? This sight window is 7½ inches, and it has been cut ⅕ inch past the center of the bow to facilitate arrow clearance. A take-down, working recurve target archery bow meeting the criteria outlined is highly recommended for beginners and experts alike.

Weight

The weight of the bow is very important. Bow weight is defined as the bow manufacturers' determination of the number of pounds required to draw the bowstring a given distance—usually 28 inches. Mass weight of the bow is the literal weight of the bow in pounds. Mass weight of a bow should never be confused with bow weight. The mass weight of a good target archery bow with a stabilizer should be in the 3- to 6-pound range. This amount of mass weight adds to the bow's shooting stability.

Due to the efficiency with which good recurve target archery bows can convert potential energy into kinetic energy, considerable force can be transmitted to the arrow, resulting in excellent arrow velocity. With the working recurves, this is accomplished at relatively low bow weights. How much bow weight is enough for each archer to attain good scores in target archery? Some guidelines can be supplied to partially answer that question, but the final answer lies in the extent or lack of muscular endurance and strength each individual has in the extensor muscles of the body, the shoulder joints, and shoulder girdles. (Physical conditioning principles for the target archer are covered in considerable detail in Chapter 8.)

Archery instructors generally agree that an archer should select a bow weight which he or she has strength enough to draw and hold without undue strain for multiple repetitions during a class or competitive situation. Generally, for most men, this means a bow weight should be found that is comfortable somewhere within a range of 30 to 50 pounds. Although adult women only have approximately 50 percent of the muscle mass seen in men, one should not deduce that a functional bow weight for all women is low. Observations by archery instructors verify that this is not the case. Strength in human beings is a product of central nervous system efficiency as well as muscle mass; therefore, many small people, male and female, can handle bow weights considered to be rather high. Generally, for most women, a bow weight that is functional and can be handled without strain should be found in a range of 25 to 35 pounds. That range does not represent the upper range for all women, because some good, competitive women archers handle bow weights higher than that range. Bow weight is a highly individual matter, and the bow weight must be "matched" to meet the anatomic attributes of the archer as well as the arrows to be shot from it.

As indicated, bow weights are determined according to the number of pounds required to pull the bowstring back to full draw for a given arrow length. Most bows are marked for bow weight at a 28-inch draw. As the draw diminishes in length, the bow weight also diminishes in pounds. Conversely, as the draw increases in length, the bow weight increases in pounds. The archer needs to know the actual draw weight for the arrow length being pulled. The recommended procedure for doing this was established by the Archery Manufacturer's Organization. This fairly simple procedure is accomplished as follows: Divide the draw weight marked on the bow by twenty, and determine how many inches, more or less, the actual draw length deviates from 28 inches. Multiply these two answers, and subtract (or add) the answer from the weight marked on the bow. The result of this simple calculation gives the archer the actual draw weight. As an example, assume that an archer has a 35-pound bow, and is actually drawing 30 inches. Thirty-five divided by twenty equals 1.75. In this example, 1.75 would be multiplied by two, which is the extra number of inches being drawn above the 28-inch mark. The resultant answer of 3.50 would be added to the 35-pound bow weight. Therefore, an archer drawing a 30-inch arrow on a bow marked 35 pounds for a 28-inch draw would actually be drawing 38.5 pounds.

It is a good idea for some beginners to learn while using a bow weight lighter than they have strength to handle. It is easier to learn shooting fundamentals with a comfortable bow weight, because the archer's concentration is not distracted due to fatigue or other physical factors. As skill increases, bow weight may be increased to meet the individual's strength and muscle endurance capabilities. This procedure is recommended in those learning situations where matched tackle is available and may be issued to the archers.

Many archers like to believe they need a very heavy bow weight. Let us consider what actually happens when the potential kinetic energy of a bow is doubled. What are the differences in terms of arrow velocity between 45- and 90-pound bows? Will arrow velocity be doubled? Tripled? Taking variable arrow weights into consideration, it has been established that a 90-pound bow only increases arrow velocity between 19 and 25 percent over a bow weight of 45 pounds. When an archer considers such factors as ease of handling, shooting over prolonged periods of time during tournaments, and accuracy difficulties, is a high bow weight really worth the extra effort needed to draw it? Most archers would answer that question in the negative. Contemporary target archery bows have excellent thrust force. This results in superior arrow velocities to handle the standard distances shot in tournaments. An arrow velocity of between 163 and 210 feet per second will generally be functional for target archery purposes.

The arrow velocity potential for today's bows and arrows is determined by calculating a ballistics coefficient based on the interrelationships of the: (1) peak weight of the bow in pounds; (2) total weight of the arrow including point, nock, and fletching in grains; and (3) draw length of the bow. Bows with draw lengths over 30 inches—stable and efficient in terms of longer application of force on the arrow nock after bowstring release—have better ballistic coefficients than bows that do not meet these scientifically based criteria. A working recurve bow with a ballistics coefficient of 0.140 would produce an arrow velocity of 210 feet per second. In terms of accuracy, flight efficiency, and trajectory, that velocity level could be better than an arrow projection of 240 feet per second. So, the choice of your ultimate bow weight is based on numerous technical and scientific factors. The greater bow weight may not be the most efficient. The efficiency of the bow ultimately boils down to three key factors: (1) design, (2) construction materials, and (3) the skill of the archer using it. The latter is the most important factor! The components of the ballistic coefficient documents the basis for matched tackle.

Let us consider some of the basic differences between the working recurve bow and the older long bow. This discussion is presented, because, unfortunately, long bows are still being issued for learning purposes in some archery classes. First, it should be noted that all bows sold as recurve bows do not have recurve actions. In order to work efficiently, it should be remembered that the bowstring of the recurve bow must actually touch the face of the bow for two to three inches at the end of both limbs. If the bow is not designed in this manner, it will respond essentially the same as the long bow. When the bowstring touches the recurve tips as shown in the bows in figures 3.5 and 3.7, this does increase the leverage potential and adds to arrow velocity. This increases the force-time relationship during energy transfer from the bow to the arrow. The total effect of the force generated by the bow and applied to the arrow via the bowstring-nock arrangement is the product of the magnitude of force with the time during which it operates. This principle is magnified, for example, within the design of bows that utilize wheels, pulleys, and cams. These compound bows cannot be used in target archery competitions. But, the modern design of recurve bows is very efficient. A recurve bow weight of 45 pounds will project an arrow at a rate of speed approximately 20 percent greater than a long bow of comparable weight. A working recurve bow tends to draw more smoothly than a long bow. This is particularly true of the modern take-down bow. These bows have very little increase of weight during the last few inches of draw. *The phenomenon of ever-increasing weight as one draws the bowstring hand toward the face is known as "stacking."* Due to the increased arrow velocity, which is derived through increased leverage, the working recurve bow tends to project the arrow on a flatter trajectory than a long bow. This aids accuracy considerably. Finally, the semicircular configuration of a long bow seen as it is being drawn tends to cause an uneven distribution of stress in the limbs. This factor also detracts from the overall efficiency and longevity of the long bow. This stress factor within the limbs does not occur within a good working recurve bow. Except for those in the hands of expert archers who have been using long bows throughout their lifetimes, the long bow should be retired to the museum! A beginning archer should definitely learn to shoot while using a good, working recurve bow.

Length

Target archers are no longer using short bows. They are simply too difficult to use. There is extreme pressure on the bowstring fingers at full draw, and this negates a smooth release of the arrow. Most target archers use bows ranging from 64 to 70 inches in length. The added bow length minimizes the pressure the fingers exert on the nock of the arrow during the draw and at release. In addition, the longer bows generally have greater mass weight. This factor helps the conditioned archer have a steadier bow hand while shooting.

The draw length or arrow length must be considered when selecting a bow for target archery:

Draw Length	Bow Length
1. 25 inches to 28 inches	64-inch limbs
2. 27 inches to 30 inches	66-inch limbs
3. 29 inches to 32 inches	68-inch limbs
4. 31 inches to 34 inches	70-inch limbs

Personal preference and kinesthetic feeling enter into bow length selection. As an example, a person with a 30-inch draw can use a 66- or 68-inch bow. Whichever length ultimately has the best feeling after shooting several arrows is the bow which should be purchased. Most professional archery shops have indoor ranges where bows may be tried prior to purchase. Also, limb lengths can be interchanged by using take-down bows.

Figure 3.9
Bow equipped with one stabilizer.

Stabilizers

One or more stabilizers can be mounted on a bow. The stabilizer can contribute to more efficient arrow flight by minimizing or negating some of the archer's fundamental shooting faults involving the bow arm. A stable bow means less twist or torque of the bow at and following release. A stabilizer is shown mounted on a target bow in figure 3.9. The stabilizer is a metal rod screwed into the back of the bow on the bow handle. The stabilizer can be adjusted for length to fit the personal preference of the archer. The number, weight, and length of stabilizers is a matter of individualized preference. Some archers prefer to use tapered stabilizers mounted on a rotor which pivots 360 degrees. This allows considerable adjustment flexibility for stabilizers. Figures 3.8 and 3.10 show a v-bar stabilizer system mounted on a bow.

A word of advice is in order regarding the use of stabilizers. *The beginner should learn basic fundamentals of shooting before mounting a stabilizer on the bow.* After the fundamentals have been learned to the extent that the archer is grouping arrows consistently, a stabilizer can then be used for a portion of all future practice sessions. However, the archer should try to correct fundamental faults without using the stabilizer. If successfully done, this will mean higher scores when the stabilizer is used in competitive situations. A stabilizer should not be used as a "crutch" to compensate for fundamental faults.

Bowstrings

Like arrows, bowstrings must be matched to specific bows as well as the requirements of the archer. Archery manufacturers make recommendations regarding what type of bowstring and how many strands should be used with specific bows.

Figure 3.10
A stabilizer system mounted on a target archery bow. (Courtesy Black Widow Bow Company, H. C. R. #1, Box 357–1, Highlandville, Missouri 65669)

Bowstrings come in varieties of Dacron, Kevlar, and Flemish. Dacron and Flemish tend to stretch too much with use, and that can have a negative effect on aerodynamics and accuracy. Kevlar string reduces the elastic component to a minimum, and it produces a good shot with an average weight bow when twelve to fifteen strands are used. Dacron strings will vary from eight strands for bows to 30 pounds to twelve or more strands recommended for bows up to 45 pounds. Bowstrings can be adjusted by twisting, but utilization of this technique should be limited to a maximum of twelve twists to minimize friction and breakage.

The middle portion of the bowstring is called the *serving*. The arrow is placed on the string or nock at a point on the serving. As can be seen in figure 3.11, two nock-locators have been mounted on the serving. The nock-locators tend to serve as the spot on the serving of the bowstring which marks the exact nocking point for the arrow. These locators insure that the exact nocking angle will be consistent from shot to shot. The added thread wrapping around the portion of the bowstring known as the serving is needed to protect the string from breakage, because this area of the bowstring receives considerable wear and tear.

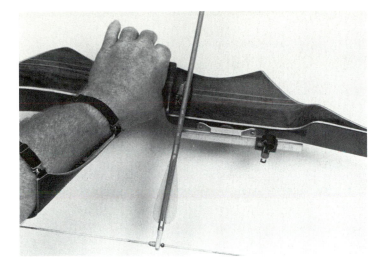

Figure 3.11
Bowstring, serving, and nock-locators.

Bowsights

The bowsight shown in figure 3.12 is used by members of the U.S. Olympic Archery Team. This target sight is equipped with a 10-inch dovetail extension. Sights of this caliber come equipped with operating features that make micrometer elevation and windage adjustments relatively easy and quick. The pointer can be moved easily and set as desired. Also, leveling the aperture with this sight can be accomplished by simply hanging the bow in a verticle position. You loosen the allen set screws at the top and bottom of the sight body. The aperture is leveled simply by turning the allen screw at the bottom left of the sight body with the key. The aperture does not move from its level position as you tighten down the screws at the top and bottom of the sight body. All of these features are important in a quality target archery bowsight. *The beginning archer should learn target archery by using a quality bowsight for aiming purposes versus shooting instinctively.* Bowsights are mounted on the bow as shown in figure 3.10.

Accessories

The archer must have protection for the bow arm and bowstring fingers. The bow arm must be protected from possible contusions due to being slapped by the bowstring in the general region of the radioulnar and wrist joints (forearm). Without protection, the bowstring fingers become severely irritated due to the constant pressure and friction exerted by the bowstring. Two common leather accessories, the finger tab and arm guard, are shown in figures 3.13 and 3.14. Both come in several sizes, shapes, and styles. These accessories are relatively inexpensive.

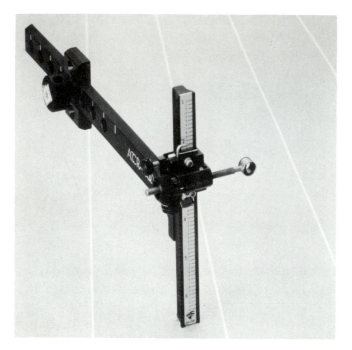

Figure 3.12
The Accra Combo 1103 target archery bowsight used by U.S. Olympic Archery Team Members. (Courtesy Accra 300)

Figure 3.13
Finger tab. (Courtesy Wilson Brothers, Route 1, Elkland, Missouri 65644)

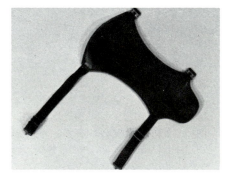

Figure 3.14
Arm guard.

Figure 3.15
Finger sling.

The finger tab is rather awkward to use at first, but it is absolutely essential for prolonged shooting during class or tournaments while using the conventional three-finger release technique. Tender skin may become blistered by the friction created when the bowstring rolls over the fingertips if a finger tab is not used. This, of course, would have an adverse effect on accuracy. The finger tab is an accessory designed to enhance shooting and accuracy. If you shoot a great deal, it may become worn, rough, or less pliable. It is necessary to change tabs when that occurs, because of possible negative impact on accuracy.

Some archers prefer shooting gloves instead of finger tabs. A shooting glove is shown in figure 4.15.

The arm guard is placed on the bow arm between the elbow and wrist. The arm guard is shown in figures 3.14 and 3.16. The lower arm in the vicinity of the wrist is an area which is "slapped" periodically by the bowstring when it is released. Shooting without an arm guard can result in serious contusions. Furthermore, following one severe blow by the bowstring on an unprotected arm, an archer has a tendency to flinch—flexion occurs in the elbow and/or wrist—when the arrow is released. These movements at the elbow and wrist are bad habits which the protection afforded by the arm guard tends to eliminate.

A finger sling is an accessory that can also help eliminate some problems during release and follow-through. The finger sling is shown in figures 3.15 and 3.16. The finger sling attaches to the index finger or middle finger and the thumb of the bow hand. It then extends across the back of the bow as shown in figure 3.16. It serves the purpose of keeping the bow from falling to the ground during release of the arrow and the subsequent follow-through. Therefore, the archer can concentrate more on the release and less on losing control of the bow.

An arrow quiver is another accessory which the archer must obtain. This is a device designed to carry arrows. There are shoulder, hip, ground, pocket, and bow quivers available. Those come in all sizes, shapes, prices, and materials. Most beginners rely upon inexpensive, ground quivers. The most commonly used quiver, however, is the hip quiver as shown in figures 3.9 and 3.17.

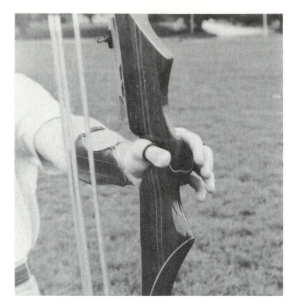

Figure 3.16
Arm guard and finger sling in use.

Figure 3.17
Hip quiver.

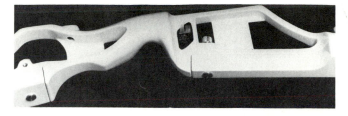

Figure 3.18
Arrow rest without an arrow.

Figure 3.19
Arrow rest holding the arrow at full draw.

Another important accessory is the arrow rest. This small device is mounted just above the arrow shelf on the bow. Its purposes are to maintain arrow position and stability from the initial nocking of the arrow onto the bowstring to the time of arrow release. There are one- and two-piece metal and plastic arrow rests on the market. For best results, the one-piece, plastic arrow rest is recommended. Arrow rests are shown in figures 3.8, 3.18, and 3.19.

A clicker is used extensively in target archery. A clicker is shown mounted on the sight window of the bow shown in figures 3.7 and 3.8. As indicated, a clicker is a shooting accessory that facilitates a consistent draw and helps the archer concentrate on aiming. The arrow is ready to be released when the archer hears the "click" of the clicker as the fully drawn arrow point passes through the clicker.

Care of Archery Tackle

The Bow

The following care and treatment of a target bow will add to its longevity and effectiveness:

1. Always unstring the bow after use with a bowstringer.
2. Place the bow in a bow case for storage purposes. In the case of a take-down bow, remove the bow limbs prior to inserting it in the bow case.
3. Lay the bow in a flat place or hang it vertically if a bow case is not available.

4. To protect the outer surface of the bow, wax it periodically.
5. Use beeswax on the bowstring occasionally to minimize fraying.
6. Do not leave the bow lying on the ground when retrieving arrows from the target.
7. Do not drop the bow.
8. Draw the bow several times to your draw length prior to actually shooting an arrow, but do not release the string at full draw without an arrow in the bow.
9. Always use a bowstringer to brace the bow.
10. A take-down bow can be stored while strung if desired. It should be hung horizontally.
11. Maintain limb and string alignments.

Arrows

The following care and treatment of arrows will add to their longevity and effectiveness:

1. Store arrows in an arrow case.
2. Wipe arrows clean after shooting.
3. Check fletching periodically and replace as needed. Fletching can be replaced at a very low cost.
4. Do not carry arrows in a tightly clenched fist. This tends to damage fletching. Place the arrows between the fingers when carrying them back from the target to the shooting line.
5. Check nocks periodically and replace as needed.
6. If an arrow is embedded in a target up to the fletching or nock, remove the arrow by pulling it completely through the target. This protects fletching.
7. If an arrow is embedded or "snaked" into the grass on the target range, remove the arrow from the grass by pulling it in the direction of its flight. This protects fletching.

Review Questions

1. Why is it advisable to become proficient in target archery prior to pursuing a specialized interest in bow hunting, bow fishing, or field archery?
2. What advantages does the working recurve bow have over earlier long bow designs?
3. What do the following terms mean when used in connection with archery: (1) cast, (2) stabilizer, (3) fletching size, (4) tackle, (5) Archer's Paradox, (6) point weight, (7) take-down bow, and (8) thrust force?
4. In FITA competition are bow stabilizers permitted? If so, are there restrictions regarding their use?
5. What is the purpose of a bowsight, bowmark, or point of aim? How do these differ? Are they permitted in competition?

6. Describe routine procedures for the care of target archery tackle.
7. Why must archery tackle be matched? What are the necessary components of matching tackle to tackle and tackle to the archer?
8. Discuss the changes in arrow construction over the years. What is the impact on target archery?
9. What should you consider in terms of selecting a bow weight for yourself?
10. How do you determine your actual draw weight?
11. What arrow velocity do you need in target archery?
12. Compare and contrast bowstring differences in terms of shooting performance.
13. What is the purpose of a clicker mounted on your bow?
14. In what sense is it true that an athlete can be no better than his or her equipment? Turn this around: Is a very well equipped person necessarily a good athlete?
15. Is this assumption true: The least expensive tackle is appropriate for the novice, but it is necessary for the champion to have exactly matched tackle?
16. After a novice in any sport has fooled around for a while and learned a little about a sport, then it is time to obtain some expert instruction. Is this sound advice? Why?
17. What is the difference between bow weight and weight of the bow? How is each determined? What is the relationship between the length of the draw and bow weight?

Fundamentals of Target Archery

4

The learning of target archery shooting skill serves as the foundation for virtually all archery sports. Target archery is one of the most demanding of all the shooting sports. Minute errors in the fundamental skills can be very frustrating for the target archer, because they lead to rather large accuracy problems. Precision and consistency are mandatory attributes the target archer must possess, and these learned habits are based on a thorough understanding of shooting fundamentals. Target archery is a challenging sport to learn, because there are numerous opportunities to err between the time the archer nocks the arrow, draws the bow, and releases the arrow on its flight toward the target. Those things most difficult to attain in life often are perceived to possess the greatest values. Therein lies some of the mystique and challenge of archery.

Some basic techniques and fundamentals of archery have been modified by champions and other participants in the sport. Such changes occur in all sports because of individual differences. Target archers, like other athletes, have numerous theories, preferences, idiosyncracies, and variations on their shooting styles. These are usually developed over a period of years of shooting in practice and competition. Although not all target archers shoot exactly alike, when their fundamental skills are analyzed, they have more similarities than differences in their performances. *Those basic fundamentals of shooting, which are generally agreed upon as the stereotype of perfect skill or mechanics for archery, are discussed in this chapter.*

Variations or modifications of basic form and style are mentioned on occasion. The beginner may want to try these variations, but this should be done only *after* becoming familiar with tackle and basic shooting techniques.

NOTE: All discussions and illustrations in this textbook pertain to the right-handed archer.

Archery and Safety

The archer should keep the following concept in mind when archery tackle is in hand: *Archery is not a dangerous sport, but the bow and arrow does have lethal potential.* As a consequence, respect should be shown for one's tackle and other human beings while on an archery range of any kind.

Safety rules vary from range to range. All rules, however, incorporate good common sense with the concept of always being aware of the whereabouts of your fellow archers. When an arrow is placed in a bow it should be pointed *only* in the direction of the intended target. The archer must know beyond all doubt that no other human being is within arrow distance of the intended target. This is easier to ascertain on target archery ranges than on field archery courses (units) or in bow-hunting situations. Practice on a target archery range is done from a common shooting line for all archers. Whistle signals are usually used to tell the archers when to shoot, stop shooting, and retrieve arrows. An archer should never move in front of the shooting line for any reason until he or she hears the whistle or signal authorizing retrieval of the arrows. Each archery instructor or Director of Shooting will post and announce range safety rules. When these rules are followed in detail, and archers show courtesy and respect for each other on the range, target archery is one of the safest of all sports.

The archer should go to the range in comfortable clothing. Loose fitting golf sweaters, long-sleeved shirts, and blouses are not recommended clothing to be worn on the archery range. That type of clothing can become entangled with the bowstring after it has been released. It is also good practice to remove such things as watches, pens from pockets, and jewelry prior to shooting. These can become entangled in the bowstring. Also, footwear should be comfortable. The use of shoes with high heels on a target range is not recommended.

From the standpoints of personal safety and proper care of tackle, the bow and arrows to be shot should be given a visual inspection prior to shooting. The bow limbs and arrows should be checked for stress fractures. The bowstring needs to be checked to see if all strands are intact and that the loops are properly notched on the bow following the bracing process. These simple observations can eliminate potential problems.

Bracing

Bracing the bow simply means attaching the bowstring to the bow in preparation for shooting. Bracing the bow can create problems for some archers, and it must be remembered that bows can also be damaged due to improper bracing techniques. *Working recurve bows should always be braced with a bowstringer.* If a bow is broken while using the older push-pull and step-through methods of bracing, some bow manufacturers will not replace the broken bows under their guarantees.

A bowstringer is shown in figure 4.1. Figures 4.2 and 4.3 show how to use the bowstringer. The bowstringer shown in figure 4.1 is equipped with two leather pockets, one longer than the other. Place the longer leather pocket on the lower tip of the bow, and place the shorter pocket on the upper tip of the bow. Turn the bow face downward, and place the left foot on the center of the bowstringer (fig. 4.2). Grip the bow firmly and pull it straight upward. At the same time, slide the loose loop of the bowstring into its notch (fig. 4.3). Check both bow notches to see that the bowstring is properly inserted prior to shooting. To unstring the bow, the above procedure is reversed. *The use of a bowstringer is simple, safe, and recommended at all times.*

Figure 4.1
Bowstringer. (Courtesy of Bow-Pal)

Figure 4.2
Bracing with a bowstringer—Step one.

Figure 4.3
Bracing with a bowstringer—Step two.

If, however, a bowstringer is not available, there are two methods for bracing a bow manually: (1) the push-pull method and (2) the step-through method. The method used by the archer depends upon the weight of the bow, design of the bow, and strength of the individual.

For most lightweight bows and archers with average strength, the push-pull method of bracing is adequate. The following is the procedure for using the push-pull method of bracing:

1. Place the lower limb of the bow against the instep of the right foot; be certain that the bowstring is placed in the notch on the lower limb of the bow.
2. Grasp the handle with the right hand.
3. Grasp the loop of the bowstring with the thumb and index finger of the left hand and slide it up the lower limb toward the notch of the bow.

Figure 4.4
A Scythian archer in the act of bracing his bow. Since early times this method has proved satisfactory for stringing short and powerful composite bows. From a kylix by the Paraitois painter, after c. 490 B.C. (From E. G. Heath, *The Grey Goose Wing*)

4. PULL with the right hand and PUSH down on the upper limb with the left hand while sliding the bowstring upward and into the bow notch. *For safety purposes, keep your face out of alignment with the upper limb.*
5. Check to see that both bowstring loops are properly inserted (fully) into each bow nock. This is a final safety precaution.

The step-through method of bracing is used more frequently than the push-pull method, especially with working recurve bows. However, this bracing technique is only recommended when a bowstringer is not available for the archer:

1. Assume an upright stance with the feet apart at shoulder width.
2. Step through or between the bowstring and face of the bow with the right leg.
3. See that the recurve of the lower bow limb encircles your left ankle.
4. Hold the handle of the bow on the upper thigh so both upper and lower bow limbs will bend.
5. Taking advantage of the leverage which this bow position allows, grasp the upper bow limb and bend it forward and downward with the right hand.
6. Move the bowstring upward, placing it in the bow notch with the left hand as the upper limb is being bent downward.
7. Check both bow notches to see that bowstring loops are properly inserted into each. Failure to insert them properly exposes the archer to danger during the shooting process.

If the bow should slip during this step-through procedure for bracing, cuffs of slacks, pantyhose, and trousers can be ripped. Steady pressure should be exerted and proper placement of the recurve around the left ankle must be checked to prevent the occurrence of that type of problem. Also, if the bow is twisted during this bracing method, it is possible to crack the bow. As can be seen in figure 4.4, variations of this bracing method have been around for a considerable period of time! If you have ever tried this bracing method while fully clothed, you might readily understand why the archer in figure 4.4 is bracing in the nude.

The actual distance from the bowstring to the handle of the bow is very important. This is known as the brace or string height. Bowyers, individuals who make bows, indicate exactly what the brace height should be for each bow. This will depend upon the length of the bow. As one example, the manufacturer's recommended string height for the bow in figure 4.2 is 9¾ to 10¾ inches for a 69-inch bow and 9½ to 10½ inches for a 67-inch bow. The archer should measure the brace height accurately after bracing the bow. A bowstring too close or too far away from the face of the bow will adversely affect arrow velocity and flight. There are times when the experienced target archer may adjust his or her brace height to compensate for individual shooting style. A higher brace height of an inch, as an example, may reduce bow shock at release and produce more stable arrow flight for some shooting styles. On the other hand, lowering the manufacturer's recommended brace height can possibly compound shooting errors and problems.

A bowstring can be rotated or twisted in some cases to make minor adjustments for proper brace heights. The twists of the string should be limited to a range of three to ten for any single adjustment. The best situation is to have a properly fitting bowstring for the proper brace height for your bow, and it should have the proper number of strands providing a bowstring diameter you can grasp comfortably.

Stance

The right-handed archer stands with the left side of the body toward the intended target. The archer's stance must be consistent from shot to shot. The exact placement of the feet on the shooting line should be marked. Golf tees provide good markers for this purpose. They can be driven into the ground to indicate heel and toe placement for both feet. This procedure enables the archer to return to the exact stance on the shooting line after retrieving arrows. Stance deviations of even a few inches can cause sighting and aiming problems, which in turn lead to accuracy problems. *Consistency* is a key word in the sport of target archery.

Figures 4.5, 4.6, 4.7, and 4.8 show four different types of foot placement which can be used by archers.

Many archers prefer the even stance shown in figure 4.5. In this stance, the shooting line is straddled and weight is evenly distributed over both feet. As can be seen, the heels and toes of the feet are aligned, and the middle of the instep of the foot should be aligned with the center of the intended target. The beginning archer may want to try this stance and determine how it feels while shooting several practice rounds. Many expert archers use this stance, but it is not the stance of choice in terms of scientific criteria relating to static equilibrium and perception of the visual field. In those terms, the open and oblique stances are better. But, individual choice is a pleasant fact of life in archery!

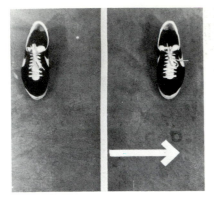 

Figure 4.5
Even stance.

Figure 4.6
Open stance.

 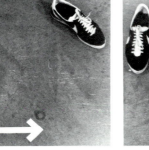 

Figure 4.7
Oblique stance.

Figure 4.8
Closed stance.

The open stance is shown in figure 4.6 and is recommended for the beginning archer during the initial learning period. The feet should be shoulder-width apart in the open stance. It is recommended that the body weight be distributed evenly on both feet. The archer should stand with both feet in such a position that an imaginary line can be drawn through the insteps to the center of the gold on the target face, as is the case in the even stance. To "open the stance," the left foot should be moved backwards approximately six inches as shown.

Once the placement of the feet have been determined for your open stance and you are comfortable on the line, foot placement should be marked. After shooting an end of arrows, you return to the *exact* foot placement each time. You may have to make adjustments after gaining shooting experience. Changing the position of the feet once the open stance is determined should not be done. The place to make motion adjustments is in the lumbar-thoracic spine, i.e., keep your stance stable and rotate the spine as needed to make the necessary adjustment.

Some expert archers use what is called the oblique stance, as shown in figure 4.7. This stance is attained by placing the toe of the left foot nearest the target on a line with the target and pivoting the left foot so it is at a forty-five-degree

Figure 4.9
Body position for addressing the target in target archery—even stance. Shooting line is straddled with the target to the archer's left.

Figure 4.10
Nocking the arrow.

angle to the target. The heel of the right foot is then placed in line with the toe of the left foot. The oblique stance allows the bow arm to remain in such a position that there will be optimum clearance of the bowstring when the arrow is released. Furthermore, with the weight distributed over the balls of the feet, total body equilibrium is enhanced. The archer in figure 4.10 is using a modified form of the oblique stance.

A closed stance is shown in figure 4.8. The shooting line is straddled and the weight is evenly distributed over both feet. The left foot is simply moved forward a few inches so a heel-toe relationship exists between the left and right feet respectively. This type of stance is not very popular among archers.

It is recommended that the beginning archer learn while using the open stance. After you have become cognizant of all of the archery fundamentals and have had opportunities to practice, various stances should be tried during the shooting process. The final stance chosen should be the one allowing the greatest degree of comfort, stability, and accuracy for the individual.

The term "addressing the target" simply means that the target archer assumes the stance of his or her choice and straddles the shooting line (figs. 4.5, 4.6, 4.7, and 4.8) to prepare to shoot. The arrows in those figures show the direction to the target. The overall body position for addressing the target is shown in figure 4.9. The right-handed archer holds the bow in the left hand, and the left side of the body is nearest the intended target. If a ground quiver is used to hold the arrows, it is placed in front of the archer in a convenient position so the arrows may be reached without changing the stance.

Nocking

Nocking the arrow is placement of the arrow in shooting position on the bowstring. This is an important step in preparation for shooting. In target archery, this is accomplished when all archers have assumed their stances on the shooting line. The archer holds the bow horizontal to the ground next to the hip nearest the target, as shown in figure 4.10. The arrow shaft is laid on the arrow rest. The arrow nock is placed on the bowstring with the index feather upward at the serving. Bowstrings should be equipped with rubber, metal, or plastic nocking points to ensure consistency of arrow placement on the string during nocking.

The archer should place the arrow nock on the string one-eighth of an inch below the nocking point. A ninety-degree angle is formed between the arrow and bowstring. This is the traditional nocking angle (fig. 4.11). The nocking position may be changed one-sixteenth of an inch or so if abnormal flight patterns are noted. However, that type of problem related to flight stability of the arrow is more likely to be the result of poor archer release instead of improper bow tuning. (See the bow tuning section in this chapter.) Skill fundamentals must be mastered in order for properly tuned tackle to be effective.

Figure 4.11
Traditional ninety-degree nocking angle.

Bow Hold

When used in conjunction with the bow hand, terms such as "holding" and "gripping" are misnomers. They tend to be misleading as far as archery skill is concerned. The archer does not hold or grip the bow as the draw is made. The bow is held while nocking and after the arrow reaches the target. During the process of shooting, the bow is actually held in place by pressure on the bow hand at the pivot point of the bow. This pressure is the resultant counterforce of the force needed to move the bowstring in the opposite direction during the draw. There is no need to literally hold the bow. *The bow should never be gripped firmly by the hand during the drawing, aiming, and release phases of shooting.* The lack of a firmly held bow minimizes torque when the arrow is released. Torque causes erratic arrow flight.

As can be seen in figures 4.12 and 4.13, the bow is placed between the thumb and index finger. The bow arm-bow hold alignment technique should be the one which aligns the middle of the bow arm with the center of the bow. That will produce better balance between the pressures exerted on the bow handle and the line-of-pull of the bowstring. This balance of the two forces tends to reduce bow twist or torque as the shot is made, and that enhances accuracy due to the fact that the bowstring travels in a straight line as the release is made. It does not throw the arrow off-line as it starts its flight.

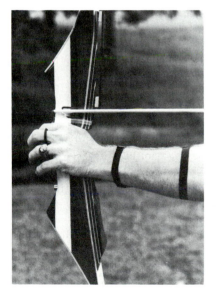

Figure 4.12
Bow hold. The archer must keep the fingers relaxed.

Figure 4.13
Bow hold—hand pressure is exerted high, low, or on the bow's pivot point depending upon the type of bow used and the archer's preference.

The grip can either be high, medium, or low in regard to the position and pressure applied by the hand to the bow in relation to the bow's pivot point. A high grip was the preference of archers who shot with the bows made primarily of wood. The high grip was needed to minimize torques. Modern bow designs have reduced (although they are not eliminated) torque problems, so more target archers now utilize medium and low grips effectively. Each archer should experiment with pressure placement of the bow hand high, on, or low in regard to the bow's pivot point. Pragmatically, the pressure placement that works and feels the best with your tackle is the one to use.

There is a tendency for the archer to let the bow pressure position slip slightly to the right during the process of shooting. This is attributable to a lapse in concentration and/or the fatigue factor. This tendency can be counteracted by a very slight counterclockwise movement of the thumb against the bow handle while extending the thumb forward toward the target.

There should be a relaxed feeling within the bow hand as much as possible. The palm of the hand should not apply pressure on the bow. The index finger may wrap around the bow, but it should not grip it. Some archers like to have the tip of the thumb and index finger touch gently as a consistency checkpoint for the bow hold, but this is a matter of personal choice. If the fingers on the bow hand are held as relaxed as possible, this will enhance accuracy. The reason for this lies in the fact that the opportunity for muscle fatigue in the forearm musculature of the bow arm is lessened considerably by not gripping. Many of the muscles that control hand gripping are located in the forearm. If they are not being contracted to grip the bow, fatigue is eliminated. This negates muscle tremor due to tiredness and helps to increase accuracy. Any deviation of the bow arm unit at the time of release, no matter how small, will have a negative effect on accurate arrow flight. Expert athletes in all sports know how to "relax under pressure" at specific times to ensure that they reach their potentials. Relaxing the important bow hold is one of these times for the archer.

Drawing

Drawing is the act of pulling the bowstring to the anchor point on the archer's face. This is analogous to cocking a pistol prior to firing a bullet. One major difference is that there are many more opportunities for human error while drawing a bowstring than while cocking a pistol. Drawing may start as soon as the arrow is nocked properly.

Controlled breathing is very important during the drawing and subsequent aiming processes. A system should be found which is comfortable for the archer during the total drawing and aiming time period. One procedure used commonly is to take a deep breath and exhale it just prior to starting the draw. Another deep inhalation is made promptly and the breath is held until the archer sees the arrow strike the target. The total elapsed time for breath-holding for most archers should be no more than ten seconds. That is the time frame for drawing, aiming, releasing, and for the follow-through.

Figure 4.14
Head rotation while addressing the target.

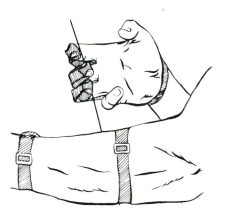

Figure 4.15
Traditional three-finger grip with shooting glove.

Some archers use a variation on this breath-holding technique. When the sightpin is in place on the target during aiming, a small amount of breath is released or exhaled. The remaining breath is held as aiming is finalized. The release is made, and breathing does not resume until the arrow is on the target. This breathing procedure tends to relieve some muscle tension. Different breathing mechanics should be tried by beginning archers until one is found that feels comfortable.

Figure 4.14 shows the very simple one-quarter turn of the archer's head toward the intended target. This seemingly simple aspect of left cervical spine rotation tends to be a definite problem for some beginning archers. It shouldn't be if the following principle is observed: *The bowstring must be drawn to the head instead of moving the head to the bowstring.* Some beginners move the head forward or flex the neck to meet the bowstring as it is being drawn. Such practices only complicate matters. The head must remain in the position shown in figure 4.14 at all times during the process of drawing, release, and follow-through.

One excellent way to maintain head position while learning is to mount a level on the bow; some bowsights come equipped with level bubbles mounted on them. If the bubble is off center, the archer should maintain the bow in a vertical position and adjust the head angle to fit the bow and string. *Levels are not legal in competition.*

Figure 4.15 shows the commonly used three-finger bowstring grip (some excellent target archers use a two-finger grip). A shooting glove is shown in figure 4.15 to protect the fingers, but a finger tab (fig. 4.16) is recommended for use over a shooting glove in target archery. Proper placement of the fingers on the bowstring prior to drawing is very important to minimize release problems. The little finger and thumb do not touch the bowstring. The remaining three fingers are placed on the bowstring with them "hooked" on the string at or slightly past the first or distal interphalangeal joints of the fingers.

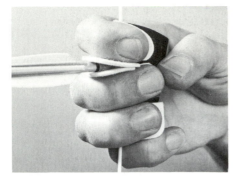

Figure 4.16
The three-finger grip while using a finger tab. Care must be taken not to exert undue or unequal pressure on the arrow nock. (Courtesy Wilson Brothers, Route 1, Elkland, Missouri 65644)

The large knuckle joints of the hand are not flexed at any time during the draw. These joints remain extended and stable at all times. The wrist is also kept straight or extended throughout the draw and release phases. The wrist should never move (flex or hyperextend) during the draw and subsequent release of the arrow.

Figure 4.16 shows the relationship between the index and middle fingers and the nock of the arrow while using a finger tab. Although this appears to be simple, position of the fingers on the bowstring next to the arrow nock is difficult to maintain as the pressure increases during the draw. The essence of the problem lies in the nature of the musculature within the hand. As fingers are flexed, it is natural for them to be drawn tightly together into a fist. This is fine for the boxer, but it creates arrow flight problems for the archer! Because the index and middle fingers are flexed and the pressure increases during the draw, the two fingers have a tendency to apply pressure on the arrow nock. Beginning archers find that the points of their arrows will wave around and fall completely off the arrow rest as the draw is made. This common problem is caused by finger pressure on the arrow nock. The archer must compensate for the gripping effect of the hand musculature prior to the draw by placing the index finger one-eighth of an inch above the arrow nock. The middle finger is placed the same distance below the arrow nock. It may seem that the arrow will become disengaged from the bowstring before the draw can be made, but this feeling will be eliminated by the use of nocking points and practice. The principle to bear in mind is: *Pressure exerted by fingers on the arrow nock should be kept at an absolute minimum prior to the draw.*

As the bowstring is being drawn, it will move from its position across the flexed distal joints of the three fingers to a position diagonal to that joint line. The amount of pressure on each of the three fingers differs. The middle finger should have the greatest feeling of pressure, and the third finger will have control

Figure 4.17
Start of the draw. To clearly illustrate finger position, a finger tab was not used.

Figure 4.18
Completed draw.

over a good percentage of the remaining force on the hand. The index or top finger has minimal pressure on it, because its role is one of control at the time of release.

The problem of pressure against the arrow nock exerted by fingers during the draw process is completely eliminated when using a release aid. This is one reason release aids have been banned in target archery. A great challenge of the sport of target archery is the ability of the archer to control this type of pressure from draw to release. Release aids eliminate a tremendous amount of human error, but, in the process, they also negate many of the aspects of target archery as a complex sport. Release aids can be used in the sport of bow hunting, and will be discussed in Chapter 6.

As the draw is started, the bow is moved from the horizontal (fig. 4.10) to a vertical position. The archer in figure 4.17 is midway through the drawing procedure. The bowstring hand is being pulled toward the anchor point on the face. During this pull or drawing action, it may be necessary for the archer to make a compensating motion within the forearm (radioulnar joint) to maintain proper string alignment and pressure on the fingers as noted above. There is a natural tendency to elevate the drawing elbow slightly during the draw. The equal and opposite motion result is the slight diagonal change of the finger-string alignment noted above. If that string position were left unchecked, it would cause some unnecessary string torque. Poor arrow flight would be the result at the time of release. That can be counteracted by rotating the forearm a few degrees clockwise (supinate the radioulnar joint) during the draw or upon reaching your anchor point. The result of that motion will move your little finger closer to your neck. The little finger should be close to the neck as seen in figure 4.19. It should not be in a position analogous to holding a tea cup at a social event!

It is essential for the archer to understand that the force for drawing the bow is provided primarily by powerful muscles on the posterior aspect of the shoulder and within the shoulder girdle. (Specific muscular detail and conditioning recommendations are presented in Chapter 8.)

The force for drawing the bow is not the major function of the musculature within the drawing arm. It is necessary that the archer keep the arm musculature as relaxed as possible during the draw. These muscles are handling external tension due to the bow weight; therefore, they are stabilizing joints of the arm. There is no need to contract them further and create more internal tension. That would be counterproductive to good accuracy. The finger grip provides a "hook" on the bow string. The shoulder and shoulder girdle muscles exert the force to move the string, and the bowstring arm is simply the lever through which the force is exerted. That is accomplished as much as possible without adding tension within the arm. This is another time when the skilled archer knows when and how to "relax under pressure." The potential for shot accuracy is enhanced, and that is the name of the game in target archery!

The completed draw is shown in figure 4.18. The bow arm and drawing arm should be studied carefully in this figure. The bow arm is abducted or raised to shoulder height. The wrist and elbow are kept extended at all times, and they remain stable or nonmoving throughout the drawing, aiming, and release phases. The bow arm will react by moving downward as the arrow is released.

The bowstring should not slap the bow arm after it has been released if the bow arm position is correct. The arm guard may be hit periodically. This can be caused by extra shoulder, elbow, or wrist movements. "String slaps" will diminish in frequency as the archer increases in skill. Some archers, however, require adjustments of their body positions to eliminate painful contusions caused by continued "string slaps" on the bow arm. If the bowstring hits the bow arm above the arm guard, the archer's stance probably should be changed to the oblique stance described previously. For most individuals this should eliminate the problem. If such a stance adjustment does not work, a bow arm adjustment should be made. The arm should always remain abducted at the shoulder joint and extended at the elbow joint as shown in figure 4.18. To make the bow arm adjustment the bow should be held in position horizontal to the ground initially. Slowly rotate the bow to the vertical position by laterally rotating the bow shoulder—move the bow counterclockwise—with the elbow extended. This may move the bow arm out of the path of the bowstring. This alignment should be checked visually prior to releasing an arrow. If that alignment adjustment does not appear to be satisfactory, the bow arm should be rotated clockwise by medially rotating the shoulder joint until the bowstring can be seen to clear the arm. This is called *canting* the bow. *(The elbow should never be flexed to allow the string to clear the bow arm.)* These bow adjustment procedures are only recommended for those people who have arm and elbow configurations that elicit continued "string slaps." The sport cannot be enjoyed or mastered if trauma occurs to the bow arm during each shot.

The alignment of the drawing arm with the arrow and bow as shown in figure 4.18 is important. If the drawing form is perfect, there will be a straight line running from the tip of the elbow through the forearm, wrist, hand, arrow nock, and shaft to the arrow point. Due to anatomic differences, it is not possible for all archers to align the drawing limb perfectly with the arrow. However, all archers should attempt to come as close as is physically possible. If this is accomplished, there will be a smoother transfer of the potential energy within the drawn bow to kinetic energy into the arrow at release. A straight alignment also facilitates a smooth release. If, as an example, the elbow is too high, it is inevitable that the index finger will exert pressure downward on the arrow nock at release. This produces erratic arrow flight. The ACTION of releasing the bowstring should produce the desired REACTION of perfect forward or linear motion of the bowstring and arrow. Any alignment error of the drawing arm during this preparation-drawing phase of the skill would cause significant arrow trajectory problems and grouping errors.

At this point, it is highly recommended that the first section of Chapter 8 be read to gain some understanding of the muscular control and forces needed as you establish a stance, nock, and draw to your anchor point. Finite control and accuracy in archery are matters of not only fine-tuning your tackle, but, more importantly, the archer must be cognizant of and fine-tune his or her own integrated neuromuscular mechanisms.

Anchor Point

The term "anchor point" means the place on an archer's face where the hand is placed with the bowstring at full draw. Anchor points are usually described as being high or low on the face (figs. 4.19 and 4.20). An anchor point on or under the mandible or jaw bone is termed low. An anchor point on or underneath the bone beneath the eye is high. Preference for a particular anchor point usually involves such factors as facial contour and type of shooting. Many field archers, bow hunters, and instinctive shooters use the high anchor point. These archers like to think they sight down the shaft of the arrow, but actually they tend to look over the arrow point. The low anchor point is used very often by target archers who rely on bowsights for aiming. Both types of anchor points can be used effectively for any kind of shooting. The archer ultimately should use the anchor point which feels most comfortable and is most consistent with good aiming.

It is recommended that the beginner utilize a low anchor point in target archery. Figure 4.20 shows a low anchor point. To learn any athletic activity, one must utilize as many senses as possible. The low anchor point involves the touch, pressure, sight, and kinesthetic senses. The index finger is placed under the chin, and pressure is applied to the mandible or jawbone by the index finger. This low anchor position on the chin allows the bowstring to bisect and *gently touch* the chin, lips, and nose. The archer must not compress the tissue on the lips and nose. For consistency, the upper and lower teeth must touch gently. The teeth should never be clenched. That type of tension is contraindicated in target archery. The

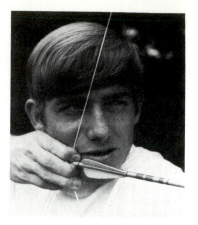

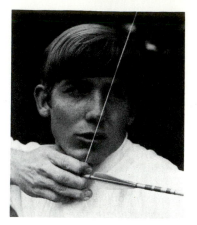

Figure 4.19
A high anchor point (to clearly illustrate finger position, a finger tab was not used). This anchor point is used most commonly by bow hunters.

Figure 4.20
The recommended low anchor point for target archery. Apply firm pressure to the chin, and the string should barely touch the nose and lips.

more one can be "relaxed" during the process of shooting the better. Static contraction of the jaw muscles has negative reactions in the degree of tension within the muscles of the neck and rib cage. The mounting of rubber "kissing buds" on the bowstring should not be done. The mild touch of the string to the lips at anchor is enough to provide the desired consistency for the draw.

Some target archers use what is termed a "side of face" anchor point if the low anchor described above seems awkward. The head is rotated toward the target as described previously. The bowstring is drawn to the point that it actually touches the side of the mouth, i.e., the right side for a right-handed archer. The chin is not moved to accommodate the string placement. The hand is anchored *under* the jaw with the index finger in contact with the side of the mandible or jawbone, similar to the low anchor position. Some archers believe that one advantage of the "side of face" anchor is the fact that the alignment of the drawing arm and arrow is easier to attain.

Some beginning archers believe that they must change the anchor point and length of draw when shooting from varying distances. This is a disastrous mistake. The anchor point and draw remain constant for all distances. Adjustments for shooting varying distances is accomplished by changing the angle of the bow arm at the shoulder joint.

Aiming

Two aiming techniques are used extensively by archers. Use of a bowsight for aiming is absolutely essential in target archery, and bowsights are also utilized by serious bow hunters who know how to gauge distances in hunting environments. (Exact distances are always known in target archery.) The most interesting and sporting aiming technique in archery is called instinctive shooting. No aiming device is mounted on the bow. Learning how to shoot instinctively is interesting, because most archers will describe their technique with slight variations.

The beginner should not be too concerned about any aiming procedure until he or she feels comfortable handling appropriate archery tackle and performing the basic fundamentals: stance, nocking, drawing, anchor point, release, and follow-through. To gain familiarity and confidence with the tackle and skill fundamentals, shooting should be performed initially over relatively short distances on the range. This eliminates the pressure to aim during the first few shooting sessions. When a general understanding of fundamentals is acquired, the archer should turn attention toward aiming and grouping ends of arrows in small patterns on the target at various distances.

Bowsight Aiming

The use of the bowsight will greatly enhance one's ability to hit the intended target; consequently, the use of a bowsight is recommended in preference to any other aiming technique. The archer must establish a bowsight setting on the bow for each shooting distance. This requires the archer to shoot a number of ends at each distance to experiment with bowsight settings. To use a bowsight, the archer places the sighting device in the middle of the intended target—gold on a regulation target archery face—and releases the arrow properly. This procedure is repeated until several ends have been shot. The archer must continually check the grouping patterns on the target face. For example, if an archer shoots six ends of arrows at a target without changing the bowsight setting and all arrows consistently group low and left on a regulation target face, the archer must move the bowsight setting device down and left for the next series of shots in order to move the grouping into the center of the target. The principle to keep in mind for bowsight adjustments is as follows. *The bowsight is always moved in the direction of the arrow grouping error.* The bowsights shown in figures 3.10 and 3.12 can be adjusted to compensate for any directional error. They can be moved left, right, up, and down to assist the archer. In the example, if the bowsight were moved properly down and left (error directions), the next end of arrows shot should group in or near the gold on the target face. This will occur if the archer executes all of the other fundamental skills properly. A perfect bowsight setting cannot compensate for a poor release!

Concentration plays an important role in the process of aiming. The total shot must be considered, i.e., each step must be performed consistently and properly leading up to aiming. There is a subjective, kinesthetic feeling the experienced archer attains when the sight pin is being moved to and held on the gold during the aiming process prior to release. Progress is made only through intensity of attention, and nothing must be allowed to interfere with concentration intensity when the sight pin is being placed on the gold. When the fundamentals are mastered, concentration controls the aiming process and the degree of scoring success one has in archery.

Does the sight pin always have to be absolutely fixed on the gold at the time of release? Each archer has adapted an aiming procedure based on his or her overall shooting style. Some do attempt perfection on every shot, striving for precise sight pin settings on the target at the instant the arrow is released. That can be frustrating at times, and it has the potential to deflate confidence. If that procedure does not work for you, move the sight pin into a target area instead of a precise spot. Release the arrow properly once the sight pin is in the boundary lines of your aiming target area. Many excellent archers use this method with good results. It removes some of the pressure concurrent with always fixating on a precise spot. Each person must define his or her target aiming areas for each specific shooting distance on the range.

One must be aware of what effect winds at different velocities and directions will have on the accuracy of arrows. Aiming rules for wind conditions differ with the archer and tackle being used. Aiming adjustments do have to be made, and the experience of shooting in windy conditions is the best teacher.

Sighting and aiming with the bow and arrow differs considerably from aiming a rifle. The rifleman tends to look down the top of the rifle barrel through a series of sights mounted on the barrel. While using the low anchor point in particular, the archer does not and should not look down the shaft of the arrow. The line of sight should be through the aiming device on the bowsight toward the intended target. The bowsight is mounted above the arrow shaft to align with the archer's field of vision. The target archery bow has an unofficial rear sighting device. The bowstring can serve this purpose.

When the archer's head is in the correct position, the archer tends to "look through" the bowstring. The string is set toward the right side of the bow as seen in figure 4.21. This avoids having the string running through the sight window

Figure 4.21
Bowstring to bow alignment used during aiming. (Bow quiver shown is used in field archery and bow hunting.)

of the bow spoiling your view. The bowsight is aligned with the center of the target. The checking of the bowstring alignment becomes automatic with experience, and most of your concentration for aiming purposes must be directed toward the sight pin. Using the bowstring alignment as a checkpoint does place the arrow in a definite direction relative to the target. The archer must be able to maintain control of the alignment between the "rear sight" and centered front sight if accurate aiming is to remain consistent. Peep sights are now available for use as rear sights on bowstrings. These are designed to be used with front mounted sights as shown in figure 3.12. However, National Archery Association rules stipulate that "a bowstring must not in any way offer aid in aiming through peephole marking or any other means."

There are archery authorities who contend that the eye nearest the target should always be closed during the act of shooting. This is a fallacy! What if the eye away from the target—the right eye for a right-handed archer—is the weak eye? Should the good eye be closed and the weak eye remain open? One would logically assume that this could have a detrimental bearing upon accuracy, and accuracy is the essence of the sport of target archery. Many fine right-handed archers shoot with both eyes open or with the left eye partially closed and the right eye open. Eye preference is a highly individualized matter. It is recommended that the beginner try shooting while using all combinations of eye openings and closures. Each archer should use the eye position which feels most comfortable and produces the best results. Some archers enjoy the sport without using either eye. They are blind! Archery is truly a sport that can be adapted for everyone.

Instinctive Aiming

Many people who hunt with rifles and bows interchangeably use high anchor points. This allows them to partially sight down the arrow shaft and over the point if a bowsight is not used. Many bow hunters do not use a bowsight, but rely upon instinctive aiming techniques. Instinctive aiming is utilized by many field archers also. There are tournaments held in field archery for bare bow and instinctive shooters exclusively. Many excellent scores are recorded in these tournaments; and the lack of mechanical aiming devices adds to the spirit of true sport.

Each archer who uses instinctive aiming usually provides a slightly different version of how this task is accomplished. Basically, the instinctive archer must have excellent eyesight and depth perception. The term "instinct" as it is used in conjunction with this style of shooting is grossly incorrect from a scientific standpoint. Through extensive practice over a long period of time, the archer increases skills related to kinesthetic awareness, conditioned responses to visual stimuli, correct reactions to wind velocities and directions, and judgment of the strengths and weaknesses of the tackle being used. These factors and others enable the skilled archer to adjust rapidly as he or she looks over the arrow point toward the intended target.

When aiming, the instinctive shooter makes several judgments regarding such things as distance to target, wind direction, and wind velocity. The archer literally perceives a space or gap between the arrow point and intended target. The bow arm moves the arrow into position for the shot. Here is where individual differences abound. Instinctive shooters approach the shot by moving the bow downward, upward, left, and right toward the target. Many, however, choose to start with the bow arm held high and move the bow downward. The release of the arrow is calculated to coincide with the visual perception of the gap being closed by the arrow point coming into view of the target. Most instinctive shooters will hold the bow motionless for a second when the gap has been closed in order to implement an efficient release. This is a "pure form of shooting," and there are many expert instinctive archers. This is particularly true in field archery and bow hunting. For target archery, the bowsight method of aiming is recommended.

Release and Follow-Through

Releasing an arrow is the most important fundamental of shooting. The key elements are: (1) relaxation and (2) concentration. The paradoxical nature of these two factors at this critical stage of shooting adds another dimension to the challenge of archery as a sport. As the reader realizes, it is extremely difficult to relax during a time of intense concentration. Both of these elements must be under complete control, however, for any degree of success in archery to be achieved.

Releasing an arrow is not the result of forceful finger extension. It is an act of relaxing or controlling muscular interaction within the bow hand, forearm, and shoulder girdle (trapezius). When the muscles controlling flexion within the three drawing fingers release some of their tension during contraction, the bowstring will move forward as a result of the pressure brought about by the bow weight at complete draw. The bowstring may literally brush the fingers away from its path if the fingers have been relaxed sufficiently. However, the finger extension usually will clear the string as it moves forward. The archer does very little muscular work at the time of release in terms of extending the finger joints. As stated previously, the main problems are *relaxation* and concurrent control of hand, forearm, and shoulder girdle muscles in conjunction with maximum *concentration* on aiming prior to and at the time of release. Extreme concentration regarding the task at hand must be accomplished by the archer from the time of nocking until the arrow is released. It is too late to concentrate when the arrow is in flight!

How can the fingers be relaxed effectively under the tension of bow weight? The key to this lies in understanding the location of the muscles and their tendons which are under the greatest tension. The muscles are within the forearm, but the tendons are located on the back of the wrist, hand, and fingers. These are the finger extensor tendons, and they are stretched as the fingers flex to grip the bowstring. The finger extensor tendons can be palpated or touched on the back of your hand. As you make a fist, you can feel the tension increase in these tendons as they are literally stretched around your knuckles. This tension is increased when the bow weight is being held by the three flexed fingers. When you are ready to release, relax the gripping fingers by concentrating on releasing tension within the finger extensor muscles on the posterior aspect or back of your hand. This "thought focus point" aids concentration and release mechanics. The archer is less likely to make extraneous motions with the fingers and hand, which would cause erratic arrow flight, if you concentrate on a specific task.

A clicker is shown mounted on the sight window of the bow in figure 3.7. A clicker is a shooting aid that has the potential to add consistency to form and enhance scores. The arrow is placed under the clicker when nocked. If the draw is made smoothly to the established anchor point, the arrow point will pass beyond the clicker in about two seconds. The clicker will "click" against the bow informing the archer—who has been concentrating on aiming—that the release can be made. The "click," like the forward motion of a hammer on a pistol, should never be anticipated. The release should be performed shortly after the "click" has been heard.

A clicker is not recommended as a shooting aid until the target archery fundamentals have been learned. The draw and the anchor point must be established. Any change of anchor point would require a clicker change. When the shooting fundamentals are consistent, have the arrow point position marked on the bow when you are at your anchor point. The clicker is then placed on the bow so only one-eighth inch of your point lies under the clicker at full draw. The "click" of the clicker is made by continuing to move the draw arm elbow backward. It is very important for the archer to understand that the drawing arm moves through its range-of-motion without interruption. The drawing elbow is moved backwards by large shoulder and shoulder girdle muscles (horizontal abductors) to the point that the clicker will be heard. The archer must never make extraneous motions with the bow arm to activate the clicker. If the clicker is mounted properly and the archer's shooting fundamentals are sound, it can be a beneficial shooting aid used to: (1) enhance shooting consistency, (2) facilitate aiming concentration, and (3) assist in the release.

The proper use of the clicker in target archery as just described has greatly enhanced scoring. The archer should practice with it to the point that clicker activation produces the proper conditioned response for release. Never anticipate!

A bow sling is recommended as an aid to help the archer during the release and follow-through phases of shooting. There are three different types of bow slings available. Any one of these will assist the archer in keeping the bow from falling to the ground after release. The type chosen is a matter of individual preference. The basic consideration in choosing a bow sling is to remember that nothing should *prematurely interrupt* the bow's movement toward the target after the arrow has been released. The function of the bow sling is to hold the bow from falling to the ground *after* the arrow is in flight beyond the bow. If the bow sling or the archer's bow hand grasps the bow at or prior to release, arrow flight will be erratic. The archer must work to ensure that this is not done, and that

Figure 4.22
Release and follow-through positions. Watch the arrow onto the target, check the positions of your bowstring hand and bow arm after release.

the bow as well as the arrow is free to move forward at release. Figure 4.21 shows the use of a finger bow sling. The finger sling is a very valuable asset in shooting. The finger sling is placed on the thumb and index or middle finger and wraps around the back of the bow. The sling enables the archer to release the arrow without worrying about the bow falling to the ground. Extraneous motions of the wrist joint are thereby minimized. The bow can be held literally after the archer sees the arrow embedded in the target.

Figure 4.22 shows proper release form. The elbow of the bowstring arm should not extend appreciably after or during the release. The bowstring hand will usually move backward in a position relatively close to the chin or neck after release. This is a natural recoil action following release. The beginner must avoid the habit of trying to release the arrow by hyperextending the wrist—moving the back of the hand toward the forearm—and allowing the bowstring to roll off the fingertips. This "plucking" of the string causes very erratic arrow grouping. Also, the elbow of the bowstring arm should never be extended during the release. The elbow should remain in the flexed position as shown in figure 4.22.

To follow-through in archery means to hold the release position until the arrow is safely embedded in the target.

The following are features of a good follow-through: (1) the fingers on the bowstring hand are relaxed, (2) head and eyes are turned toward the target, (3) the bow arm is extended toward the target, and (4) the bow hand is gripping the bow with the help of the finger sling. Why is follow-through important? It is absolutely essential for consistent performance and minute accuracy. If there are any unusual movements observed in the follow-through phase of shooting, those movements were probably initiated prior to and continued through the release phase. Obviously, this is contraindicated as far as archery accuracy is concerned.

Figure 4.23 shows the important phases of archery fundamentals from nocking to follow-through.

a   Nocking

b   Drawing

c   Low Anchor Point

d   Release & Follow-through

Figure 4.23
Nocking through the follow-through in archery. NEVER UNDERESTIMATE THE COMPLEXITY OF
SOMETHING THAT APPEARS TO BE THE EPITOME OF SIMPLICITY!

Scoring

Target archery competition is conducted in *rounds*. There are numerous championship and nonchampionship rounds, and these are discussed in Chapter 5. Each round is different in terms of the number of arrows to be shot at the various designated distances. A set number of arrows are shot during each round before the archers are allowed to go to the target, score, and retrieve the arrows. That set number of arrows (usually 3, 5, or 6) is called an *end*.

There are two target faces used for scoring purposes in outdoor target archery rounds. The 122 centimeter (48 inch) target face is used at distances of 90 meters (98.46 yards), 70 meters (76.58 yards), and 60 meters (65.64 yards). An 80 centimeter target face is used in rounds when distances of 50 meters (54.70 yards) and 30 meters (32.82 yards) are used. The center of the target should be fifty-one inches above the ground, and the target face is inclined away from the shooting line twelve to eighteen degrees.

The official target archery faces are divided into five concentric color zones. These scoring rings are each colored differently. From the center or bull's eye outward they are gold, red, light blue, black, and white. Each of these concentric colored rings is divided into two equal halves for scoring purposes. (The exact center of the gold is marked, and it is known as the "pinhole.") The ten concentric rings on the target face are used for scoring as follows: inner gold, ten points; outer gold, nine points; inner red, eight points; outer red, seven points; inner light blue, six points; outer light blue, five points; inner black, four points; outer black, three points; inner white, two points; outer white, one point.

Indoor rounds are shot at shorter distances. This requires the use of smaller target faces. Distances of 18 meters (19.69 yards) and 25 meters (27.35 yards) are common indoor distances. A 40 centimeter target face is used at 18 meters, and a 60 centimeter face is used at 25 meters.

Two archers on each target act as scorekeepers. Each archer tells the scorer the values of his or her arrows starting with the highest values first. Scores plus the number of hits per end are written on the score sheet, as shown in figure 4.24. High scores are recorded first for each end.

All arrows are to remain in their places embedded in the target mat until they have been scored and verified by the designated scorekeepers. Pulling arrows from a target mat mounted on a tripod stand should be done with caution. First, check to see that no one is standing behind you as arrows are pulled from the target. An arrow nock in the eye can be traumatic. The arrow should be grasped and pulled by the shaft near the target face with one hand. The other hand should provide a counterforce for the pull by being placed against the target mat (fig. 4.25). This simple procedure eliminates the embarrassing and costly experience of pulling a target full of arrows onto the ground.

If an arrow is embedded in the target mat up to its fletching or nock area, it should be removed by pulling it completely through the mat in the direction of its flight. That practice keeps the fletching or vanes from being damaged or torn from the shaft. If an arrow "snakes in the grass" or lies horizontal to the earth and covered with grass, it should also be removed by pulling it forward through the grass.

SCORECARD
SCHOLASTIC ROUND

Name **Al Trombetta**

Class **Archery Techniques**

40 yards						Hits	Score
9	9	9	9	9	9	6	54
9	9	7	5	3		5	33
7	7	7	5	3	1	6	30
9	9	9	7	7	7	6	48
Distance Score						23	165

30 yards							
9	9	9	9	9	9	6	54
9	9	9	9	7	7	6	50
9	9	7	7	5	5	6	42
9	9	7	5	3	1	6	34
Distance Score						24	180
Total Score						47	345

Figure 4.24
A sample scorecard for the Scholastic Round.

Figure 4.25
Arrow values are given to the scorer by the archer to whom the arrows belong. The scorer and other archers assigned to the target verify the scores. After all arrows have been scored, they are removed from the target. (Bud and Linda Clay)

There are several scoring variations to account for atypical arrow hits and other unusual situations. Arrows which rebound from the *target face* can be scored in several ways if they are witnessed. The most common procedure used for competitions other than international or national tournaments is to score these rebounds as seven points. A rebounding arrow can also be scored according to where it impacted upon the target face if it is witnessed.

The classic situation whereby one arrow impales another arrow already embedded in a scoring arrow on the target face is awarded the same value as the struck arrow. The ultimate tight group would be to have the first three arrows shot into very close proximity to the "pinhole," with the final three arrows embedded into the shafts of the first three arrows. The score would be sixty points. That would be one definition of perfection in the sport of target archery.

Arrows which strike other arrows already on the target and deflect are scored in various ways. If an arrow deflects from an arrow on the target face and sticks in the target, it is scored according to the target area where it lies. For example, an arrow that rebounds from an arrow shaft embedded in the outer gold or yellow and enters the target in the inner light blue is scored six instead of nine points.

In the case of an arrow rebounding completely off the target after hitting an arrow on the target, it would be scored the value of the arrow hit. However, it needs to be witnessed, and the damaged arrow must be identified. If both criteria were met using the example above, the rebounding arrow would be given a score of nine after deflecting off an arrow already in the outer gold ring.

Holes are marked during competition. If an arrow is witnessed as passing completely through the target mat, it is given the value of the unmarked hole on the target. This happens often in school situations when mats become worn due to excessive use. One option used in these situations is to score the arrow as a seven if it passed through a scoring ring on the target face and the hole could not be identified.

A baseball thrown by a pitcher which hits the ground in front of the plate and bounces through the strike zone of the batter can be called a strike or hit by the hitter. The analogous situation in archery whereby an arrow hits the ground, rebounds, and sticks in the target face does not score or count as a hit for the archer.

If an archer becomes confused and shoots an end of arrows on other than his or her assigned target for that round, the score of those arrows does not count. Hits are not recorded for the arrows, because they did not hit the correct target.

As noted on the example scorecard in figure 4.24, all hits are also recorded. A hit is scored for any arrow receiving a score from one through ten. An arrow embedded in the skirt or petticoat of the target face or the archery stand is not recorded as a hit. The hits are important to break ties when they occur. Three criteria are used to break ties for individual competitors: (1) the archer with the greatest number of hits is the winner; (2) if hits are also tied along with the score, the archer with the most tens wins; or (3) if hits and tens are tied, the archer with the most nines wins. If they are still tied, the Director of Shooting will declare that they were truly equal in skill for the round shot.

Common Grouping Problems

To group one's arrows consistently in the ten ring of the target regardless of the distance being shot represents the ultimate in target archery. The frustration of the sport is the fact that arrows do not always group according to the desires of the archer. The main source of help in regard to consistent grouping and fundamental adjustments must come from the individual's archery instructor or coach. However, when such help is not available, the following *teaching or coaching suggestions* for self-help can be quite valuable. Pragmatically, the archer who does not have a teacher or coach should try the suggestions and utilize the one(s) which correct the problem. In regard to the suggestions listed below, the assumption is made that the archer is using matched tackle.

Arrows Grouping Left

1. Check your stance. You may have inadvertently rotated your body slightly to the left. Place your entire body in line with the target with good weight distribution over your stance.
2. Adjust your bowsight to the left.
3. Check your bow grip. Do not involve the fingers in the gripping process; push with the bow hand; use a finger or bow sling.
4. The anchor point may have been moved to the right. Make certain the string placement is consistently touching the same facial areas and is aligned with the center of the bow.
5. Nock with the index feather skyward in the nocking position.
6. The bow may cant to the left during aiming and release; consequently, check to see that the bow is held perpendicular to the ground instead of being rotated counterclockwise during the shooting phases.
7. Check the position of the elbow on the bow arm; the elbow should be fully extended at all times from nocking through follow-through. You may be flinching or flexing the elbow at release.
8. Check to see that you are not applying too much pressure on the nock of the arrow during the draw and release with the index and middle fingers; allow an extra space between the gripping fingers and arrow nock.

Arrows Grouping Right

1. Check your stance; align your body with the target instead of rotating it to the right.
2. Adjust the bowsight to the right.
3. Adjust your grip to eliminate any possibility of a clockwise torque of the bow during release.
4. Check to see that your string alignment has not moved to the left; align the string to touch the middle of the nose and lips.
5. Concentrate on extension only of the finger (interphalangeal) joints during release. Any extraneous action such as plucking the string or pushing the string inward will cause a grouping error to the right.
6. Make certain that the bow is held perpendicular to the ground and not canted counterclockwise.

Arrows Grouping High

1. Check your stance for an even weight distribution, as opposed to placing too much weight on the leg away from the target.
2. Adjust your bowsight upward.
3. Make certain you are not pushing against the bow grip with the entire palm or heel of the hand.
4. Keep your mouth closed; upper and lower teeth should be touching—not clenched—from the time you reach your anchor point through release; check the anchor point to see that it has not moved to a lower position on your face. The hand must maintain contact with the jaw.

5. Make certain that a ninety-degree string-arrow nock position is attained during nocking. A low nocking point causes the arrow to go high. Place nocking points on your serving if they are not being used at the present time.
6. Do not inhale during the drawing, aiming, or release phases; breathing should be done before nocking, and you should exhale after the arrow is in the target.
7. Push through the bow at all times from drawing to follow-through; do not raise (abduct) the bow arm at release.
8. Take time to aim so your release will coincide with the bowsight intersecting the desired target spot instead of releasing above the target.
9. Check the bowstring fingers to make certain that the pressure is distributed with minimal pressure on the index finger.
10. Keep the wrist stabilized and extended at release so no extraneous motion occurs in that joint.

Arrows Grouping Low

1. Check your stance and make certain that weight is not being distributed over the foot nearest the target.
2. Adjust your bowsight downward.
3. Rotate the head toward the target and draw the string to your face without flexing your neck and moving the head toward the string.
4. Draw to your regular anchor point, making certain that all facial points are contacted with the string hand; an incomplete draw will reduce arrow velocity and cause the arrows to go low on the target.
5. Check to see that you have not nocked above the ninety-degree angle.
6. Hold your anchor point until the arrow is in the target. Allowing the string to move forward—"creeping"—prior to release reduces arrow velocity.
7. Check your grip to make certain that you are not applying pressure to rotate the whole bow toward the target.
8. Maintain the correct bow-arm position without lowering it (adducting the bow-arm shoulder) until the arrow is in the target.

Bow Tuning

If the archer understands and executes the shooting fundamentals properly and continues to have grouping problems, the bow may need to be tuned. Tuning a bow for an individual archer determines that arrows shot from the bow are correct for true flight. Arrows are checked for correct spine. Nocking points are evaluated, along with arrow rest placement, pressure point position, and string height. Tuning is a very individualized process, i.e., a bow properly tuned for one archer may not be satisfactory for another archer. The purchase of matched tackle is very important, as noted. Skilled archers should use a bow tuning method on several bows and ends of arrows prior to purchase to determine or validate the matched status of the arrows to the bow, and both to the archer's style of shooting.

There are several bow tuning methods. The Eliason Method is described; this method was developed by Edwin Eliason. Adjustments of arrow flight patterns must be made in the vertical and horizontal planes, and bow tuning methods determine what types of adjustments are needed.

To determine vertical plane adjustments, the archer needs to shoot several ends of his or her fletched arrows while aiming at the same spot. The shooting should be at a distance of 10 or 20 meters, depending upon the skill level of the archer. Beginning archers should use the closer distance. Once a grouping pattern has been established, an *unfletched arrow* is shot, using the same aiming spot.

The relative position of the hit of the unfletched arrow on the target to the fletched arrow group is very significant for making an accurate adjustment of your nocking point. If the unfletched arrow hits *above* the fletched arrow group, raise your nocking point until the grouping patterns coincide. Conversely, if the unfletched arrow hits below the fletched group, lower your nocking point.

To determine horizontal plane adjustments, follow the same shooting procedure, using fletched arrows and an unfletched arrow. You should determine the left or right deviations of the unfletched arrow hits in relation to the fletched arrow grouping. This is necessary to evaluate spine. If the unfletched arrow hits to the right of the fletched grouping pattern, the spine of the fletched arrows being shot is too weak. Conversely, if the unfletched arrow hits the target to the left of the fletched grouping pattern, the fletched arrow's spine is too stiff. New arrows may have to be purchased, or the archer can make several other adjustments until satisfied with arrow flight.

The following are possible bow tuning adjustments when it has been found that the *spine* of your arrows is *too stiff*. Arrows may need to be lengthened, or heavier points be placed on the existing arrows. The arrow plate may need to be moved to the right, or the spring tension on a compressible pressure point should be softened. In regard to the bow itself, adding a stabilizer may help. Decreasing the mass weight of the bow, increasing the bow weight, and/or increasing the string height may prove to be beneficial in alleviating horizontal fluctuations of arrows.

The following are possible bow tuning adjustments when it has been found that the *spine* of your arrows is *too weak*. The arrows may need to be shortened, or lighter points need to be placed on the existing arrows. The arrow plate may need to be moved slightly to the left, or the spring tension on a compressible pressure point could be increased. If a stabilizer is on the bow, try shooting without it. Increasing the mass weight of the bow, decreasing the bow weight, and decreasing the string height may prove beneficial.

Bow tuning helps to minimize or eliminate vertical and horizontal arrow flight deviations. It should be remembered, however, that the archer must have achieved good shooting fundamentals in order for bow tuning adjustments to be effective. Bow tuning is ineffective when used in conjunction with or to rationalize poor shooting fundamentals.

Review Questions

1. Make a list of important safety precautions to observe when on the range. Beside each rule, indicate the chief reason for it.
2. What systems have been found effective in controlling breathing during the draw and aiming? Which one works best for you?
3. How is target archery scored? What is the point value of each of the concentric rings on the target?
4. Name several common causes of arrows consistently grouped to each of the following, respectively: the left, the right, high, low.
5. Describe the recommended procedure for bracing a bow.
6. What are the implications of shooting with an improper brace or string height?
7. What is the recommended stance for target archers? How can you ensure stance consistency?
8. Describe the ways in which the bow may be held. Provide the rationale for your bow hold.
9. Discuss what occurs between your fingers, the bowstring, and the arrow nock during the draw. How can you counteract pressures on the arrow and fingers that will be counterproductive at the time of release?
10. How do you anchor? Why?
11. What are the guiding principles for using the target archery bowsight for aiming? What is your eye preference?
12. Describe the use of the clicker, your release, and follow-through.
13. What is meant by the term "bow tuning"?
14. When is it appropriate in target archery for you to nock your arrow; shoot; stop shooting; retrieve your arrows? Why?
15. For what reasons is a bowstringer recommended?
16. Why should all target hits be recorded (as well as the score)?

Target and Field Archery Sports

5

The purpose of this chapter is to provide an overview of the sports and activities archers pursue once they have a grasp of the fundamentals of shooting. Target archery includes not only the traditional forms of competition most people associate with the sport, but it also includes such activities as crossbow competition, clout shooting, flight archery, and competition for handicapped people. Field archery offers a variety of activities with relationships to target archery, bow hunting, and bow fishing. You may want to learn more about one or more of the archery sports after being introduced to them in this chapter.

There are three principal controlling organizations for archers: (1) National Archery Association, Incorporated, of the United States (NAA); (2) National Field Archery Association of the United States, Incorporated (NFAA); and (3) Fedération Internationale de Tir a L'Arc—International Archery Federation (FITA).

The oldest of these organizations is the NAA. It was founded in Chicago in 1879. According to the NAA Constitution adopted in August 1982, "The corporation is organized and shall be operated exclusively for educational and charitable purposes and to perpetuate, foster, and direct the practice of the sport of archery in connection with the educational and charitable purposes of this corporation and to raise funds for carrying out these purposes." The NAA is recognized as the sports governing body for archery in the United States. The NAA headquarters are now located at the Olympic Center in Colorado Springs, Colorado. *(Appendix B contains addresses of archery organizations.) The U.S. Archer* is the official publication of the NAA.

The NFAA was founded in 1939. According to the NFAA constitution, some of the organization's major purposes are, "To foster, expand, promote, and perpetuate the practice of field archery and any other archery games as the association may adopt and enforce uniform rules, regulations, procedures, conditions, and methods of playing such games. To encourage the use of the bow in the hunting of all legal game birds and animals, and to protect, improve, and increase the sport of hunting with a bow and arrow." This organization has a strong interest in conservation as it relates to bow hunting and bow fishing. *Archery* is the official publication of the NFAA.

The FITA was organized in 1931. This is the organization that promotes and encourages target archery throughout the world. The FITA organizes and arranges for regional and world championships in target archery. Records are processed through this organization. Target archery organizations of the various countries are affiliated with the FITA; this is necessary in order to coordinate national, regional, and international competitions. The FITA determines amateur eligibility for such tournaments. The NAA is affiliated with the FITA.

Target Archery

Target archery, like competitive road running, swimming, and cycling, is divided into functional age and sex groups for meaningful competition. Virtually any individual, regardless of sex or age, can compete in local, school, and state tournaments. The competitive classifications are shown in table 5.1. An archer may elect to shoot in a higher age classification, but may not shoot in a lower classification.

To encourage proper archery instruction, competition, and motivation for boys and girls, the NAA has an active Junior Olympic Archery Development Program (JOAD). Some of the World Class archers who represent the United States in national and international competitions started in this program. In addition to the JOAD program, the NAA also has a very active College Division, which encourages intercollegiate archery competition for men and women. Traditionally, there have been very strong intercollegiate archery programs in the West and Southwest areas of the United States. The annual NAA Intercollegiate Ranking Program for men and women indicates, however, that excellent individual archers are found throughout the United States.

Table 5.1 Competitive Age and Sex Classifications for Target Archery Tournament Rounds

Males		Females	
Men	18 years old or over	Women	18 years old or over
Boys		Girls	
Intermediate		Intermediate	
	15 to 18 years old		15 to 18 years old
Junior		Junior	
	12 to 15 years old		12 to 15 years old
Cadet		Cadet	
	Less than 12 years old		Less than 12 years old

Championship Rounds

The NAA has twelve approved championship rounds designated for competitions. The James D. Easton Round is recommended as the Team Round. An archery team consists of eight archers; however, only the combined score of the best four archers from a team is calculated as the team's total score for a competition. The archer with the best overall score for any round is the individual champion even if that person competes on a team.

The outdoor FITA Round is shot twice in individual and team competitions such as the World Championships and the Olympic Games. The FITA Round distances for men and women are very demanding—see table 5.2. For men, the longest distance is 90 meters (98.46 yards), and the longest distance shot by women is 70 meters (76.58 yards). If you have never shot those distances and want to gain some understanding of the challenges of target archery, it is recommended that you set up a 122 centimeter target at each of those distances, shoot, and score thirty-six arrows. At 90 meters, the best men in the world average about 8.90 for each arrow shot. The best world class women average close to 9.00 for each of the thirty-six arrows shot at 70 meters! If you have attempted those distances, you should have considerable appreciation for those feats.

Some men and women now shoot *above* 1300 for the single FITA Round—1440 is possible. The world records are considerably above 1300, but if you shoot a score of 1300 even, that means the average value for each of the 144 arrows was 9.03! One fantastic thing about archery is the fact that you do not have to average 9.03 per arrow or better to enjoy the sport. That, of course, would be great! But, in the pursuit of excellence there are many inherent values within the pursuit itself. Therein lies part of the mystique of this multifaceted sport.

Table 5.2 Examples of World Class Scores for the Single FITA Round

Distance	Total Arrows	Possible Score	Actual Score	Average Per Arrow
LADIES				
70 meters	36	360	328	9.11
60 meters	36	360	338	9.39
50 meters	36	360	335	9.31
30 meters	36	360	356	9.89
FITA Round	144	1440	1331	9.24
GENTLEMEN				
90 meters	36	360	322	8.94
70 meters	36	360	342	9.50
50 meters	36	360	345	9.58
30 meters	36	360	357	9.92
FITA Round	144	1440	1341	9.31

Table 5.2 is presented to show the reader who has not been involved with target archery a few of the actual scores that have been attained in World Class competition. These scores represent: (1) what can be accomplished in the sport, (2) a challenge to beginning and intermediate archers, and (3) potential motivation for people who like to pursue excellence! If someone else in the world has done it, why can't you? Can you be the first person to ever shoot a perfect score at 30 meters? 70 meters?

Table 5.3 presents relevant information for the outdoor and indoor NAA Target Archery Championship Rounds.

A competitive round of target archery is controlled by a Director of Shooting. Judges are assigned targets and work under the supervision of the Director. The longest distances are shot first. In order to adjust to range and environmental conditions, archers are allowed to shoot a total of six sighter arrows prior to competition. No other trial shots in any direction are allowed on the range during the competition. The archer must be emotionally, physically, and psychologically ready when he or she steps onto the target archery range.

Table 5.3 NAA Target Archery Championship Rounds

Round		Distance	Arrows Per Distance	Total Arrows	Target Size	Total Points
OUTDOOR						
FITA	Men	90,70m	36	144	122cm	1440
		50,30m			80cm	
	Women	70,60m	36	144	122cm	1440
		50,30m			80cm	
Junior Metric		60,50m	36	144	122cm	1440
		40,30m			80cm	
Cadet Metric		45,35m	36	144	122cm	1440
		25,15m			80cm	
900 Metric		60,50,40m	30	90	122cm	900
Junior 900		50,40,30m	30	90	122cm	900
Cadet 900		40,30,20m	30	90	122cm	900
James D. Easton						
	(Team)	60,50,40m	20	60	122cm	600
Collegiate 600		50,40,30m	20	60	122cm	600
Collegiate 720		50,40,30m	24	72	80cm	720
Clout	Men	165m	36	36	15m	180
	Intermediate Boys	165m	36	36	15m	180
	Women	125m	36	36	15m	180
	Intermediate Girls	125m	36	36	15m	180
	Juniors	110m	36	36	15m	180
	Cadets	110m	36	36	15m	180
INDOOR						
FITA Round I		18m	30	30	40cm	300
FITA Round II		25m	30	30	60cm	300

The Director of Shooting controls the contest by using a whistle to inform the archers when to start and stop shooting. A time limit of 2½ minutes is given to release an end of three arrows. Two blasts on the whistle is the signal for the archers to move from the waiting line to their positions on the shooting line. They address their targets. One blast of the whistle starts the 2½ minute shooting period for three arrows. Several short blasts indicate that all shooting must stop, because an emergency exists.

What type of tackle may the target archer use in competition? Compound bows may not be used. Bows must be of the classic designs such as the long bow (fig. 5.2) or recurve bow as seen in figure 3.7. The bowstring may have a serving and one or two nock locators. However, neither the serving nor the nock locators can be positioned to function as a rear sight device for the archer. An arrow rest is allowed for its specific purpose, but may not be positioned or used for aiming. One bowsight of the type shown in figures 3.7 and 3.12 are allowed. A bowsight may not include level devices, prisms, lens, or electronic gadgets. Stabilizers are approved. Arrows must be marked with the archer's name, initials, or insignia, and all of the arrows must be the same colors of fletching, nock, and crests. No release devices may be used or built in to finger protection accessories. Other accessories such as clickers, bracers, bow slings, and quivers are allowed. If the archer wears glasses, the glasses may not be modified in any manner to assist in the aiming process. All of these items, and more, are checked by the Director of Shooting and the judges prior to the contest.

Nonchampionship Rounds

There are numerous nonchampionship rounds which have been used for years. Some of these are excellent rounds to shoot in club, school, and class competitions. They are shot on the regulation 122 centimeter target face. A few of these rounds are listed below:

York Round

72 arrows at 100 yards
48 arrows at 80 yards
24 arrows at 60 yards

Columbia Round

24 arrows at 50 yards
24 arrows at 40 yards
24 arrows at 30 yards

Junior Columbia Round

24 arrows at 40 yards
24 arrows at 30 yards
24 arrows at 20 yards

Scholastic Round

24 arrows at 40 yards
24 arrows at 30 yards

Team Round

96 arrows at 60 yards—men
96 arrows at 50 yards—women

National Round

48 arrows at 60 yards
24 arrows at 50 yards

Junior American Round

30 arrows at 50 yards
30 arrows at 40 yards
30 arrows at 30 yards

Western Round

48 arrows at 60 yards
48 arrows at 50 yards

Hereford Round	Saint George Round
72 arrows at 80 yards	36 arrows at 100 yards
48 arrows at 60 yards	36 arrows at 80 yards
24 arrows at 50 yards	36 arrows at 60 yards
Windsor Round	*Saint Nicholas Round*
36 arrows at 60 yards	48 arrows at 40 yards
36 arrows at 50 yards	36 arrows at 30 yards
36 arrows at 40 yards	
Albion Round	*American Round*
36 arrows at 80 yards	30 arrows at 60 yards
36 arrows at 60 yards	30 arrows at 50 yards
36 arrows at 50 yards	30 arrows at 40 yards

Note: To change from yards to meters, multiply by 0.9144.

The York Round was used in national championship competitions for years in Great Britain and America. The distances are demanding. This was especially true for the type of tackle used during the nineteenth century. The American Round was used to establish national men champions in the United States starting in 1911. A York Round champion was also named. For several years after 1914, the national championship was based on the combined scores of double American and York Rounds. Over the years since 1879, the American women's championship has been determined by the use of the Columbia and National Rounds. The FITA Round for international competition came into vogue in 1956. It is now used extensively to determine numerous outdoor and indoor championships.

The Olympic Games

Target archery has been included in the agenda of several Olympiads during the twentieth century. Records indicate that medals were awarded in archery at the Olympic Games in 1900 at Paris, 1904 in St. Louis, 1908 in London, and 1920 in Antwerp. The sport was not revived for Olympic competition until the 1960s. Target archery was included in the 1968 Olympic Games as a demonstration sport, and it became an official gold medal sport starting with the 1972 Olympiad held in Munich. That event, highly significant to the sport of target archery, has resulted in an increased interest in target archery as an amateur sport throughout the world.

Figures 5.1 and 5.2 show some of the men and women archers who were involved in the 1908 Olympic Games. These illustrations are interesting, because they give us a chance to compare and contrast the type of archery tackle that was used in World Class competition in 1908 with tackle available to archers today. The long bow is predominant in both illustrations. The use of the long bow in this type of competition today would be almost unthinkable. It is instructive

Figure 5.1
The Fourth Olympiad of 1908 held in Shepherd's Bush Stadium in London. The men shot the York Round. The central figure in the light suit is the British gold medalist, W. Dod. (From E. G. Heath, *The Grey Goose Wing*)

Figure 5.2
The women competitors shooting the National Round at the 1908 Olympic Games. (From E. G. Heath, *The Grey Goose Wing*)

Figure 5.3
The shooting line and spectator's stadium at the 1984 Olympic Games. Photo by *The U.S. Archer.*

to compare and contrast the type of clothing worn by the competitors in 1908 with the type of clothing worn today. Also, the rather erratic arrow grouping shown in figure 5.2 would not place the archer very high in contemporary competition.

There was tremendous interest in the sport of target archery at the Games of the XXIII Olympiad held in 1984 in Los Angeles, California. (The actual competition site for archery was in Long Beach, California.) This interest was demonstrated, in part, by the fact that the competition was observed daily by over 9000 spectators in a sold-out stadium (fig. 5.3). The reader should compare figures 5.1 and 5.3 to see the difference between spectator interest in archery between the 1908 and 1984 Olympic Games. Interest in archery has also resulted in better shooting quality as demonstrated by the excellent scores which were shot during the Games (fig. 5.4). More interest in archery throughout the world has produced more elite archers who shoot better scores in competition.

Figure 5.5 is provided to allow the reader to compare and contrast the clothing, tackle, shooting stance, and equipment used by elite archers circa 1984 and 1908. Takedown, recurve bows equipped with sights and stabilizers are in vogue in 1984 compared with the long bows used in 1908. The reader should also compare the shooting stance of the archer on the line in figure 5.1 with the stance used by the archer in figure 5.5. The stereotype of stance mechanics has changed considerably over the past seven decades.

The NAA conducts tryout tournaments to select the men's and women's teams which represent the United States in national, World, and Olympic competitions. Archers are provided coaching, and some elite archers are receiving the benefits of having their shooting skills scientifically and technically analyzed by exercise scientists at the Olympic Center in Colorado Springs. Sophisticated analyses are

Archery	★	Games of the XXIII Olympiad	★	Men		
1 19A PACE	USA	641 6 10A DE KONING	BEL	613	ARROWS SHOT	072
2 18A MCKINNEY	USA	628 7 15B RUKIMIN	INA	612		
3 20A GO BJERENDAL	SWE	617 8 9C MATSUSHITA	JPN	605	WORLD RECORD	70M
4 12B POIKOLAINEN	FIN	614 9 19C YONG	CHN	602	SINGLE ROUND	339
5 8C YAMAMOTO	JPN	613 10 9A VERVINCK	BEL	601	THIS ROUND	331
★ ★ ★ ★ ★		Long Beach, California	★ ★ ★ ★ ★			

Figure 5.4
The men's scoreboard during the Games of the XXIII Olympiad showed the competitors scores in progress. Photo by *The U.S. Archer.*

Figure 5.5
Two Olympic archers on the shooting line at the 1984 Games. Photo by *The U.S. Archer.*

made involving the archer, his or her tackle, and the interrelationship of the two while shooting. These relate primarily to the anatomic kinesiology, biomechanic, and physiologic parameters involved in shooting. High speed cinematography is utilized extensively, as well as other physics instruments to measure and evaluate such elements as the forces and velocities contributing to or detracting from the archer's skill. This scientific information is communicated from the exercise scientists to the archers and coaches, to be synthesized with the technical aspects of shooting. The merging of scientific theory with the technique or practice of archery has the potential to increase skill at all levels of competition, but it is especially needed at the Olympic level.

To determine amateur status and eligibility, the NAA is governed by the eligibility rules of the FITA and the International Olympic Committee. These rules are very specific, ranging from the maximum value of trophies or prizes retained by the archer to the uses of medical and doping substances. An archer desiring to be a member of an Olympic team must meet the amateur status criteria.

There are organizations for professional archers. The NAA and NFAA provide Professional Divisions for shooting activities. The Professional Archery Association was founded in 1961. Names and addresses of all types of archery associations are provided for you in Appendix B. You are encouraged to contact any or all of these organizations to learn specifically what they offer the archer.

The United States' archers have performed very well in Olympic competition. Currently there are archery programs in place to continue instruction, development, and recognition of young archers. With good instruction and diligent practice, the individual reading this book could possibly develop into a potential archery champion of national and international caliber within a period of one to two years. This is not impossible if the individual has tremendous intrinsic motivation toward this type of goal. A young adult or adult with the proper attitude, interest, aptitude, and motivation could possibly earn a position on the Olympic team in archery. To represent one's country on an Olympic team is one of the highest honors an individual can obtain. It is both fitting and proper that archery, one of the oldest sports, is now a part of the Olympic Gold Medal Sport's agenda.

Crossbows

Crossbows have been a part of the history of man for over 2400 years. The Greeks developed a form of crossbow about 400 B.C., and the Chinese were using crossbows in battles as early as 341 B.C. The military use of these bows as weapons was very popular from the eleventh to the sixteenth century. They gradually declined as weapons of war with the onset of firearms. But, humans remain fascinated by the crossbow today. As a result, there is a growing interest in the use of the crossbow in sport. There are opportunities to use the crossbow (fig. 5.6) in such diverse activities as flight shooting, hunting, field shooting, and match competition. There are numerous state, national, and international championships organized to accommodate the interests of crossbowmen. These activities

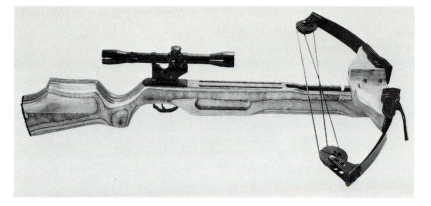

Figure 5.6
A modern compound crossbow; one of many designs used by archers for hunting, field, match, and flight competitions. (Courtesy Precision Shooting Equipment, 2550 North 14th Avenue, Tucson, Arizona 85703)

are organized under the auspices of several crossbow associations around the world. (The names and addresses can be found in Appendix B for the reader who wishes to learn more about crossbow activities.)

Just as the FITA is the major international controlling organization for target archery, the Internationale Armbrustschutzen Union (IAU) serves an analogous function for crossbow shooting. The IAU has nineteen affiliated members representing large and small countries throughout the world. Match crossbow competitions and Field crossbow shooting are controlled by the IAU and its affiliates.

The main difference between Match crossbow shooting and Field crossbow shooting lies in the clothing allowed to be worn by the Match competitor. He or she can wear leather gloves, boots, and shooting jackets, whereas the Field crossbow archer dresses like the Target archer in NAA competition (fig. 5.3). All Field shots must be made from the standing position, and all competition is on outdoor ranges. Match competition, on the other hand, may include indoor as well as outdoor targets. The indoor targets may be as close as 10 meters. The International Field Crossbow Round requires a standard 80 centimeter FITA target face. Ninety arrows are shot; therefore, a perfect score would be 900. Thirty arrows are shot from 65 meters, 50 meters, and 35 meters respectively. *The better men and women shooters will have scores at or above 800* for this round. That gives you some idea of what is being accomplished.

The NAA conducts crossbow championships on an annual basis. Most of the rules of target archery also apply to crossbowmen, but the two always compete separately. Field shooting at outdoor targets is done with bows of 80 pounds or less. Fifty pounds is recommended for indoor competitions. No mechanical aids can be used to draw the bows unless the individual is handicapped physically.

The arrows shot from crossbows are also called bolts. The crossbowman cannot use a magnifying sight, but prismatic sights and level bubble sights are allowed. Binoculars and scopes may be used to locate hits on the target.

The reader interested in the crossbow is referred to the Bibliography for references on this fascinating part of archery. The National Crossbowmen of the U.S.A. is the United States affiliate of the International Armburst Union. The U.S. Match–Crossbow Shooting Association is also affiliated with the IAU. Both of these organizations would be good contacts for readers interested in learning more about crossbow activities. Addresses are in Appendix B.

Clout Shooting

Historically, clout shooting can be traced at least as far back as the period of English archery prior to The Hundred Years' War. Clout shooting has been used in many wars throughout history. The archers shot great volleys of arrows into the air in clout fashion toward their opponents. This was an early and effective form of aerial bombardment. The reader can readily understand the apprehension of a soldier as a volley of arrows numbering in the thousands suddenly descends into his area. In addition to being an effective killing technique, on numerous occasions the arrival of the arrows caused panic among the ranks.

From that historic origin of one use of archery in war there has evolved the fascinating sport of clout shooting. As noted in table 5.3, the Clout Round is now an official NAA Target Archery Championship Round. The target in clout shooting is laid out on the ground. Its outer circle measures 15 meters (49.20 feet) in diameter. It is divided into five concentric scoring zones with each measuring 1.5 meters (4.92 feet) in width. The *Clout* is a brightly colored flag placed on a wooden pole 19.69 inches above the ground in the center of the target. The scoring values of each scoring zone starting from the center outward are five, four, three, two, and one. Arrows that stick in the clout flag are given the value of five.

Target archery tackle is used for the Clout Round. As you see in table 5.3, the Clout Round distances vary based on the sex and age level of the archer. The longest distance is 165 meters (180.4 yards) for men and intermediate boys, and the shortest distance is 110 meters (120.34 yards) for junior and cadet boys and girls. Ladies and intermediate girls shoot from 125 meters (136.75 yards). All of these distances are challenging, and the distance adds "spice" to the clout shoot. You are given only six practice or sighter arrows prior to beginning the Clout Round.

The Clout Round consists of 36 arrows. All arrows are shot from the single distance specified for your age and sex. A perfect score would be 180, but that is easier said than done! Clout shooting is an intriguing part of the sport of archery.

Flight Archery

Most people think of archery in all of its forms as placing the emphasis on accuracy. That is true with perhaps the lone exception being flight archery. Flight shooting places the premium on *how far* an arrow from a bow or crossbow bolt can be projected. This sport has great appeal to individuals who are fascinated by the physics and biomechanics of the specialized bows constructed specifically for flight shooting. The sport demands an understanding of trajectories and aerodynamic properties of arrows and bolts. The physics involving the interrelationships between the mechanical system of the bow, its kinetic and potential energy capabilities, and the forces acting efficiently on the arrow to put it into flight are all fascinating aspects of this sport. All of that knowledge regarding the tackle of flight shooting must be integrated with the proper techniques of shooting in order to attain the desired maximum distances. That is a challenge!

What is the farthest an arrow has ever been shot by a human without benefit of fuel, explosive devices, or air currents in a recognized flight shooting event? As it should be, that record is held by "The Father of Flight Archery," Harry Drake (fig. 5.7). The record was established in 1988. *He established a new World Crossbow Flight Record of 2047 yards, 2 inches, or 1.16 miles!* Harry Drake has also shot an arrow from an unlimited footbow 2028 yards, i.e., 1.15 miles! Those are amazing feats.

In competition, shooters are allowed a maximum of four rounds of flight consisting of six arrows each using any type or weight or combination of types and weights of the several varieties of bows sanctioned.

Competitions are held separately in flight archery involving "Regular Flight" and "Broadhead Flight." A regular flight bow may be designed with a special handle and overdraw capabilities, but any recurve bow may be used in "Regular Flight" events. The arrows are a minimum of fourteen inches in length from the floor of the nock to the tip of the point. They are designed with a barrel shape, and the vanes are small. The "Broadhead Flight" competition involves the usage of unaltered broadhead points as used in bow hunting. There are standards for men and women, which specify the minimum weights of the broadheads.

Flight competition is divided according to age and sex. Men and Women (fig. 5.8) categories are for people eighteen years of age and older. Intermediate and Junior categories are for ages twelve through seventeen years. The Cadet level of competition includes children eleven years of age and under. There are also divisions for "amateurs" and "nonamateurs" in this sport.

There are several bow classifications used in flight archery. Compound bows are divided into specific weight divisions plus an "unlimited" division for each age and sex group. In addition, there are competition classifications for crossbows and primitive bows. Broadhead flight shooting might also include recurve and longbow events.

Table 5.4 provides the reader with a few examples of the distances achieved with specific bows in flight shooting. It is a very interesting and challenging archery sport that you may want to try.

Figure 5.7
Harry Drake, "The Father of Flight
Shooting," using a 25 kg flight bow in a NAA
Flight Championship. (Courtesy of *The U.S.
Archer;* photo by Bob Rhode)

Figure 5.8
Flight shooting includes competitive
categories for women and men. Sherrie
Reynolds is shown using a compound flight
bow in competition. (Courtesy of *The U.S.
Archer;* photo by Bob Rhode)

Table 5.4   Examples of Flight Shooting Distances Attained With Different Types of Bows

Bow Category	Archer's Name	Distance Yards-Feet-Inches
MEN		
Unlimited Footbow	Harry Drake	2028 - 0 - 0
Unlimited Longbow	Don Brown	345 - 1 - 7
50.0 lb. Primitive Bow	Daniel Perry	295 - 2 - 3
Unlimited Compound Bow	Bert McCune, Jr.	1159 - 2 - 6
Crossbow	Harry Drake	2047 - 0 - 2
Unlimited Primitive Bow	Daniel Perry	283 - 2 - 7
WOMEN		
18 kg Flight Bow	Sherrie Reynolds	740 - 1 - 8
Unlimited Longbow	April Moon	212 - 2 - 7
Unlimited Compound Bow	April Moon	807 - 1 - 3
Unlimited Flight Bow	April Moon	1039 - 1 - 1
Footbow	Arlyne Rhode	1113 - 2 - 6

For further information on flight shooting, the reader may want to write to the NAA Flight Shooting
Committee—see Appendix B.

Figure 5.9
Former U.S. National Wheelchair Champion, Robert Norvelle, follows through after a shot. He has shot 2307 for the Double FITA Round. (Courtesy of *The U.S. Archer;* photo by Raenel Jones)

Archery for the Handicapped

The people and organizations that govern archery have long recognized the fact that this is one sport that can involve virtually everyone. The NAA rules specifically stipluate that no handicapped archer shall be barred from a tournament unless his or her mechanical aids provide an advantage over the other archers or the shots cannot be made within the time sequence. Archers in wheelchairs can shoot on the line from their chairs. There is also an organization for wheelchair archers, The National Wheelchair Athletic Association (see Appendix B for the address). This organization is involved with competitions in archery and other sports at the state, regional, national, and international levels (fig. 5.9).

Archery as a sport can be adapted to meet the special needs of people with various types of disabilities. This is done in many school situations and can also be accomplished within the environment of a yard at home. With some thought and ingenuity, archery tackle can be modified for use by people with all kinds of dysfunctions. As one example, blind people can enjoy target archery by simply placing sound indicators on the targets. Each shot can be scoped for the archer, and he or she is informed about the arrow placement on the target. It is then up to the blind archer to make kinesthetic sense adjustments for aiming the next arrow.

The National Wheelchair Athletic Association makes very few adaptations or special accommodations for the target archers in their competitions. Their events are not separated by classification of the disability except in the cases of some quadriplegics. If a quadriplegic can shoot without a mechanical release, he or she competes in regular archery rounds. If a mechanical release is needed due to upper limb weakness or some other dysfunction, quadriplegics with this situation in common compete against each other in a separate division of each round. For shooting stability, novice quadriplegic archers who use mechanical release aids may be strapped into their wheelchairs during the first year of competition only. These archers may also receive help in nocking their arrows. All of the other challenging and difficult aspects of the sport must be met by the archer.

Jim Cowart, an adapted physical education specialist with the Alameda Schools in Hayward, California, is a professional who has modified archery tackle so his students can enjoy the sport. Figure 5.10 shows an adapted archery bow in use by a student with some neuromuscular limitations. The bow is mounted on a camera tripod, and a release aid (Stuart Hot Shot Release) was placed where the student could trigger it. The teacher or another student makes the draw and loads the string into the release aid, but the physically handicapped student must make the all-important vertical and horizontal aiming adjustments allowed by the camera tripod. When the student has the aiming alignment desired, the release aid is triggered by the finger motion. The arrow is on its way, and the student has the pleasure of knowing that he or she has plotted its trajectory. If the

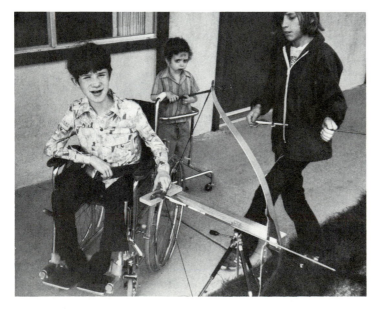

Figure 5.10
A student with muscular dystrophy enjoying the sport of archery by using an adapted bow with a mechanical release device. (Courtesy Jim Cowart, Schools of Alameda County, Hayward, California 94501)

arrow does not go where it was intended, the handicapped archer must go through the same mental processes and make the necessary aiming adjustments in the same manner as any other archer.

Tackle modifications can be made to handle most problems the handicapped person would have in archery. If the student cannot keep or control the arrow on the bowstring, the serving can be increased in circumference or the plastic arrow nock may be narrowed. If the student cannot keep the arrow on the arrow rest while drawing, the Bear Arro-Guide arrow rest may be modified with a strip of plastic to contain the arrow without having a negative affect on its trajectory and velocity. Jim Cowart has utilized these modifications with success for his adapted physical education students.

The compound bow has considerable potential for people with neuro-muscular strength and endurance problems. One of the main features of this type of bow is the fact that it eliminates the stacking effect at full draw. This means that a person with moderate strength can hold it at his or her anchor point without too much difficulty, because the bow weight has been minimized at full draw. A stronger student or instructor can draw the bow, but the handicapped student can hold it at full draw, aim, and release. Therefore, the compound bow has the potential to allow many handicapped individuals to deal with the main problems which make archery a sport. There should be target archery tournaments for handicapped people, allowing them to use compound bows. There should be one division with release aids, and one division without them.

There should be opportunities for handicapped archers to participate in virtually all aspects of archery. That not only includes target archery, but clout shooting, flight shooting, and field archery as well. *Archery can be a sport for everyone who enjoys it!*

Field Archery

Field archery is different from target archery primarily due to the fact that a target course is laid out in wooded and open areas. Field archers walk the course. Twenty acres make an ideal field archery course, while shooting distances range from fifteen feet to eighty yards. The size and type of target face are determined by the distance being shot. A field course consists of fourteen targets; these are called a unit. Two units or twice around one unit constitutes a round in field archery. Figure 5.11 is a diagram of a typical field archery club with a 14-target basic unit. These units are usually developed to simulate hunting conditions.

The NFAA has 50 chartered associations and more than 1200 affiliated clubs. These clubs have a membership representing over one hundred thousand archers. The clubs hold many local tournaments throughout the year for members. Each state holds a field archery championship, and these are well attended. The National Field Archery Championship Tournament draws from 500 to 1000 competitors annually.

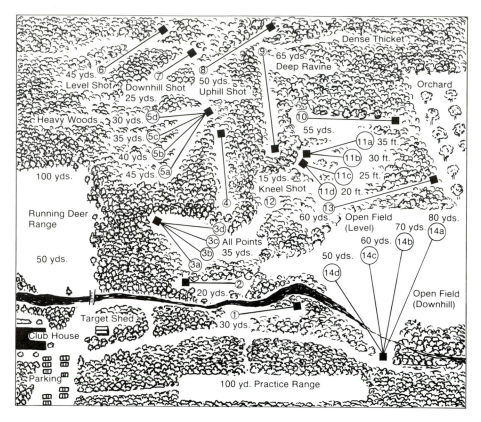

Figure 5.11
A field archery club with a 14-target basic unit.

The NFAA is dedicated to bow hunting, bow fishing, conservation, the preservation of large and small game animals, and to the promotion of a wide variety of competitions. The organization of the NFAA is structured to administer to the needs of the archers interested in these areas. (See Appendix B for the NFAA address.)

Shooting Equipment

The type of tackle that can or cannot be used by the field archer depends upon the style of shooting used. There are six styles in field archery: (1) freestyle, (2) freestyle limited, (3) barebow, (4) competitive bow hunter, (5) bow hunter freestyle, and (6) bow hunter freestyle limited. Compound, long, and recurve bows are all legal in field archery. Table 5.5 summarizes some of the major differences between shooting styles and the use of sights, release aids, stabilizers, and nocking points. Other equipment differences also exist regarding broadheads, arrow rest, clicker usage, and other equipment.

Figure 5.12
Interchangeable arrow for broadhead and field point use. A field archery point is being screwed into the shaft.

Table 5.5   Field Archery Shooting Styles and Legal Equipment

Style	Sight(s)	Release Aid	Stabilizers	Nocking Point
Barebow	No	No	Yes	Yes
Freestyle	Yes	Yes	Yes	Yes
Freestyle Limited	Yes	No	Yes	Yes
Competitive Bowhunter	No	No	One	Yes
Freestyle Bowhunter (5 points & peep)	Yes	Yes	One	Yes
Freestyle Limited Bowhunter (5 points & peep)	Yes	No	One	Yes

Since most field archers are interested in bow hunting and/or bow fishing, the total weight of the arrow needs to approximate the arrow weight when it is fitted with the broadhead point. Practice with broadheads or shooting with them at field archery targets can be impractical because of the damage they inflict. Field points are made to match the heavy weight of the hunting broadheads used by the archer. A threaded bushing can be fitted into the arrow shaft. Field points and broadheads can be used interchangeably. A single set of arrows can be used for field archery practice and hunting if the weights are matched perfectly. This setup is shown in figure 5.12. The field points are much easier to use for most regular practices. Broadheads should be used for practice before hunting season and to tune the hunting bow.

Divisions of Competition

Age and sex divisions are established in field archery to allow for equitable competition. In addition, the NFAA has a sophisticated handicapping system designed to be an equalizer for archers with different abilities. The divisions for competition plus the handicap system make competitions very interesting for all competitors.

The Adult Division is for men and women eighteen years of age and older. Archers who are sixteen and seventeen years of age compete in the Young Adult Division, and the Youth Division is for archers ages twelve through fifteen. Cub archers are under twelve years of age. There is also a Professional Division for men and women eighteen years of age and over. All of these divisions of competition and the styles of shooting noted previously provide opportunities for competition at the National and Sectional tournaments. An additional division is added for archers fifty-five and over at National tournaments. This is known as the Senior Division. It is optional at Sectional and State levels.

In addition to these divisions of competition, the NFAA now has a program in place to accommodate the needs and interests of young people under the age of eighteen who shoot with compound bows. This activity is known as the NFAA Junior Bowhunter Program. It provides a special award system plus competition for junior compound shooters. It is designed to help interested and motivated young archers into competitions at the State, Sectional, and National levels. Guidance is also provided for young people who want to develop their hunting skills or who desire just to pursue the sport of field archery. The program offers Indoor and Outdoor Field and Animal Rounds. These are the Freeman Bowhunter Round, Indoor Round, Animal Round, and Field Round. Achievement level scores for patches and awards are established for each of these rounds based on the shooting styles: (1) barebow, (2) freestyle limited, or (3) freestyle. What may or may not be used with these styles of shooting is outlined for you in table 5.5. The NFAA Junior Bowhunter Program helps the young archers get started in the sport correctly, and that is an important factor.

Official NFAA Rounds

The number of arrows shot, targets, shooting positions, rules, and scoring differ widely between field archery rounds. There are thirteen official NFAA Rounds. Eight of these are shot outdoors, and the remaining five are indoor rounds:

Outdoor

1. Field Round
2. NFAA Expert Field Round
3. Hunter Round
4. Animal Round
5. 15 Target "300" Field Round
6. 15 Target "300" Hunter Round
7. 15 Target "300" Animal Round
8. NFAA International Round

Indoor

1. NFAA Indoor Round
2. NFAA Indoor Championship Round
3. NFAA Freeman Round
4. Freeman Bowhunter Indoor Round
5. Flint Bowman Indoor Round

Generally, the target faces used for most of the outdoor rounds are 65, 50, 35, and 20 centimeters in diameter, based on the distances to be shot. Targets for the various rounds have different configurations, and the animal rounds use animal targets only. These targets are placed in four diminishing size groups. Animals such as elk and moose are in the largest group while ducks and jack rabbit targets are in the smallest group. The diversity of the outdoor rounds and their placement within the shooting unit help make field archery challenging.

The indoor rounds have targets of various sizes and designs. They are 40, 35, 20, and 16 centimeters in diameter, depending upon the round. Animal targets may be used instead of the 40 centimeter target face in the Freeman Bowhunter Indoor Round. Twenty yards is the greatest distance shot in the first four indoor rounds listed above. Thirty yards is the greatest distance shot in the Flint Bowman Indoor Round. These distances make indoor shooting popular.

Awards

Any effective organization has a system to recognize the efforts of its members. The NFAA has a good awards system ranging from NFAA Membership Pins to the Compton Medal of Honor. The latter award is recognized as the most highly esteemed honor in all archery. NFAA bow hunters gain recognition by qualifying for the following game awards: (1) Art Young Big Game Awards, (2) Art Young Small Game Awards, (3) Bow Hunter Pin, (4) Expert Bow Hunter Pin, (5) Master Bow hunter Medal, and (6) the Diamond Buck Award for the largest deer based on antler measurements.

If a field archer telescopes an arrow during a round when the arrow is lodged in the highest scoring area of a target, he or she would be eligible for entry into the Fellowship of Robinhood. And, on a less prestigious note, a field archer who commits an unwitting error or "boner" while hunting becomes eligible to enter The Order of the Bone! Recognition is also given in the NFAA Bowfisher Program to those archers taking the largest carp and gar during the year. The Bowfisher Program is discussed in Chapter 7.

Field archery, like other archery sports and activities, is a challenging and fulfilling endeavor. It can be enjoyed throughout a lifetime from "Cub" to "Senior" Division status.

Review Questions

1. What are the three main organizations for archers?
2. What equipment and tackle modifications are illegal in target archery competition?
3. How does the NAA contribute to the development of archers for the Olympic Games?
4. How does a field archer qualify for the Fellowship of Robinhood and The Order of the Bone?
5. Describe the programs and competitions promoted through the NAA.

6. What would be a good, competitive score for the FITA Round?
7. In target archery during a round, what does several short blasts on the whistle by the Director of Shooting indicate?
8. What are names, functions, and purposes of the organizations that control crossbow activities?
9. Describe the differences between match and field shooting with crossbows.
10. Compare and contrast clout and flight shooting.
11. What distances are attained in flight shooting with the various types of bows? What is the longest distance ever recorded for an arrow shot from any type of bow? How long would it take you to run that distance to retrieve the arrow?
12. Describe the ways in which archery may be used by handicapped archers and the levels of competition for handicapped archers.
13. What are the international controlling organizations for target archery, field archery, and crossbows?
14. Describe the programs and competitions promoted through the NFAA.
15. What are the six shooting styles used for competition by the NFAA?

Bow Hunting

6

The sport of bow hunting has become increasingly popular in the last few years. Its gain in popularity is documented by the increasing numbers of archery hunters who register for license and permits with the official wildlife agencies (see Appendix A). As one example, in 1971, 6412 archery hunters went after deer in Arizona. By 1987, that number had increased to 16,132 archers who went into the field bow hunting for deer. During this same time period in Arizona, archers seeking permits to hunt elk increased from 659 to 3469. These same trends have been observed in other states.

There are numerous reasons given by hunters for using the bow and arrow as primary hunting tools. One of the most common is that the inherent challenge of bow hunting has rewards that cannot be met by any other hunting methods. The bow hunter is limited to very close ranges and has to understand thoroughly the animal's habits as well as its environment in order to be successful. Seasons set by state game and fish departments are generally longer for archery than for firearms. This gives the archer a chance for more time in the field. Also, there is a wider variety of small and large game animals that can be hunted, and this makes the sport more attractive. Many archers indicate that they prefer the relatively uncrowded conditions found in the field during the bow hunting seasons. Unfortunate hunting accidents are not likely to occur during bow hunting seasons; however, they are fairly common during firearm seasons.

With the increase in the number of people participating in archery activities and particularly bow hunting, there has been a corresponding increase in the refinements of archery tackle. Competition between the many archery companies has resulted in a wide selection of fine bow hunting equipment. With the large number of specialized hunting products on the market, the process of selecting equipment can become a confusing task. Because of this, it is necessary to have a basic understanding of bow hunting tackle, so the correct decisions can be made when purchasing archery equipment.

If the archer chooses good tackle, with slight modifications, it can also be used for various forms of archery. The principles for purchasing hunting tackle are almost the same as those for buying target archery tackle discussed in Chapter 3. There are, however, decided differences between target archery and bow hunting tackle. *The individual who wants to participate in bow hunting exclusively should purchase tackle designed specifically for bow hunting purposes.*

Hunting Bows

The modern hunting bows are a far cry from the bows our ancestors used or the ones found in primitive societies today. Bows that have provided food and protected primitive people for centuries look like toys when compared to current bow hunting equipment. Though the primitive hunting bows were not as efficient, the individual who used them possesed excellent hunting skills. Also, those people had a motivational factor that most bow hunters today do not have—hunger!

Bows used commonly for modern hunting include the crossbow, straight bow (long bow), recurve, and compound. Each step in this progression represents an improvement in the ability of a bow to transfer its potential energy into kinetic energy. While it is virtually impossible to make a bow that is 100 percent efficient, the best designs of today's bows are reaching an energy storage efficiency in the range of 80 to 84 percent.

Crossbows

The crossbow is one of the romantic weapons of archery. The legend of *Wilhelm Tell* helped romanticize the crossbow. Most people know what a crossbow is but have never seen one outside of a museum. A quality crossbow camouflaged for bow hunting is shown in figure 6.1.

The use of the crossbow as a legal hunting implement has gained momentum in the past several years. Some states now allow its use for a few of the larger game animals as well as for varmint and bird hunting. As with recurve and compound bows, specific criteria are set by state game and fish commissions specifying the poundage of the crossbow, the length of the bolt, and the size of the

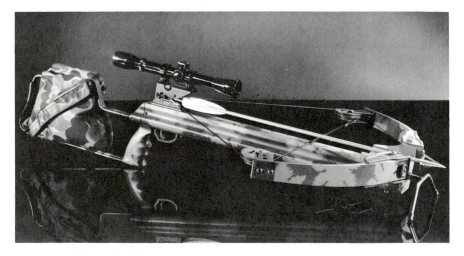

Figure 6.1
A hunting compound crossbow camouflaged and ready for use with a broadhead on the bolt or arrow. (Courtesy Precision Shooting Equipment, 2550 North 14th Avenue, Tucson, Arizona 85703)

actual broadhead. In Arizona, for example, a hunting crossbow must have a minimum draw weight of 125 pounds and shoot at least a 16-inch bolt. The bolt must be tipped with a broadhead that has a metal cutting edge of at least ⅞ of an inch in length.

If you are interested in bow hunting with crossbow, keep in mind that state regulations do vary regarding the legal use of the crossbow. You must contact the appropriate wildlife agency in the area you wish to hunt *prior* to going into the field. They will supply you with the latest rules and regulations pertaining to crossbow hunting.

The modern crossbow has gone through several design changes in recent years. The newer generation of crossbows of the type shown in figure 6.1 use the same mechanical devices as the compound cam bows for increasing arrow velocity. They also use modern construction materials that can withstand the added stresses on the limbs and elsewhere. These factors make the modern crossbow highly efficient for use in target archery and bow hunting.

Long Bows

Long bows such as those shown in figures 5.1 and 5.2 can be used for hunting. However, they are rarely used any more, since they are mechanically inefficient, as discussed in Chapter 3, when compared to recurved and compound bows. If you use a long bow for hunting, the emphasis must be placed on the term *hunting*. The bow hunter who uses the long bow must be an excellent stalker and hunter with indepth knowledge of the game being sought. Some legendery archers of the past, Howard Hill, Dr. Saxton Pope, and Art Young, used the long bow effectively in the field. It can be done. If you desire "true sport" while bow hunting, the long bow may be the bow for you.

Recurve Bows

The recurve principle has been known for a long time but was not fully utilized until modern materials were developed. Plastics and adhesives have made it possible to laminate layers of material that will remain intact under the stresses that a bow is exposed to during the shooting process. With a working recurve bow, the tips will point away from the archer when unstrung. However, when braced, the tips are pulled back and will usually point upwards with the string contacting the belly of the bow for at least two inches. If the string does not contact the bow in this manner, the bow will not work to its best mechanical advantage. A takedown recurve hunting bow is shown in figure 6.2. The bow is equipped with a covered bow quiver, brush buttons, and string silencers.

The conventional recurve bow will stack its weight as the string is drawn to the anchor point. The peak weight of the bow increases, and there is added pressure on the drawing hand fingers. Most people begin with bow or draw weights that they can handle comfortably and then grow into higher poundage equipment. It makes no sense to purchase a bow that is too heavy in terms of poundage. This will only cause accuracy and technique problems that may be hard to unlearn.

Figure 6.2
A take-down recurve hunting bow equipped with a covered bow quiver, brush buttons, and string silencers. (Courtesy Black Widow Bow Company, H. C. R. #1, Box 357-1, Highlandville, Missouri 65669)

Famous bow hunters such as Fred Bear and Doug Kittridge used the recurve bow extensively in past years and added to its popularity. Recurve bows in the hands of experienced archers like these have taken the largest and most dangerous animals found in the world. The recurve bow was the primary choice of most archers until the mid-1970s. Since that time it has lost some of its status to a new generation of bows called compounds. However, many bow hunters surveyed indicated that they were returning to the use of the recurve bow after using compound bows for several years. The general feeling was that the recurve bow made hunting more of a sport than using the compound bow.

Compound Bows

The compound bow is by far the most popular hunting tool of the modern bow hunter. A check of recent entries into the Pope and Young Records for trophy class animals shows that most were taken by this type of bow. The two-wheel compound bow seems to be the most popular. An example of a two-wheel bow and the terminology for the compound bow are shown in figure 6.3.

As discussed in Chapter 2, the compound bow was invented in January 1966 by H. W. Allen specifically to make bow hunting more efficient. One of his early models is shown in figure 6.4. The reader can gain some understanding of the

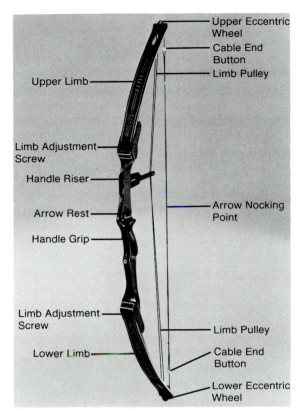

Upper Eccentric Wheel

Cable End Button

Limb Pulley

Upper Limb

Limb Adjustment Screw

Handle Riser

Arrow Nocking Point

Arrow Rest

Handle Grip

Limb Adjustment Screw

Limb Pulley

Lower Limb

Cable End Button

Lower Eccentric Wheel

Figure 6.3
A two-wheeled bow with compound bow terminology. (Courtesy Precision Shooting Equipment, 2550 North 14th Avenue, Tucson, Arizona 85703)

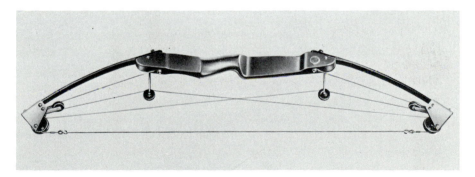

Figure 6.4
An early model (c. 1970) of the Allen Compound Bow. (Courtesy of Allen Archery, 201 Washington Street, Billings, Missouri 65610)

evolution of the compound bow by comparing and contrasting figure 2.11, which shows the original model, with other compound bows shown in this chapter and elsewhere.

The compound bow generates greater foot-pounds of energy than composite bows due primarily to the eccentric pulleys which can be seen on the bows in figures 6.3 and 6.4. This pulley system allows peak pull weight poundage at mid-draw. This effect has two advantages:

1. There is no stacking effect in a compound bow at full draw. The peak poundage is at mid-draw.
2. At release, the poundage increases to peak, and this gives a major increase in foot-pounds of energy for application to the arrow.

The compound bow, when drawn, has a "peak" weight and a "let-off" weight. In most cases, compound bows, because of their eccentric wheel design, will have a "let-off" weight of approximately 30 to 50 percent. This means that if you shoot a 60-pound compound bow with a 50 percent "let-off" factor, the actual weight held on the fingers at full draw will be 30 pounds. As you can see, this could be advantageous in a situation where the hunter would have to hold in a fully drawn position for any length of time.

The newer cam wheel compounds are essentially the same as the regular compounds, with the exception of the wheel designs. Instead of a round wheel at the tip, there is a cam-shaped device. These bows generally produce faster arrow velocities than eccentric compounds and recurves of the same poundage. The advantage in this faster cam-type bow lies in the arrow trajectory. If the arrow velocity is higher, the amount of drop is less. This means that the margin for error, due to arrow drop, is decreased. At close ranges the estimation of distances is not as crucial with a cam compound as it is with a recurve bow. An error of 5 yards in estimating distances of 30 yards or less will usually result in a kill shot. This same error with a recurve bow of lower arrow velocity may result in a missed shot or a wounded animal.

Bow Weight

Hunting bows have higher draw weights than their target bow counterparts. While the minimum draw weights used for target bows are set by personal preference, the draw weights for hunting are established by state game and fish departments. Generally, a hunter must use a minimum bow weight of 40 pounds. This is to ensure that the arrow penetration is sufficient for killing game. Most experienced archers use higher draw weights than this for hunting. It is recommended that poundages of 45 to 60 pounds be used on game animals up to deer, and bow weights ranging from 60 to 80 pounds be used for larger game animals such as elk.

Bow hunters, like target archers, need to select and shoot bows they can handle. The choice of bow weight will depend on several things: (1) experience, (2) muscular strength, (3) the type of game you plant to hunt, and (4) state game laws. When selecting a hunting bow you should choose the heaviest weight you can handle with ease and comfort. If this means that you are comfortable with a 40-pound bow, then this is exactly what you should shoot. Do not make the common mistake of purchasing a bow that has excessive poundage, because it will be difficult to shoot. Start with a lighter bow and work up as you become stronger and more experienced.

Bow Length

The length of the bow for hunting is a very important consideration. Some archers believe that a short bow length is most desirable in the hunting situation. Their argument usually centers around the fact that the shorter bow is less cumbersome in heavily wooded and foliaged areas. This may be true, but how many times does a good bow hunter confine himself or herself to hunting in heavy brush? In these circumstances, it is virtually impossible to shoot accurately with any length bow. The arrow will strike limbs or leaves, and as a result it will not find its mark because of deflections and loss of velocity.

A more serious negative factor in regard to the short bow is the sharp angle created for the archer against the bowstring and arrow. The angle at the nocking point tends to compress the fingers of the bowstring hand so tightly that a smooth release is very difficult when using the conventional three-finger grip. A longer bow, 64 inches, has longer limbs and a longer bowstring; consequently, the angle created at the nocking area at full draw is greater than the same angle for a shorter bow. This allows a smoother release when using the traditional three-finger grip. The most common lengths for hunting bows range from 58 to 64 inches.

Hunting Arrows

The arrow is the single most important piece of tackle the bow hunter must consider for accuracy. Many beginning bow hunters make the mistake of purchasing a good bow and then try to shoot mismatched arrows. This only leads to frustration and many a missed shot because of inconsistent arrow flight. Most beginners will do better by starting with a lower quality bow and shooting matched arrows than they will with a top-of-the-line bow shooting a quiver full of arrows that have different lengths, spines, and weights. Exact matching of arrows is essential for any type of bow hunting success.

The fiberglass arrow became popular because it offered qualities that were improvements over the older wooden arrow shafts. Fiberglass arrows can be purchased as matched sets having the same spine, length, and weight. So, if one of your hunting arrows is damaged or lost, it would not be difficult to obtain an exact replacement. Another consideration which has influenced people to use fiberglass is that they are almost unbreakable. A deflected shot which would shatter a wooden arrow or bend an aluminum one would do little or no damage to a fiberglass shaft. Also, unlike wooden arrows, fiberglass shafts are impervious to wet weather conditions. They will not warp. The only real drawbacks in using fiberglass arrows are in the areas of cost and weight.

Aluminum is by far the most popular material used for hunting arrows. (Graphite arrows are also becoming popular with bow hunters.) Many bow hunters choose this material over wood or fiberglass because it offers excellent accuracy. This is accomplished because aluminum arrows can be matched exactly to each other in terms of spine, weight, and length.

Aluminum arrows can be purchased to match any type of bow or bow weight. To help with this process the manufacturers have developed charts that assist with arrow selection using the variables of draw length, bow type, bow weight, and let-off. These shafts are made of high strength tubular aluminum that comes in different diameters and wall thicknesses. By varying the diameter and wall thickness of a shaft, different spines can be obtained. (Aluminum shafts usually have four numbers imprinted on them that indicate the diameter and wall thickness. For example, an aluminum arrow that has the number 2117 tells you that the shaft diameter is 21/32nds and the wall thickness is 0.017 of an inch.) In most cases, the bow hunter will have several shaft sizes to choose from when using any particular bow weight.

Archers are so concerned with accuracy that most do not mind the drawbacks of shooting with aluminum arrows. One of the major annoyances is that, unlike fiberglass, aluminum shafts often bend when deflected off an object. If the bend is not too drastic or too close to either end of the shaft, the arrow can be straightened by using an arrow straightener. Most archery shops have this tool and will straighten arrows for a minimal charge. (Many serious bow hunters, who use aluminum shafts, will invest in a precision arrow straightener because of the convenience of being able to straighten bent arrows in the field. Also, an arrow straightener will pay for itself if a person does much field practice or hunting.)

Another aspect of hunting arrows deals with the crossbow bolt. The "bolt" (fig. 6.1) is the term for the projectile used in a crossbow. Bolts are shorter than regular hunting arrows, but they are usually shot at much higher draw weights. This is evident when looking at the minimum allowable draw weights used for hunting. Most states set *minimum* draw weights for recurve and compound bows at 40 pounds as compared to crossbow minimums of 125 pounds.

The rationale for setting the higher draw weights for crossbows lies in the relationship between the speed of the bolt and its weight. A lighter projectile shot at a higher velocity should penetrate as well as a heavier object shot at a slower speed. Here again, the concern is for good arrow penetration so a properly placed shot will result in a successful hunt—not a wounded animal!

Arrow Fletching

Fletching material is generally made of either turkey feathers or plastic vanes. Most hunters choose the plastic variety simply because they are more durable and hold up well in poor weather conditions. A plastic vane subjected to a rain storm will still shoot with good accuracy. Also, plastic vanes do not make as much noise during arrow flight. This reduces the probability of spooking or alerting the animal during the critical moments between arrow release and impact.

Turkey feathers are still used by bow hunters who favor a natural material over a synthetic substitute. Some hunters claim that shooting turkey fletched shafts will give a faster arrow flight and flatter trajectory. The chief drawbacks to using turkey fletching are that moisture affects them and they do not wear as well as plastic vanes. Wet turkey feathers will drastically alter the flight of the arrow, making accurate shots very difficult.

Another consideration in dealing with arrow fletching is the length. In most cases, the fletching used for hunting is longer than that used for target archery shafts. This is due to the differences in the total weight of the arrow. Since a hunting arrow is heavier and uses a different point, it needs longer fletching to stabilize it during flight. Fletching used for hunting arrows range from 4 inches to 5½ inches in length, depending on the number of vanes and total weight of the arrow. Most hunters experiment with these factors to determine which combinations work the best for them. (See fig. 3.3.)

The number of vanes to be put on an arrow shaft has aroused considerable debate among archers. Some individuals prefer a three-vaned arrow while others like four vanes. The proponents of the three-vaned arrows claim that this arrangement results in more efficient arrow stabilization during flight. An arrow that utilizes three vanes usually has two set at 120 degrees and the other is set at 90 degrees out from the bow. The odd vane is called the "cock feather" and is usually of a different color. When nocking an arrow to the string, it is essential to make sure that the "cock" or index feather is facing out; otherwise it can brush against the arrow rest or riser section of the bow and throw the shot off. Hunters who use the four-vaned shafts usually do so because they do not want to have to concern themselves with making sure that the "cock feather" is pointing outward before taking a shot. This is an advantage in a situation where the hunter does not want to drop the eyes from the target in order to nock an arrow. The four-vaned arrows are glued to the shaft at 75 degrees and 105 degree angles.

There are several other types of fletching used by bow hunters but one of the most common is the flu-flu. A flu-flu (fig. 3.3) utilizes oversized fletching material in order to create wind resistance and shorten the arrow's flight distance. This makes them effective at close ranges but their velocity drops off very fast as distance increases. Hunters use these arrows on small animals such as squirrels and birds. A missed shot at a tree squirrel with normal fletching usually results in a lost arrow. The chance of recovery with a flu-flu fletched arrow is much greater.

Vanes are glued to the shaft in two ways: (1) helical and (2) straight. It is recommended that hunting arrows use the helical fletching because it helps to spin and stabilize the heavier projectile.

Just as with all other aspects of archery, the type of material, length, weight, and number of fletching used on the arrow shafts should match as closely as possible. Mismatching any of these can cause accuracy problems that are not directly related to the human factor.

Bow Hunting Points

Before proceeding with a discussion of modern arrow points, let us regress somewhat and evaluate the bow hunting tackle of the American Indian. Obviously, these people were highly successful as hunters. Their survival over thousands of years in primitive territory testifies to their skill. Hunger tends to be a major motivating factor for developing bow hunting skills.

The Navajo Indian drawing his bow in figure 6.5 would have had less trouble obtaining game if he and other Indians would have had bows like those shown in figures 6.2 and 6.3. Points like those shown in figures 6.7 and 6.8 instead of the Indian points seen in figure 6.6 would have also helped.

The Navajo and other Indian tribes developed very effective composite bows made with a backing of layers of sinew. The arrow points used by American Indians differ appreciably from those utilized by contemporary bow hunters. If the reader takes the time to compare and contrast figure 6.6 with figures 6.7 and 6.8, these differences will immediately become apparent. Figures 6.7 and 6.8 show four popular hunting points.

Figure 6.6 shows a variety of Indian arrow and spear points that were found in the northeastern part of Missouri. Most individuals would assume that all of the points shown in figure 6.6 are arrow heads. This would be an erroneous assumption. The point on the extreme right in the picture and the point on the extreme right of the upper row are both spear points. The large, 4¾-inch-long "beaver tail" point on the right side of the picture was used on a shaft of a spear. The upper right point is also a smaller, 3¼-inch-long spear point. The remaining are arrow points ranging in length from ¾ inch to 3 inches. These were actually attached to the ends of wooden arrow shafts. The small, ¾-inch-long arrow point in the lower row on the left side, is called a bird point. One theory about bird points indicates that they were made and used by smaller children who utilized them with light pulling bows and shot them at birds. In other words, they were

Figure 6.5
A Navajo Indian and his bow hunting tackle. (From E. G. Heath, *The Grey Goose Wing*)

Figure 6.6
Indian arrow and spear points from the collection of Loyd Howell, Wyaconda, Missouri 63474.

Figure 6.7
Three different types of broadheads.

Figure 6.8
Close up view of a modern three-bladed insert type of broadhead. Broadheads must be RAZOR SHARP!

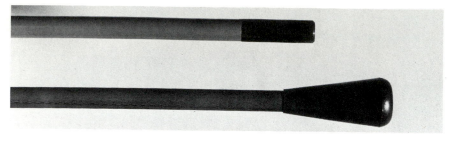

Figure 6.9
Blunt hunting points.

considered to be functional toys used by Indian children. The unnotched arrow in the upper row is a war point. These arrows were shot into enemies. When the shaft was pulled, the arrow point remained within the body of the individual who was shot. Obviously, this posed serious ramifications in terms of removal, compounded by the perils of infections which could be lethal if the penetration by the arrow itself failed to kill the individual who was hit. This particular war point is 2½ inches in length.

Today, bow hunting points are designed in all shapes and sizes, depending on the intended purpose. Most bow hunters incorporate inserts with their arrows, thus allowing them to change a point by simply screwing one out and putting another one in its place, as seen in figure 5.12. There are other methods, but this one is the fastest and most versatile.

Field tips are utilized for practice and on some small game animals. They come in various weights and shapes. Most bow hunters try to match the weight of their field tips to the weight of their broadheads. It is better to practice with tips that are of the same weight as your broadheads, because you get accustomed to the arrow trajectory and only minor adjustments are needed if a sighting device is used.

Blunts, as seen in figure 6.9, are favorite tips for hunting small game. They are made of rubber or metal, and usually slip on or screw in the shaft. These tips kill by the force of impact. The shocking power of a blunted arrow is usually enough to cause death instantaneously to the smaller game animals such as rabbits or squirrels.

There are other types of arrow tips that are manufactured or homemade, to be used for bagging small game. Some incorporate field tips that have a piece of wire brazed through them, and others use spring wire protruding in four directions. These tips also work on force of impact and are devastating on small game. Archers who hunt birds have developed a tip that has four wide loops of wire that can clip a bird in flight. By looping the wire, a wider area is created in which the bird can be hit as the arrow passes. A direct hit is not necessary to bring down the bird with this kind of tip (fig. 6.10).

Broadheads are the only legal tips that can be used on large game species. Most state game and fish departments require broadheads to be at least ⅛ of an

Figure 6.10
Bird hunting requires a special point with wire loops in order to hit the bird in flight. (Courtesy *Bow and Arrow Magazine*)

inch in width and have metal cutting edges. The key to the broadhead's effectiveness depends on one factor—*sharpness*. Since a broadhead kills by hemorrhaging, it is absolutely essential that the cutting edge is RAZOR SHARP (fig. 6.8).

It is important to remember that an arrow point will not always kill an animal, because the blood vessels will not be lacerated to the extent of allowing a steady, unobstructed blood flow. The dull arrow point will tear tissue instead of cutting. A torn blood vessel will constrict to act as its own protective mechanism against hemorrhage. The bow hunter who is attempting to kill does not want this to occur. The animal struck in this fashion will have a tendency to continue moving great distances and become lost to the hunter. The American Indian had this problem while bow hunting with the type of tackle shown in figures 6.5 and 6.6. Unlike the contemporary bow hunter, the American Indian was better at trailing and finding the stricken animal. An archer shooting a dull arrow must strike a vital organ most of the time to kill the game animal, but this is not necessarily true if a razor-sharp arrow is used. Such a hit in a large muscle group, for example, will clearly sever arteries, veins, capillaries, and other blood vessels in the area. This will cause hemorrhage sufficient and fast enough to result in death rather quickly. The bow hunter merely follows the trail of blood from the stricken animal until it collapses from asphyxiation. Most large animals are taken with the bow and arrow by using the hemorrhage technique.

One way to tell a novice from the serious bow hunter is by the sharpness of the latter's broadheads. Knowledgeable hunters will not step into the woods with broadheads they could not shave with! It is the responsibility of the hunter to see that this critical factor is not overlooked.

There are two basic types of broadheads, the ones which need to be hand sharpened and the ones which use razor inserts. If you do not know how to hone an edge to razor sharpness, it is recommended that the insert type be used so you will be assured of effective cutting edges (fig. 6.8). If you prefer to hand sharpen your broadheads but have had difficulty getting the desired edge, the following suggestions will help make the task easier. The tools needed for this sharpening job are two files, one cowhide strop, and some jewelers rouge. The strop is made from a piece of leather, using the rough-out side. That is securely glued to a 10- to 12-inch piece of 2 × 4 board by means of contact cement. The sharpening process is started by putting a rough edge on the broadhead with a 10-inch mill bastard file. Once the edge is formed and the tip chiseled, it is reworked lightly with an 8-inch mill bastard file. The final step puts the desired cutting edge on the broadhead. It consists of putting jewelers rouge on the cowhide strop and moving the edge away in long strokes. This is repeated until the edge is sharp enough to shave with. Sharpening your blades adds a personal touch to the hunting experience.

There are many quality broadheads offered today, and most of them are more than adequate for bringing down game as long as they are sharp and hit a vital area. You should talk to as many experienced bow hunters as possible before making a choice.

Bow Hunting Accessories

A quick look into any well-stocked archery shop will show many different devices available to bow hunters to improve their chances of being successful on a hunt. Many of these accessories can be used for either bow hunting or target archery. Devices, discussed in Chapter 3, such as finger tabs, arm guards, and arrow rests fall into this category. Hunters, however, need some additional tackle which is specific to bow hunting. This includes such items as special quivers, mechanical releases, string silencers, and hunting sights.

The arrow quiver is probably one of the most necessary accessories in terms of safety and convenience. There are three common quivers in use today: (1) the hip quiver, (2) shoulder quiver, and (3) bow quiver. The hip and shoulder quivers are generally used in field practice where the archer does not have to be concerned with brush or other obstacles. *The bow quiver is the most popular and recommended method of carrying arrows in a hunting situation* (fig. 6.2). It is attached directly to the bow by means of springs or screws. Bow quivers come in different models capable of carrying from 4 to 16 arrows. Each individual should decide on what capacity quiver will fit his or her needs.

The single most important safety consideration is that the broadheads be covered and tightly secured inside the bow quiver so they will not jar or vibrate loose. Some of the early clip-on bow quivers did not cover or secure the broadheads. Several serious accidents occurred when archers inadvertently touched these razor-sharp points. Falling on an uncovered bow quiver could be fatal while in the field.

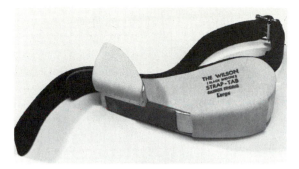

Figure 6.11
A release device that utilizes a strap. (Courtesy Wilson Brothers, Route 1, Elkland, Missouri 65644)

Figure 6.12
The Allen Hunting Release designed for use with compound bows. (Courtesy Allen Archery, 201 Washington Street, Billings, Missouri 65610)

Mechanical releases are used by some bow hunters to eliminate elements of human error caused by the fingers upon loosing the string for a shot. These are designed in many shapes and have evolved through several steps. Some of the first releases were made of a piece of rope or strap which was wrapped around the string and held with pressure from the thumb (fig. 6.11). These were very useful on bows of lower draw weights, but are difficult to handle on higher weighted bows. Other releases, like the one in figure 6.12, were developed to handle this problem. They utilize mechanical mechanisms of either hook or rope.

Figure 6.12 shows a hunting release device for a compound bow. The front hook is attached to the bowstring as shown in figure 6.13. The release is held in the palm of the hand, with the draw pressure distributed over the heel of the hand on the rear butt plate. Vigorous gripping is not needed, and the thumb is placed below the release. The index finger is placed on the trigger. After the draw has been made, the forward end of the release is placed on your anchor point. (Fig. 6.13 can be used as a reference for using the type of release shown in fig. 6.12.) There are two rubber beads mounted on the bowstring, along with the

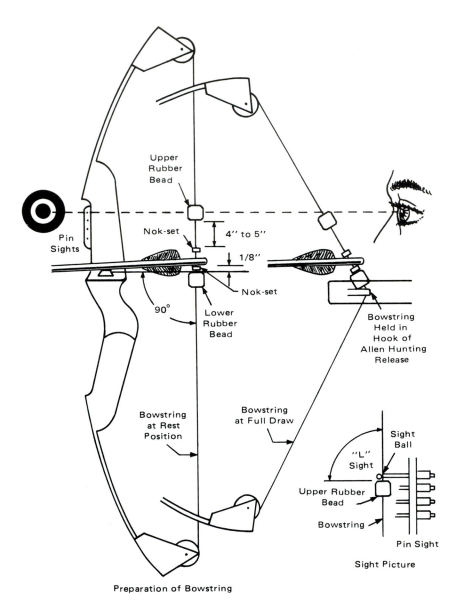

Upper Rubber Bead

Pin Sights

Nok-set

4'' to 5''

1/8''

Nok-set

90°

Lower Rubber Bead

Bowstring Held in Hook of Allen Hunting Release

Bowstring at Rest Position

Bowstring at Full Draw

Sight Ball

"L" Sight

Upper Rubber Bead

Bowstring

Pin Sight

Sight Picture

Preparation of Bowstring

Figure 6.13
Aiming and using the Allen Hunting Release with a compound bow. (Courtesy Allen Archery, 201 Washington Street, Billings, Missouri 65610)

nock-sets. At full draw, slide the upper bead to the line of sight across the top of the bead to the point where the sight ball appears as shown in the "sight picture." When the proper alignment is made and the sight pin is on target, the arrow is released by squeezing the trigger with a steady force. There must be *no motion* of the bow when the arrow is released.

Although these mechanisms can improve accuracy, it is important to note that many arrows have been accidentally released before the archer was ready. Common sense dictates that you thoroughly familiarize yourself with the release and be especially aware of where the tip of the arrow is pointing as the bow is drawn.

String silencers serve one function, and that is to dampen the sound of release. There are many variations to choose from. The type seen in figure 6.2 is commonly referred to as "cat whiskers," and is used by many hunters. Other common types include rubber buttons, yarn strands, or rubber burrs. The cost of this accessory is nominal and well worth the price if it allows the hunter a chance at a second shot or keeps a spooked animal from jumping.

The vast majority of bow hunters view the bowsight as a vital accessory. The hunting bowsight is usually calibrated in 10-yard increments starting at 10 yards and moving out to as much as 60 yards depending upon the skill level of the archer. While 60-yard shots at a game animal are not unduly difficult for experienced bow hunters, it is highly recommended that beginners should limit their shots to distances of 40 yards or less.

Archers who use bowsights for hunting are commonly called "pin-shooters." The reason for that name lies in the fact that pinlike devices are used as target locators. An example of a pin bowsight is seen in figure 6.14.

The pins on a bowsight can be adjusted up and down or left and right to meet the requirements of each archer. Pin spacing will differ from bow hunter to bow hunter depending on equipment and technique.

Sighting in a bowsight for accuracy at various distances is not difficult. Just remember to move the pin in the direction of the miss. For example, if your arrow hit high-right from where you aimed, your corresponding adjustment would be to move that pin up and to the right. After a few adjustments, you should be hitting your target, i.e., hitting with that pin at that distance. Each pin on the sight must be adjusted for accuracy at a specific distance chosen by the archer.

For the bow hunters who use pins, it is imperative that they practice judging distances. Bowsights are useless unless the person shooting the bow can make precise distance estimates, and execute proper shooting fundamentals.

The overdraw is another accessory that has gained in popularity with bow hunters in the last few years. A compound bow equipped with an overdraw system allows the archer to move the arrow rest closer to the shooter (fig. 6.15). The overdraw accessory allows the bow hunter to shoot a shorter arrow at a higher velocity. The resulting flatter trajectory makes errors in judging distance less critical. As a result, accuracy is enhanced. The overdraw accessory appears to be most important to bow hunters who use pin-type bowsights for aiming.

Figure 6.14
A pin-type bowsight used by hunters. Note the sturdy guard to protect the pins. (Courtesy Precision Shooting Equipment, 2550 North 14th Avenue, Tucson, Arizona 85703)

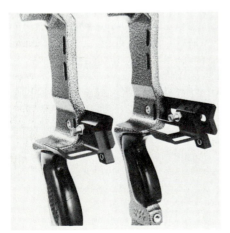

Figure 6.15
Example of an overdraw system. Note how the arrow rest on the right is moved toward the archer to increase the overdraw. (Courtesy Precision Shooting Equipment, 2550 North 14th Avenue, Tucson, Arizona 85703)

Figure 6.16
Camouflage helps conceal Dave Brilhart while bow hunting.

Figure 6.17
Blending in with the surrounding environment is the objective of camouflage.

Camouflage clothing and paint are considered necessary items for bow hunting. The very nature of archery demands that the hunter move extremely close to the quarry before releasing an arrow. The ideal shots are less than 30 yards in distance. To do this, the human shape must blend into the surrounding terrain to such a degree that the animal cannot discern it as seen in figure 6.16.

Camouflage clothing is made in many patterns and color variations. The bow hunter should consider both the time of year as well as the type of terrain when choosing the color of camouflage to be used.

To be totally camouflaged means that all reflective surfaces and exposed body areas must be dulled so large color patterns are broken up. This can be accomplished by applying "camo paint" to face and hands. The reflective surfaces of the bow can be covered by using nonglare paint or tape. Some bow hunters even paint leaf patterns on their bows to make them blend into the surrounding vegetation. The archers in figures 6.16 and 6.17 are suitably camouflaged for the lighting, foliage, terrain, and season of the year.

Techniques

Preparation for a bow hunter begins long before the opening day of the hunting season. All tackle must be checked and organized for the trip. The bow hunter should have an ongoing physical conditioning program using the program presented in Chapter 8. Practice should be held on a regular basis. If possible, trips into the area to be hunted should be made prior to the season in order to scout or look for intended game. All of these preparations take considerable time, thought, and effort.

Although shooting techniques for the bow hunter are very similar to those outlined in Chapter 4, the information in this section is primarily for recurve and compound bow hunting. The main variation is the anchor point. Most bow hunters will use a side-of-the-mouth anchor or a high anchor point as seen in figure 4.19. Some bow hunters like to anchor with the arrow at eye level so they can aim down the shaft in a manner similar to aiming with a firearm. The anchor point ultimately chosen is a matter of personal preference, because good hunters have been known to use a wide variety of anchor points. There are also stance differences between bow hunting and target archery, and these will be discussed in this section.

Prior to the start of the hunting season, target practice is absolutely essential. If the archer has been shooting with target or field points, a switch should be made to the heavier broadheads or hunting points for preseason target practice. Flight trajectories of arrows equipped with broadheads differ considerably from trajectories of arrows equipped with target or field points. During this preseason target practice, bowsight adjustment for hunting distances will have to be made. Traditionally, these are the shorter distances of 10, 15, 20, 25, and 30 yards.

All shots made in the field will not be like shots on the target range; consequently, it is a good idea to practice periodically before the bow hunting season starts on a field archery range. The good bow hunter practices on both target and field archery ranges by taking shots while in unusual positions.

For this reason, three-dimensional targets are available for numerous animals. Shoots are held using these targets strategically placed on field archery units. These events put the archer in practice situations similar to those encountered during the hunt. Archers may practice taking shots at these targets using a variety of stances which may be necessary during the bow hunt. An example of this is shown in figure 6.18 where the archer is taking a shot from a kneeling stance at a deer target.

The 3-D animal shoots are of great value because they help archers become aware of weaknesses in their techniques or inaccuracies in the estimation of yardage between them and the target. Once a problem is known, it can then be remedied with practice before the season starts. And, these shoots are fun!

If you plan to hunt game in mountains or hilly terrain, there should be practice shooting both at uphill and downhill angles. Those are entirely different situation than shooting over a flat surface. The arrow will tend to rise above the line of sight when it is shot from an extreme angle either above or below the imaginary level line of horizontal sight. The greater the degree of angle away from the horizontal level, the greater the amount of rise of the arrow. *In shooting situations, this means that you have to take off yardage for uphill and downhill angles depending on the steepness above or below the horizontal plane.* The degree to which this is done depends on the archer and the tackle being shot. So, if you are going to hunt in the hills, it is best to practice in hills ahead of time and become accustomed to making these necessary adjustments in aiming.

Figure 6.18
A three-dimensional animal target shoot allows Dave Brilhart the opportunity to practice
potential bow hunting situations.

Regular target practice must also be a routine ritual for the bow hunter. When using broadhead points, hay bale targets like the one shown in figure 6.19 are desired. Target archery shooting techniques are used.

The bow also needs to be checked to make sure that it is properly tuned. A bow is out of tune when arrows do not fly in a straight line. Any wobbling or yaw at the rear of the shaft is generally an indicator of a tuning problem when the arrow spine is incorrect for the bow. These problems usually derive from plunger or nocking point irregularities. Movement of the arrow to the left and right during flight is an indicator that plunger adjustment is needed. If the arrow flight motion is up and down, the nocking point needs to be adjusted.

The bow tuning procedure discussed in Chapter 4 can be used, but the hunting arrows and points to be used in the field must be shot during the tuning process. And, the bow must be equipped for hunting with the various devices you may use, such as stabilizers and bow quivers.

Shooting a bow and arrow when fatigued is vastly different from shooting when rested. It is entirely possible that the bow hunter may get the best shot of the year while very tired. The conditioned hunter can handle this situation much better than the individual who is "out of shape." Regardless of the physiologic condition of the bow hunter, anyone can become tired while performing the type of work one must do while in the field. Consequently, bow hunters should know how to compensate during shooting for the feeling of being tired. The best way to accomplish this is to practice shooting when fatigued as well as in the rested

Figure 6.19
Larry Rogge utilizes regular target practice with bow hunting tackle in preparation for a javalina hunt in Arizona.

state. Many bow hunters make the mistake of never practicing while tired. This type of illogical practice would be analogous to a football coach never having his team work out and execute their skills while feeling the stress of competition and prolonged neuromuscular activity. Such a team would find the going very rough in the last few minutes of the fourth quarter of a football game. The archer who has never experienced shooting while fatigued would also be hard pressed to kill a game animal if the situation presented itself in the field when he or she was extremely tired. Some practices should *follow* conditioning as discussed in Chapter 8 when you are tired.

The bow hunter should practice judging distances constantly throughout the year. This can be done almost anywhere. As an example, while walking pick out a sign, tree, person, or object, and estimate its distance. When this has been done, count your steps as you move toward the object selected. Judgment of distance will improve steadily through such practice. Why is this important to the bow hunter? If a bowsight is used as recommended, it will help gauge distances more precisely when in the hunting environment. Thus, the bowsight setting can be used more accurately and this can lead to more game.

Like the Indian of yesteryear, the bow hunter must become very familiar with the game being sought. Eating and drinking habits must be known, and the bow hunter must be very familiar with the habitat of the animals being pursued. It is a good idea to go into the hunting area on foot a few weeks prior to the hunting season to study or scout intended game. As an example, a deer herd may be observed for several days. Their eating, drinking, and bedding habits can be observed if the individual is an excellent hunter. Some people are so good at this that they actually choose the deer to be shot prior to the opening day of the season. This takes considerable patience, knowledge, and hunting skill. Many hunters of the "instant hunting school" are in such a hurry to kill their game that they fail to enjoy the hunt.

An important part of any hunt is the fine art of stalking or seeking out game animals. This is more critical in bow hunting than gun hunting, because the bow hunter must get closer to the game animal to make the kill. Most deer, for example, are killed with the bow and arrow at distances ranging from 10 to 35 yards. The gun hunter, on the other hand, routinely kills deer with high-powered rifles at distances of over 100 yards.

The good bow hunter shoots the deer while the deer is in a nonmoving position. To obtain that type of shot, the bow hunter must be an excellent stalker with an intimate knowledge of both the deer and the environment. In addition, such factors as habits of the animal, common noises and scents in the area, wind direction changes by time of day, animal camouflage techniques, and animal movements must be thoroughly understood by the bow hunter.

The bow hunter must also face one fact prior to stalking game animals. Regardless of cleanliness, the human body has odors atypical to those in the hunting area. These odors come from skin, breath, hair, and human habits such as the use of tobacco and liquor. If the hunter does not hunt into the air currents, the chance for success will be diminished. Every animal will know that a predator, a human being, is in the area. The hunter should try to eliminate all odors of civilization. This can be accomplished in part, through a study of wind patterns. Wind patterns differ, depending upon the time of day and nature of the terrain. These should be studied, preferably prior to the opening of bow hunting season. If this is not possible, it will take some very astute observations on the part of the bow hunter to study these patterns while in the process of hunting. Odors from the hunter should be minimized by using nonscented soap, and refraining from the use of tobacco and liquor while on the hunt.

There is a great sport associated with bow hunting which actually depends upon specialized noise. This sport is known as *varmint calling*. This is a sport utilizing noise to attract predatory animals. The predator hears the noise made by the hunter thinking it is an animal in distress. The game animal becomes the stalker, and the bow hunter actually becomes the hunted object. This can be very exciting, especially when the predator is in the big cat family!

The varmint caller uses a hand-built or commercially built device to attract the predator. The sound of the call is not like any emitted by any particular animal; however, it does resemble the squeal of many animals in distress. The noise attracts the predator, because he associates the crying sound with previous experiences while on a hunt. The motivating drive for the game animal is hunger. When the predator gets within a few feet of the area where the bow hunter is camouflaged, the hunter releases the arrow. This is seen in figure 6.20. The distance of the shot depends largely upon the type and size of the predatory animal stalking the bow hunter; the extent of his or her intestinal fortitude and courage; and the ability to shoot accurately under pressure. It can be exciting!

Figure 6.20
How close a predatory animal gets to a varmint caller depends upon several factors related to the bow hunter. (Courtesy *Bow and Arrow Magazine*)

Wounded rabbit calls are very effective on predators such as coyotes, bob cats, foxes, and occasionally, the mountain lion. This type of call, when used correctly, can also be used to attract adult javalina by imitating the sound of their young in distress (fig. 6.21). Other types of call are used on game as small as quail and as large as bull elk. Turkey calling has become very sophisticated over the years.

Some cities have game calling clubs which meet monthly to practice and to exchange ideas on the art of calling. These people are experts, and they are usually more than happy to share their experiences and skills with others.

Noise can be used in many situations to the bow hunter's advantage. Many hunters believe that they should be absolutely quiet at all times on the hunt, but it is virtually impossible to be quiet in all hunting situations. Noise that is not typical of the environment should be avoided as much as possible when stalking. However, noise can be used to flush game out of thick, brushy areas where a shot would be very unwise, since a shot usually panics the animals and causes them to move rapidly in several directions. A shot while the animals are moving would probably be wasted. Noise can be used, however, to flush birds from their hiding places in high grass or bushy areas. This is common practice in hunting birds such as quail and pheasant with the bow and arrow (fig. 6.10). Hitting a bird on the wing with an arrow is a real challenge!

Excessive talking and noises associated with human beings should be avoided as much as possible. A broken twig may alarm an animal, but animals in a wooded area are familiar with such noises. They usually respond by looking intently in

Figure 6.21
Bow hunting for javalina is a popular pastime for archers in the Southwestern deserts. (Courtesy Jerry Day, Arizona Game and Fish Department)

the direction of the sound. The best thing to do following such a noise is to remain motionless for a few minutes. A grazing animal who has heard such a sound will return to eating after assuring himself that a predator is not stalking in the immediate area.

It may seem obvious, but the bow hunter must know how to see the animal being sought. This takes considerable practice and experience. In their natural habitat, animals are capable of hiding or camouflaging themselves very effectively. The untrained eye can miss seeing a potential shot. Some animals, especially birds such as pheasant and quail, depend upon their cover and camouflage for protection even more than on their movement abilities. There are no secrets for spotting game animals. The bow hunters should know the coloring of the animal being sought and how these colors change with the seasons. They should also know how the colors blend with the foliage in the environment where the hunt will take place. Anytime a bow hunter walks through a forest or wooded area, he or she should practice on this skill by trying to observe every detail in the area. This practice will help develop field awareness. (It is also recommended that one listens to the natural sounds of the area you hunt.) A good set of binoculars will help in locating game; these are considered essential by most bow hunters.

A bow hunter who has located and stalked an animal to within bow range must know how to distinguish a good shot from a poor one. It is essential to know where to place an arrow so it will penetrate a vital area. Many an animal has been lost due to ignorance on the part of the archer regarding the anatomy of the animal being hunted. (It is recommended that animal targets with the vital organs of animals outlined be used for some practice sessions prior to the hunt.)

Knowing the anatomy of the hunted animal is important because the most effective shots put the arrow in the lung and heart vicinity. Bow hunters should also familiarize themselves with the locations of major bones, arteries, liver, stomach, and kidneys. A razor sharp broadhead shot into or through the chest cavity will cause severe bleeding, easy tracking, and almost always result in a successful hunt.

Once the shot has been taken, the bow hunter has to make a judgment regarding whether or where the animal was hit. This decision will dictate the plan of action for tracking. Most archers look for blood or try to recover the arrow to help give them clues regarding the nature of the hit.

The color of blood can tell the archer if the arrow severed a vein or an artery. Blood that comes from a vein is dark red in color whereas blood from an artery is bright red. If it is known for certain that the chest area was penetrated, the plan of action is to wait for at least 30 minutes to one hour before trailing. The animal will usually bed down a short distance from where it was hit and die. Some beginning hunters make the mistake of trailing too soon and end up chasing the wounded animal all over the woods!

If the animal were gut shot, the plan of action would be much different. Even though gut shots are always fatal, they are hard to trail and the animal takes much longer to die. In this case, the archer should wait anywhere from five to six hours before starting on the animal's trail. A gut shot animal that is pushed can travel miles before it is exhausted enough to bed down.

There are several situations where the best plan of action is to follow the animal immediately. These include muscle hits, leg hits, and situations where darkness or bad weather is approaching.

Before following a trail, be sure to mark the spot from which the shot was taken and the spot where the animal was hit. Blood is easy to follow, but sometimes the flow stops. In that case, the archer will have to rely on other clues such as prints, scuffmarks, and broken vegetation. Be patient and do not overlook any signs, because trailing can take hours of tedious searching and concentration. One should not give up the trailing task until all possibilities have been exhausted.

When an animal has been recovered, it needs to be field dressed as soon as possible so the meat can cool. This helps keep it from spoiling, especially in the warmer climates. Special care should be taken during the field dressing process, because there is always the possibility of cutting one's self.

For information regarding legal game and bow hunting, season dates, license fees, lottery systems for various species, and other matters, the official state wildlife agency must be contacted. Addresses are listed in Appendix A. There are all kinds of exciting species to hunt which can bring satisfaction to the bow hunter. One example is shown in figure 6.22.

Table 6.1 includes several examples of game taken with the bow and arrow in the United States, Mexico, and Canada.

Figure 6.22
The enjoyment of a successful antelope hunt shows on the face of Jack Frazier, an expert bow hunter. (Courtesy of Jack Frazier)

Table 6.1   Examples of Game Animals Taken with Bow and Arrow in the United States, Canada, and Mexico

Alaska Brown Bear	Javalina
Alaska-Yukon Moose	Mountain Caribou
Antelope	Mule Deer
Barren Ground Caribou	Musk Ox
Bighorn Sheep	Polar Bear
Bison	Quebec-Labrador Caribou
Black Bear	Rocky Mountain Goat
Canada Moose	Roosevelt Elk
Columbian Blacktail Deer	Sitka Blacktail Deer
Coues Deer	Stone Sheep
Cougar	Whitetail Deer
Dall Sheep	Woodland Caribou
Grizzly Bear	Wyoming-Shiras Moose
Jaguar	Yellowstone Elk

The Pope and Young Club is the organization responsible for maintaining, recording, and determining the authenticity of the Bowhunters Big Game Records of North America (see Appendix B for the address). This club appoints and maintains official measurers across the North American continent. These highly qualified people score outstanding big game animals taken with the bow and arrow. The scoring procedure is based on well-established criteria. It is a challenging task to qualify a game animal you have taken with the bow and arrow for a Pope and Young documented big game record. That is as it should be in this sport! The Pope and Young Club is open to bow hunters who have proven themselves in the field over the years, accepted the challenges, and adhere to the principles of fair chase. Beyond the documentation of game records, there is a keen interest on the part of members in maintaining the integrity of the wildlife heritage.

For the individual who likes to hunt, bow hunting can occupy many leisure hours. The game animals can be as small as quail or as large as an elk. The environment can range from the wilderness of Canada to the deserts of the Southwest area of the United States. Bow hunting is for the adventurous individual who respects nature, sport, conservation principles, and is a lover of the great out-of-doors and wilderness areas.

Review Questions

1. What are the several types of bows commonly used for hunting and what is their order of energy storage efficiency?
2. In purchasing hunting tackle, which is more important, the quality of the bow or the arrows? What are the advantages and disadvantages of fiberglass and aluminum arrows?
3. Describe the accessory tackle specifically designed for bow hunting and indicate any points important to remember regarding safety and utility.
4. Assume that you are planning a bow hunt. What preparation is necessary in regard to tackle, conditioning, practice, site of the hunt and quarry?
5. Under what circumstances should the bow hunter trail the wounded animal: immediately, after 30 minutes to an hour, or after 5–6 hours?
6. Describe the use of the pin-sight commonly used by bow hunters. What techniques can the archer use to enhance his or her judgment in estimating distances? What aiming adjustments must be made between shots made over level ground versus shots taken up and down hills?
7. How does an overdraw accessory mounted on a hunting bow work to the advantage of the archer?
8. What is varmint hunting and how does it differ from deer hunting with the bow and arrow?

9. Discuss the rationale for the guideline that broadhead arrow points must be razor sharp.
10. What animals in the area where you plan to bow hunt constitute "legal game"? What is the best way in which to obtain the *definitive* answer to that question?
11. Cite reasons that substantiate the statement that bow hunting provides challenges and rewards that are not present in other hunting methods.
12. If the compound bow can generate more foot-pounds of energy than composite bows, and if the compound bow is now the most popular hunting tool of the bow hunter, why are some hunters returning to the use of the recurve bow?
13. What devices do the bow hunters need in addition to those customarily used for target archery and why?
14. Can one's judgment of distance be improved? If so, how? Can one improve sight or hearing? If not, how can one learn to be more observant when bow hunting?
15. Why is stalking more critical in bow than in gun hunting?

Bow Fishing

7

The purpose of this chapter is to introduce the reader to the exciting sport of bow fishing. There are many challenges to be met in this sport, and the type of aquatic animals that can be taken with bow and arrow are rather diverse. They range from minnows and small goldfish (carp) to rather large and violent sharks. It can be exciting!

Bow fishing is a sport with great appeal for people who enjoy archery and angling. It is a wholesome mixture of both sports with some of the aspects of harpooning added. Bow fishing is not new, because primitive people have used the techniques for years to acquire fish, frogs, and other aquatic animals for food. However, bow fishing as a sport is relatively new as compared to target archery. It is gaining in popularity especially as people discover that the sport exists, because bow fishing is a challenging adventure.

The National Field Archery Association has encouraged and supported bow fishing for many years. Recognition of prize fish and articles appear periodically on bow fishing in the NFAA magazine, *Archery*. The number of people who bow fish for avocational purposes is growing.

Bow fishers can ply their skills on rivers, lakes, ponds, and oceans. The size of the "rough fish" sought adds to the excitement of the sport. On the average, the species legalized for bow fishing are much larger than most game fish taken with rod and reel. The smallest of the common "rough fish" approved for bow fishing are the bowfin and shortnose gar; these average about 5 pounds as adults. The largest of the "rough fish" sanctioned for bow fishing outside of ocean water is the alligator gar. The largest on record weighed 302 pounds, and it was over 7 feet in length. The record alligator gar taken by a bow fisher weighed 212 pounds. Sharks often exceed 200 pounds, and the giant sunfish found in the Pacific Ocean ranges in weight from 50 to 1000 pounds. If you fish, think about the excitement the last time you landed a 10-pound game fish with a rod and reel. Now, imagine having your arrow hooked into a 200-pound shark and think of the challenge it would be to pull the fish into the boat or onto the shore (fig. 7.1). Therein lies some of the adventure and intrigue of bow fishing as a sport.

Figure 7.1
Three brown sharks taken by Robie Davis and his father, J. Robert Davis. The sharks were taken while bow fishing the bays on the Maryland coast. (Photo courtesy of J. Robert Davis, R.F.D. 4, Box 380, Spearin Road, Salisbury, Maryland 21801)

If you are an angler, the process of obtaining bait can be rather dull. Simply stated, you dig for earthworms or purchase your bait in a variety of forms from a store. Obtaining some bow fishing bait can be very exciting! Some people use stringrays as bait for bow fishing for shark. They shoot the bait first and then go after the big stuff! Figure 7.2 will give you some idea of the difference between this type of "bow fishing bait" and the typical bait of the angler!

As stressed throughout this book, if you have an interest in bow fishing, the first step is to perfect your target archery shooting fundamentals as discussed in Chapter 4. Those shooting skills serve as your foundation; they are prerequisites to almost all other archery sports. Some modifications are made in shooting technique as you switch from target to bow fishing tackle, but drawing and release mechanics remain the same. If you are accurate during target range practice, you will increase the probability of taking more pounds of fish once you get into the bow fishing situation. Ideally, practice should progress from standard target archery targets to moving, simulated fish targets submerged beneath the water.

The changes in tackle design in recent years have helped to make bow fishing more popular. In the past bow fishers have used all types of ingenious gimmicks to attach: (1) line to bow and arrow, and (2) crude reels to bows. Hand-wrap reels were improvised and mounted on bow backs. Hand-wrap reels (fig. 7.1) were eventually manufactured and placed on the market. These remain popular with many, but the spin cast reel attached to a short bow fishing rod which mounts on the back of the bow has minimized some of the line handling problems and made bow fishing much easier (see figs. 7.3 and 7.4).

Figure 7.2
Bill Johnston and Robie Davis with a 100-plus-pound southern stingray taken off the Del Mar Va Peninsula in Maryland. (Courtesy *Bowfishing* Magazine, P.O. Box 2005, Wausau, Wisconsin 54401)

Bow hunters are turning to bow fishing as an "off-season" activity. The summer is not a game animal season, but it is a good time of year to go after many of the "rough fish" on rivers and in lakes. The hunter can keep the skills honed as well as gain recreationally through the sport of bow fishing.

"Rough fish" such as carp, gar, and buffalo are usually relegated to "garbage status" by gourmets. Game fish such as trout, bass, and bluegill are preferred eating. The resourceful bow fisherman can learn many ways to prepare, cook, and eat the carp, gar, and other fish that have been caught. These fish can be a valuable and savory food source. They may be prepared for frying, broiling, smoking, and canning. Due to the large number and pounds of fish that may be taken by the bow fisherman in most states, the "rough fish" can supplement the diet and the diet budget for the family if a taste is acquired. People do prepare, cook, eat, and enjoy these fish. (A review of table 7.1 will show a wide variety of legal species for bow fishing.)

Conservation departments in the various states look at the harvest of "rough fish" taken by bow fishers as a positive conservation practice. These fish are large, as noted, and they tend to be prolific reproducers. As a result, natural ecological balance can be disturbed, especially in those areas where few, if any, predators exist for the "rough fish." If bow fishing increases in popularity, some fish populations may have to be monitored carefully for conservation purposes on the rivers and lakes across the country that generate the most interest to bow fishers.

Figure 7.3
A hunting recurve bow rigged for bow fishing with a spinning reel and short rod mounted on the back of the bow. (Courtesy Black Widow Bow Company, H. C. R. #1, Box 357–1, Highlandville, Missouri 65669)

There are several bow fishing tournaments and activities each year across the United States. These are increasing the general public's awareness that the sport exists. These tournaments are sponsored by local clubs, organizations, national archery organizations, and nationally known archery manufacturing companies. The competitors vie for trophies, merchandise, and large cash prizes.

Tackle

Any bow may be rigged for bow fishing. However, hunting bows, recurve and compound, are most commonly used and best suited for this purpose. The draw weights for hunting bows tend to be higher than target bows, an important consideration when going after the larger species or when trying to propel an arrow through a few feet of water. Minimum bow weights of 50 pounds are recommended for bow fishing. This will produce an adequate amount of arrow projection force to handle most situations. Lighter bow weights, however, can be used with success when bow fishing in shallow water or when shooting fish that are barely submerged. The archer who cannot handle higher bow weights should rig his or her bow for bow fishing and go. There will be numerous opportunities to

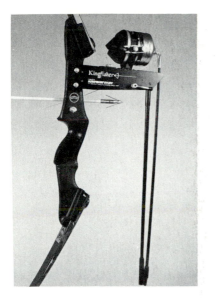

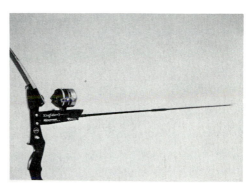

Figure 7.4(a)
The "Foldin' BoRod" mounted on the bow. The folded position is maintained while fishing, aiming, and shooting.

Figure 7.4(b)
A trigger mechanism extends and locks the bow into position when the fish is hit. (Courtesy of Corley's Bowfishin' Stuff, 727 Holiday Lane, Claremore, Oklahoma 74017)

shoot. If a dorsal fin is seen or the fish is swimming a few inches below the surface, shooting skill and not bow weight becomes the critical factor. Bow fishing gets exciting at that point regardless of the strength, age, or sex of the participant!

An excellent recurve hunting bow is rigged for bow fishing in figure 7.3. The bow has a short rod and bow reel adapter rod mounted on the back of the bow. The bow reel adapter screws into the stabilizer hole, and the rod fits into the adapter. The adapter is needed to hold the spinning reel, as shown in figure 7.3. As noted previously, this type of rod and reel set-up, as compared to the older hand-wrap reels, has made bow fishing easier. The rod provides better leverage for playing the fish, and, with the spinning reel, line tangle is minimized. There is a good line recovery on missed shots and better recovery of fish once they are shot.

Another type of bow fishing rod is shown in figure 7.4. This rod was designed by Wilbur Corley for use when bow fishing for fish ranging in weight from 10 to 100 pounds. As shown in figure 7.4(a), the rod folds when not in use. This makes the total bow and rod easy to use while bowfishing, aiming, and shooting. The fishing line runs from the spinning reel through the eye of the rod, and it is attached to the arrow. You can use lighter line and have the advantage of using a drag on the line. When you shoot and hit a fish, it is at that time that you pull the trigger and extend the rod as shown in figure 7.4(b). The rod, made of tubular

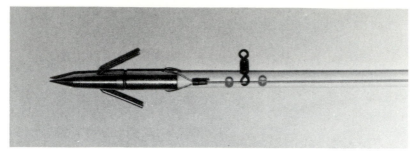

Figure 7.5
A cable mounted on the arrow for attaching the bow fishing line eliminates the problem of too much line lying on the shooter's arm while drawing. (Courtesy Ron Skirvin, Shure Shot, P.O. Box 748, Stevens Point, Wisconsin 54481)

fiberglass and very flexible, locks automatically. It remains in the extended position until the fish is landed. The rod then is folded back into the position shown in figure 7.4(a), and you are ready to start bow fishing for another "big one."

Aluminum arrows can be used to bow fish; however, *solid fiberglass arrows are recommended*. They are durable and the heavier mass weight is needed to increase accuracy as the arrow penetrates the water enroute to the fish. Arrows should be 30 inches in length, because the line must be kept away from the bow hand.

One way to ensure this is to attach a cable to the arrow as shown in figure 7.5. The line attaches to the swivel that runs the length of the cable. This means that only a few inches of the line is off the reel, i.e., the distance from the reel to the front of the bow or arrow rest. That eliminates the long length of line that could lie across the shooter's arm as the arrow is drawn. That is a problem the bow fisher encounters when using some line attachment procedures. It interferes with shooting.

Rubber fletching may or may not be used. Arrow flight is minimal in bow fishing. White is the desired color for arrows. It is recommended that several extra arrows be taken on each trip, because nocks and points do break.

There are several bow fishing arrow points on the market. Which of these points is "best" depends on personal preference, and that may change, depending upon the fish being sought. All of the bow fishing points are barbed; some of these barbs are retractable, allowing for easy removal, while others have stationary spring steel barbs. There are also four pronged "gig points" for shooting frogs.

The retractable barbed arrow points are usually preferred over the nonretractable variety; they are much easier to recover. One barbed arrow is shown in figure 7.6. This is a heavy point which helps in terms of penetration, opening to 2¾ inches across the tips to provide holding power during fish retrieval. The point is removed by simply twisting the shaft counterclockwise. The point is kept within the fish as the shaft is rotated, and the barbs reverse their position while still inside the fish. The arrow can be removed easily without disrupting the line. These positions of the barbs are shown in figure 7.6. This type of point is recommended for fish with "soft skin" such as the suckers and bowfin.

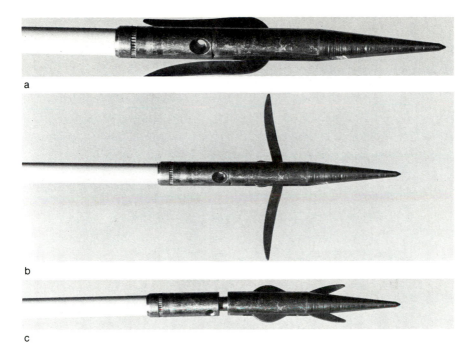

a

b

c

Figure 7.6
A retractable "sting-a-ree" bow fishing point: (a) shooting position, (b) open position to gaff the fish, and (c) point adjustment to remove the arrow from the fish.

Another type of arrow point is shown in figure 7.7. This is a newer design made of steel with a one-piece rotating barb. This eliminates the need to remove the point from the arrow once the fish is landed. The barbs rotate forward by unscrewing the point three-fourths turn while holding the arrow. A spring lock washer between the point and adapter prevents accidental release. This point attaches to a threaded adapter epoxied to the arrow shaft. Figure 7.8 shows a bigmouth buffalo taken with the arrow point shown in figure 7.7.

Bow fishing line is made of braided nylon and monofilament. The choice of which to use lies with the archer. The most commonly used, however, is braided nylon. The poundage test of the line is important, with choice usually ranging from 50- to 100-pound test line. Which poundage used depends upon the size of the fish one expects to encounter. If you go out with line too weak and large fish are found, the trip could be a great disappointment. However, it can be an adventure and test of your fishing skills to land heavy fish on relatively light test line. It is recommended that 50- to 70-pound test line be used in one reel and a second reel be loaded with heavier or lighter line, depending upon the anticipated fish size for the locale being fished. Also, maximum line length for the reel being used is important. Fish will run upon arrow impact, and line length is important to enable the bow fisher to control the extent of this movement. There are times when it is better to use lighter and longer line rather than heavier and shorter

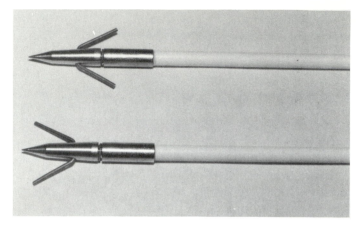

Figure 7.7
The Shure Shot point with one-piece rotating barb design. (Courtesy Ron Skirvin, Shure Shot, P.O. Box 748, Stevens Point, Wisconsin 54481)

Figure 7.8
Wisconsin bowfisherman, Ron Skirvin, with his 43-pound bigmouth buffalo. (Courtesy *Bowfishing Magazine*, P.O. Box 2005, Wausau, Wisconsin 54401)

line. Line should be examined periodically for damage caused by friction against such things as abrasive skin, teeth, or boat hulls. Weak lines will snap, and thus fish are lost.

The line is usually attached to a leader of heavy braided nylon by a strong swivel. The leader should be about 30 inches long. It can be used to hold as the fish is being lifted into the boat or dragged on to the beach or shore.

Major Accessories

Bow fishers may use the same "minor accessories" as the target archer and bow hunter: finger tab, arm guard, bow sling, etc. (fig. 7.3). In addition, they must have some "major accessories" to place them close to the fish being sought. The largest financial outlay is for a boat and wading gear.

Some of the best and most interesting bow fishing can be done while walking rough marshlands, shallow edges of lakes and rivers, swamps, and flooded fields. Boats either cannot enter these areas, or they are difficult to handle in those situations. Also, boats can be noisy and create greater water disturbance than a man or woman moving slowly through the shallow water. Chest waders are an absolute essential for this part of bow fishing. Wading will be productive for bow fishers during the spring spawning time. In addition to the excitement of shooting the fish, there is always the added adventure provided by water snakes, deep and unseen holes, insects, sunshine, and electrical storms. You have to love it!

If a bow fisher plans to pursue the sport in earnest on a regular basis on rivers and lakes, a modified, flat-bottomed boat will prove to be a valuable asset. Bow fishing on rivers and lakes can be done in a variety of boats ranging from canoes to row boats. However, boats of that type and like the one shown in figure 7.9 are not recommended. Canoes, kyaks, and regular keeled small boats tend to be unstable. As a result, they sway and can tip when the archer stands to shoot or bring in the fish.

A bow fishing boat should be stable, i.e., set relatively low in the water to minimize sway when the archer stands on the bow or stern to shoot. The archer must stand to: (1) visually hunt for the fish to be shot, (2) execute the shooting fundamentals, and (3) obtain the correct shooting angle to hit the fish. These actions cannot be performed properly while seated.

There are numerous flat-bottomed, aluminum fishing boats on the market which can be modified to meet the needs of the bow fisher. Ken Brown described such a modification in his excellent book on bow fishing—see Bibliography. The boat for bow fishing needs to be modified to include front and rear shooting platforms, an electric trolling motor with foot control to guide the boat while standing on the platforms, below deck storage areas, as well as night navigation and hunting light. The boat and platforms are wide enough to provide stability and minimize the possibility of capsizing when archers are hunting and shooting fish. For moving from place to place when not fishing, an outboard motor with steering wheel is included. These features are part of the prototype of a good bow fishing boat for lakes and rivers. From the standpoint of monetary expenditure, the boat and a

Figure 7.9
Landing a carp from a boat not designed for bow fishing. (Courtesy *Bow and Arrow Magazine*)

Figure 7.10
Jim West (*left*) and Michael Shore aboard Jim West's customized bowfishing boat—Ramboat. (Courtesy *Bowfishing* Magazine, P.O. Box 2005, Wausau, Wisconsin 54401)

trailer to haul it are the most expensive equipment items needed for bow fishing on lakes and rivers. But, the boat can also be used for a wide variety of recreational activities other than bow fishing.

The state-of-the-art boat for bow fishing is shown in figure 7.10. This boat was modified by Jim West. He started with a Lowe "Husky John" Boat and gradually built himself a highly specialized boat for bow fishing. Some of its features are:

1. Eighteen feet long, 7 feet at the beam, and 24-inch high sides.
2. Welded aluminum hull.
3. Two stable shooting platforms; the forward platform is 5 feet above the water—highly desired in terms of shooting angles.
4. Holders for extra arrows attached to each platform.
5. Nine built-in storage compartments:
   a. Two for storage for camping gear.
   b. Two for bow fishing equipment.
   c. One for wiring.
   d. One is a tool box.
   e. One for life jackets and fire gear.
   f. One live well.
   g. One for food cooling.
6. V-8 Chevrolet engine bored to 406 cubic inches.
7. Dominator jet pump for propulsion—navigation is possible in as little as two inches of water.
8. Depth finder, videocamera set-up, AM/FM radio with cassette tape player.
9. Burglar alarm system.

Any reader interested in details regarding this boat should read the articles by Paul T. Shore listed in the Bibliography.

Bow fishing on the ocean requires a seaworthy boat or ship, but most bow fishers are not wealthy enough to afford a ship as a "fishing accessory." However, ships can be chartered by groups or individuals directly or through travel agencies for ocean bow fishing trips. The travel and charter costs are not inexpensive, but the money spent can provide considerable excitement when one contemplates landing shark, rays or sunfish. Sighting, shooting, and landing a large shark or sunfish on an ocean vessel bobbing up and down on the water is a challenge, and it can add excitement to a vacation.

Legal Species for Bow Fishing

Because of extensive environmental, political, and ecological differences between states, bow fishers should never assume that a specific species is legal. A license is required in most states to bow fish, and each state clearly defines the species for legal bow fishing. It is the responsibility of the archer to know that list and the fishing limits. These laws change, so the bow fisher desiring to fish in any given state should know the current game laws and obtain a license. One should never assume that a legal species in one state will be legal in another state, e.g., Colorado allows trout to be taken by bow fishers, while New Mexico, its neighbor to the south, only allows gar, carp, buffalo, and bullfrogs to be taken in its waters. Carp is probably the most common fish so taken (fig. 7.9).

Most of the areas in the United States and Canada restrict the legal species to the so-called "rough fish." The most common are:

Alligator gar	Bowfin	Shortnose gar
Bigmouth buffalo	Carp	Smallmouth buffalo
Black buffalo	Longnose gar	Spotted gar

Table 7.1 is provided simply to show the reader the diversity of legal species which may be taken in the United States. It must be recognized that all species named in table 7.1 are not found and are not legal in all states. If you are planning to bow fish or hunt in a specific locale in the United States or Canada, you are well advised to contact the official wildlife agency where your trip will take you. Ask them to give you the latest game regulations. *The names, addresses, and phone numbers of the official wildlife agencies in the United States and Canada are listed for you in Appendix A.*

Table 7.1 Legal Species for Bow Fishing Throughout the United States

Aholehole	Gar (Spotted)	Quillback
Ama'ama	Gasperpou	Rays
Awa	Goldeye	Redhorse
Bass (Largemouth)	Goldfish	Salmon (Atlantic)
Bass (Smallmouth)	Hardhead	Salmon (Kokanee)
Blackfish	Herring	Saugeye
Blowfish	Kala	Shad
Bowfin	Lamprey	Sharks
Buffalo (Bigmouth)	Ling	Skates
Buffalo (Black)	Manini	Squawfish
Buffalo (Smallmouth)	Minnows	Stingrays
Bullhead	Moanu	Suckers
Burbot	Moi	Sunfish
Carp	Mullet	Toads (Oyster)
Catfish (Channel)	Muskellunge	Trout
Catfish (Flathead)	O'io	Tullibee
Chub	Omilu	Turtle (Soft-shell)
Ciscoe	Opelu Kala 'Opakapaka	Turtle (Snapping)
Drum	Paddlefish	Uha
Eel	Papio	Uku
Frogs	Perch (Rio Grande)	'Ula 'ula
Gar (Alligator)	Pickerel	Ulua
Gar (Longnose)	Pike (Northern)	Weke
Gar (Shortnose)	Pike (Walleye)	Whitefish

State game laws must be checked annually to determine legal species for each state.
See Appendix A for names and addresses of official wildlife agencies.

Technique Suggestions

This section describes some of the more important shooting fundamentals for bow fishing as well as presenting some suggestions for making the experience more rewarding. Bow fishing, like any skill practiced outdoors, has many variations. These are only learned through experience. Practical experience following study and directed practice of fundamental concepts are the best teachers of bow fishing.

The nocking, drawing, anchoring, releasing, and follow-through shooting fundamentals are the same as those practiced in target archery. Obviously, the stance for the bow fisher must be modified, depending upon the position of the fish in relation to the archer. The release cannot be hurried in the excitement of the moment. The three fingers relax and extend as in target archery to let the string move forward in a straight line without causing unnecessary deflection of the arrow. This appears to be easy, but the excited bow fisher who has sighted a "big one" will periodically try to help the bowstring move by plucking it or pushing the bow at release. One must refrain from doing this. Target practice plus experience in the field helps to minimize these undesired reactions. Target practice should be done with field points which weigh the same as the fishing point.

Aiming presents unique problems in bow fishing. From the standpoint of physics, water and air are both fluids. But, water presents an entirely different set of problems for the bow fisher than looking at a land target through the air. A land target does not appear distorted; the distance to a target is either known exactly as in target archery or can be readily estimated by the experienced bow hunter. The bow fisher, on the other hand, must deal with the refraction of the sun's light rays as they penetrate the water in the immediate area of the fish. (It is best to wear good sun glasses to increase visual acuity, especially on bright days.) It is difficult to evaluate the depth of the fish in the water, because the light rays have a tendency to bend downward. This means that the fish will actually be closer to you than it looks.

As a result of these factors aiming is made more difficult in bow fishing because you cannot aim directly at the fish. *The aim must be at a point below the fish.* The aiming point below the fish is dependent upon (1) the depth of the fish in the water and (2) the distance the bow fisher is away from the fish at the time of the shot. Ken Brown, an expert from Oklahoma, recommends that one inch be allowed for every five feet of distance between the archer and the target, and the archer should allow one inch for each foot the fish appears to be below the surface of the water. The aiming point would be four inches below the fish for a side shot from fifteen feet when the fish was one foot deep in the water. Most shots by good bow fishers are made at relatively close distances.

You may hit the fish if you follow the aiming directions, though certainty is not guaranteed, because fish simply will not hold still for any predictable length of time to allow time for a good shot. The bow fisher has problems with the water, aiming, and moving fish, but these difficulties help to make bow fishing a challenging and exciting sport. The bow fisher can derive considerable personal satisfaction when these problems are overcome and the fish is landed.

Figure 7.11
Two expert bowfishermen, Rob Davis and Bob Alexander, display their pride after landing a lemon shark that weighed 212 pounds and measured 8 feet 11 inches in length. (Courtesy J. Robert Davis, R.F.D. 4, Box 380, Spearin Road, Salisbury, Maryland 21801)

In figure 7.11, satisfaction and pride of accomplishment can be seen on the faces of two expert bow fishermen, Rob Davis and Bob Alexander. They have landed a 212-pound lemon shark which measured 8 feet 11 inches in length. They fish the bays between the barrier islands and the mainlands of Delaware, Maryland, and Virginia from May until September. They hunt stingrays (fig. 7.2) to use as bait to draw the sharks close for a shot. Both are exciting game. Aiming and shooting a large fish is only half of the excitement. What you do with a fish that weighs more than you do is the other half!

It is not a good idea to always drag large fish such as those shown in figures 7.11 and 7.13 into a boat. They can cause serious problems, including capsizing small boats. If they are brought on board alive, the thrashing about can cause injury, loss of equipment, and damage. Therefore, it is best to make certain the fish is dead prior to bringing it aboard the boat. In the case of large fish, it is best to haul them alongside the craft and beach them if possible rather than trying to lift them into the boat. J. Robert Davis recommends this procedure for sharks: he utilizes an innertube as a flotation device attached to the line and arrow. His shark rig is reinforced with steel cable to help control the fish. This improvised rig is seen in figure 7.12.

Once the fish has been landed, the problem is what to do with it? As noted, the fish legal for bow fishing are edible. There are many ways to prepare them for human consumption. The most popular edible rough fish is probably the carp.

Figure 7.12
A steel cable rig attached to a fishing arrow and innertube flotation device used in fishing for and landing sharks. (Courtesy J. Robert Davis, R.F.D. 4, Box 380, Spearin Road, Salisbury, Maryland 21801)

Figure 7.13
Wilbur Corley with an alligator gar, which weighed 123 pounds 6 ounces. The fish was taken on a river in south Texas. (Courtesy Wilbur Corley, 727 Holiday Lane, Claremore, Oklahoma 74017)

If you land a "big one" of any species, it could make a nice trophy mounted on the wall of your den to document the fact that not all big ones get away. Finally, fish not eaten make excellent fertilizer for home gardens. They should never be left on the bank to rot.

Bow Fishing Activities

Beyond the bow fishing activities of individuals, there are numerous organized activities conducted each year. These activities are sponsored by local archery clubs, national archery organizations, and manufacturers of archery tackle. Tournaments are conducted in many states and throughout the world.

National Field Archery Association Bowfisher Program

This program is designed to promote bow fishing as a sport and to recognize the accomplishments of bow fishers throughout the country. To be involved in this program, you must be a member of the NFAA. Patches are given to participants in the NFAA Bowfisher Program, and there are patch awards to indicate the type of fish taken. Carp and gar are the approved species.

The NFAA Bowfisher of the Year awards (plaques) go to the individuals who can document that they have landed the largest fish. There is one award for carp and one for gar. Winners are determined by weight of the fish, and the catch must be fully documented to the satisfaction of the NFAA Bowfisher Committee.

The NFAA also keeps records of who holds the distinction of having taken the largest carp or gar while using bow fishing techniques. To hold a NFAA Bowfisher Record, you must be a member of the NFAA. Record keeping and review of the records are done on an annual basis. If no records are broken during the year, the old records stand for the next year. There is a procedure for documenting catches and fish weights.

The NFAA Bowfisher Program Records are as follows:

Carp:	Lance Sullentrop	51 pounds
Gar:	Lance Sullentrop	157 pounds

These records have held since 1988.

Minimum Bowfisher Catch Objectives

Bowfishing magazine, when it was in publication, started a citation program for recognizing bowfishers who landed fish of minimum weights for specific species. (See Table 7.2.) This was an excellent idea. It is recommended that the standards established by Paul T. Shore continue to be utilized by bowfishers as desired catch objectives. For example, if you land an alligator gar above 100 pounds, you know that your catch is special.

Table 7.2   Bowfishing Magazine Citation Program Standards

Fish Species	Minimum Weight (Pounds)
FRESHWATER	
Alligator gar	100
Bowfin (grindle)	10
Buffalo	32
Carp	30
Gaspergou (freshwater drum)	15
Gold fish	3
Longnose gar	28
Paddlefish	35
Shortnose gar	7
Spotted gar	8
Sucker	5
Tilapia	4
SALTWATER	
Cownose ray	50
Flounder	3
Mullet	3
Shad	2
Shark	100
Sheepshead	4
Stingray	75

Bow Fishing Tournaments

There are numerous bow fishing tournaments held throughout the world each year. People of all ages enter for cash and other prizes provided through entry fees and sponsors. Prizes are awarded for the largest fish taken and for the highest weight total during the day or days of the tournament. There are competitive opportunities for teams as well as individuals in these tournaments. They are growing in numbers in a fashion analogous to the regular angling tournaments.

One of the better known bow fishing tournaments is the Annual Bowfishing Championship held at Clear Lake in Northern California. This is a carp shoot with lucrative cash and merchandise prizes. It is a two-person team event. The winning team is determined by the overall weight of the carp taken during the time allowed. Winning teams have taken as much as 847 pounds during the two-day competition! A cash prize is also awarded to the individual who lands the largest carp. The Fish and Game Department welcomes this type of tournament, because carp tend to multiply rapidly and upset the ecologic balance in waters such as Clear Lake.

Bow fishing, like other archery activities, can be satisfying as an individual endeavor or as a social activity to be enjoyed with friends. It is a sport that can provide many hours of recreation throughout a lifetime for the active participant who enjoys combining archery and fishing interests.

Review Questions

1. Describe in detail the arrows recommended for bow fishing.
2. Itemize the minor and major accessories that a well-prepared bow fisher should have.
3. Describe the aiming techniques that have proved successful in bow fishing.
4. Which of the species listed in table 7.1 are currently legal for bow fishing in your state, and what are the fishing limits?
5. What type of bow and rod rig would you use for bow fishing? Why?
6. Which type of bow fishing point would you use? Why?
7. Discuss the criteria you would use to purchase or to modify an existing boat for bow fishing.
8. How would you prepare for bow fishing for shark, and what techniques would you use to catch and land one that weighs more than you do?
9. What programs are available to recognize the efforts of bow fishers, and how do these programs operate?
10. Beyond the competitive and avocational aspects of bow fishing tournaments, what are some of the other benefits derived?
11. Why does aiming in bow fishing present problems not encountered on land?
12. What would be your aiming point for a side shot at a fish from a distance of 10 feet when the fish appears to be 2 feet below the surface?

Physical Conditioning for the Archer

8

Archery, like most sports, places physiologic demands on the individual. *Good physical conditioning increases the probability of success for an athlete in any sport. Archery is no exception to this axiom.* Competitive target archers are athletes. Bow hunters should also prepare themselves physiologically for their hunting seasons with intensity similar to that of many athletes in their preseason workouts.

The purpose of this chapter is to provide physical conditioning guidelines for serious target archers, field archers, and bow hunters. Exercises are presented and discussed with some anatomic detail. The archer needs to know what muscular exercise can and cannot do for you. Therefore, the exercises are described to show the archer how they should be performed; what muscles are exerted; how those muscle groups relate to archery performance; how intense, frequent, and for what duration they should be used; what outcomes can be expected through use of exercises at prescribed intensity, frequency, and duration levels.

Specificity of conditioning is unique for each sport, although there also are common exercises used in a wide variety of exercise programs. The emphasis taken to condition the archer differs considerably from conditioning programs designed for long distance runners or football players. Each sport places different demands on various body systems. *Different muscles are not necessarily used from one sport to the next, but muscle groups which cause motion are used differently.* Motions vary between sport activities in terms of their velocities and direction. A baseball pitcher, as an example, must be trained to move his throwing limb at maximum velocity in a precise direction in order to be effective. An archer, on the other hand, must train to hold the bow arm unit at maximum steadiness at a specific angle from drawing until the arrow is in the target. The exercises described in this chapter focus on the specificity of training for the target archer, field archer, and bow hunter. With reference to specific conditioning, there are even some differences between these archery sports to consider.

Muscle Analysis of Shooting

This brief anatomic analysis of shooting is presented for two reasons: (1) to help the serious archer gain a better understanding of specifically what needs to be conditioned and (2) to reinforce the learning of some of the shooting fundamentals presented in Chapter 4. It is highly recommended that the reader refer back to Chapter 4 and figure 8.1 as needed to relate the motions and techniques of the stance, the bow arm, drawing arm, and release to the muscle functions described below.

149

a   Nocking

b   Drawing

c   Low Anchor Point

d   Release & Follow-through

Figure 8.1
The shooting sequence in archery.

Stance

There are more common conditioning considerations between target archers and bow hunters than there are differences. The common bond is the fact that these archers must develop good levels of muscle strength and endurance in the large muscle groups which maintain the body in its stance or shooting position. The muscle groups which perform the function of extending the major joints at the ankles, knees, hips, and spine are called the *anteroposterior antigravity muscles*. These are shown in figure 8.2. Strength development in these antigravity muscles is indispensable for the archer, because steadiness in the shooting stance is the foundation upon which shooting accuracy is based. It is a well-known fact that even slight tremors or deviations of the extended body and bow arm segment will adversely affect arrow flight and accuracy. Both are essential to target archers, field archers, and bow hunters. Therefore, whatever the purpose is, conditioning the anteroposterior antigravity muscles for optimum strength should have the highest priority. A good level of strength in these muscle groups, which extend the major joints of your body, will increase the probability for success on the target range or in the field.

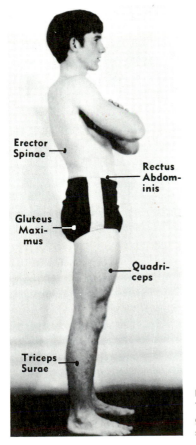

Erector
Spinae

Rectus
Abdom-
inis

Gluteus
Maxi-
mus

Quadri-
ceps

Triceps
Surae

Figure 8.2
The anteroposterior antigravity muscle groups form the foundation for stance stability.

The shooting stance is a bilateral, weight-bearing position with the major joints extended. This can be observed in figure 8.1. As a result, the static stability of the stance is maintained by this weight-bearing force and adjusted as needed by muscle contractions within the antigravity muscles, as shown in figure 8.2. The *triceps surae* are the large posterior calf muscles (*gastrocnemius* and *soleus*), which extend or plantar flex the ankle. The *quadriceps femoris* muscle group on the front of the thigh extend the knee, and the large buttocks muscle (*gluteus maximus*) extends the hip. The spinal column is maintained in the erect or extended position by the deep back muscle group known as the *erector spinae*. If an archer has a tendency to lean backwards, the abdominals or stomach muscles tend to counteract that negative motion of the spine. The *erector spinae* muscles will extend the spine of the archer if he or she has a tendency to lean forward or flex the lumbar-thoracic spine. Those two large muscle masses located anterior and posterior to your spine provide constant force-counterforce to maintain the extended spine needed for shooting. Fortunately, all of the antigravity muscle groups do not need to work maximally to maintain the erect shooting stance. They do work as needed to maintain alignment of body segments and equilibrium. The stronger they are the more efficient they become in accomplishing that task.

The importance of the antigravity muscle's strength and muscle endurance is most significant for those last few arrows shot during a target archery tournament, or for the hunter's shot at a trophy animal after he or she has been hiking and climbing in the mountains for several hours. Fatigue can have a negative effect on accuracy. The conditioned archer minimizes that factor, thus increasing the chance for success. There is an old saying in athletics that "You make your own breaks." Being in condition is part of that.

The Bow Arm

The conditioning needs are basically the same for the target archer, field archer, and bow hunter in terms of the functions of the bow arm segment and drawing arm. The bow hunter may on the average draw greater bow weights, but strength and muscle endurance development in the arms, shoulders, and shoulder girdles should greatly exceed the demands of bow weights used by all archers. The individual using a large bow weight requires more strength than an archer who draws a lighter bow weight.

Some of the arm, shoulder, and shoulder girdle musculature used to hold and draw the bow are shown in figures 8.3 and 8.4. These are the superficial muscles, i.e., those you can palpate or touch on yourself or on a cooperating adult. It is recommended that the archer find a cooperating archer and literally feel these muscles as they contract during the draw and while holding prior to release. This will facilitate understanding of the drawing process and the need for conditioning specific muscle groups. Once applied such knowledge can enhance scoring on the archery range.

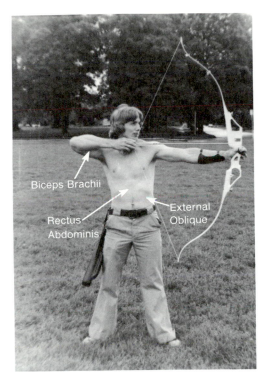

Figure 8.3
Anterior, superficial muscles. (Superficial muscles can be palpated or touched.)

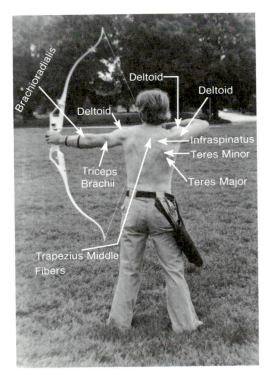

Figure 8.4
Posterior, superficial muscles.

The bow arm segment (left arm for the right-handed archer) is vital to accuracy in archery. Muscles must be strong enough to minimize motion in this arm at the time of release. Furthermore, the muscle endurance must be good enough to shoot for long periods of time, e.g., 144 arrows in a FITA Round.

As can be seen in figures 8.3 and 8.4, the bow arm segment is held in an extended position involving the wrist and elbow. After nocking, the bow arm is raised from the side (shoulder joint abduction) about ninety degrees as seen between figure 8.1(a) and (b). That motion is accomplished mainly by contraction of the large shoulder or *deltoid* muscle. The deltoid must be strengthened to perform that function. But, more importantly, it must contribute considerable stabilizing force through release to help hold the literal weight of the arm as well as the mass weight of the bow in space. Any deviation of the bow arm segment at or just prior to release will have a negative impact on accurate arrow flight. Both deltoid muscles must be strong with a good level of muscle endurance.

The *triceps brachii* is also a very important muscle within the bow arm segment, because it must keep the elbow in the extended position as shown in figures 8.3 and 8.4. Maximal contraction of the muscles in the bow arm is not necessary, and it would be contraindicated. As indicated in Chapter 4, the skilled archer relaxes as much musculature as possible while the *triceps brachii* and *deltoid* muscles exert the most critical forces.

There are thirteen large muscles that surround the wrist joint. These make up the muscle mass of your forearm, and they help keep the wrist extended by contributing some stabilizing contraction as the archer moves the bow arm into and holds the anchor position waiting to release. It is a serious mistake to maximize static or isometric contraction of these bow arm muscles. As noted, relaxation is the key. One must take advantage of the external forces provided by the bow to assist in maintaining extensions of the wrist and elbow joints. As noted in Chapter 4, the wrist is never flexed or hyperextended during the shooting process. Your forearm (radio-ulnar joint) remains stable in midposition (handshake position) between supination and pronation throughout the shooting sequence.

The Drawing Arm

The drawing arm segment (right arm for a right-handed archer) must have adequate strength and muscle endurance to handle the archer's bow weight during numerous draws, e.g., 288 times during a double FITA Round competition. From a competitive perspective, it is very important to the archer that the last draw should feel as easy as the first draw. The key to this is to condition the muscles most involved for the draw, and learn how to relax the remaining draw arm muscles as much as possible.

A key point to remember regarding the draw: *the major muscular force and finite control of the draw lies in the shoulder joint and shoulder girdle and not in the arm.* We tend to focus on the arm, because it is the moving segment. The *biceps brachii* and other elbow flexors do contribute some force during the draw. But, the draw is the result of contractions by musculature within the right shoulder joint and right shoulder girdle. The drawing arm segment transfers the muscle forces to the bowstring as it is brought to the anchor point. Scientifically, the total motion of the drawing arm is the result of: (1) elbow flexion, (2) horizontal or diagonal abduction of the shoulder joint, and (3) shoulder girdle adduction or retraction.

The force to cause the shoulder motion is provided by the *deltoid, infraspinatus,* and *teres minor* muscles. These superficial muscles are shown in figure 8.4, because of their location, some archery instructors advise students to concentrate on using "back muscles" during the draw. The force to cause the shoulder blade to move toward your spinal column during the draw (shoulder girdle adduction) is caused by contraction of the *trapezius* muscle fibers, as shown in figure 8.4, plus the rhomboid muscles attached to the shoulder blade *beneath* the *trapezius.* If you feel a partner's back during a draw, you can palpate the superficial muscles. By providing a *concentration focal point,* this will give a better perception of the draw when you do it. Also, palpate the biceps brachii in the upper arm. It will be tense, but its force contribution for the draw is not as significant as the other muscles mentioned.

Conditioning for the draw arm segment must be designed to develop adequate strength and muscle endurance levels in the very important "back muscles" of the shoulder girdle and shoulder joint. In addition, the elbow flexors need specific work to provide their force contribution to the draw.

As the drawing arm is moving the bowstring and hand into the anchor position, the shoulder blade (scapula) is being rotated upward to accommodate the head of the humerus of the arm at the shoulder joint. This motion of the scapula is the result of muscle contractions by the *serratus anterior* and parts of the *trapezius.* Once your anchor point is set, the serratus anterior stabilizes or holds the scapula in position. Muscular stability of this type is very important to the shooting process, and the muscle stabilizers in this segment and elsewhere also need attention in the conditioning process.

The Release and Follow-Through

The key muscle force component of the release is the final one-eighth inch movement of your arrow through the clicker prior to release. This very important motion is accomplished by concentration on your "middle back muscles." Specifically, the middle fibers of your trapezius muscle are conditioned to contract and *gently* move your shoulder blade toward your spinal column (scapular adduction). That moves the arrow past the clicker. When the "click" is heard, the string fingers are ready to extend allowing the string to move forward and the arrow to release. As mentioned in Chapter 4, the extension of your finger joints (interphalangeal joints) *is not* the result of muscle contraction on the part of most archers. The external force for release is caused by the string as you relax the tension within the finger flexor musculature, i.e., the "three-finger hook" around the string (fig. 4.16).

During the follow-through, you simply watch the arrow flight to observe any erratic motion. You may exhale and inhale at this time and watch the arrow until it strikes the target. There will be a slight "recoil motion" of the draw arm, and the bow arm may drop a few degrees.

Fitness Guidelines

Physical fitness is usually considered to include four parameters: (1) strength, (2) muscular endurance, (3) cardiovascular endurance, and (4) flexibility. Flexibility guidelines are not presented in detail. Due to the nature of the sport of archery, total body flexibility is not considered to be a high priority fitness factor for success. Lack of flexibility in the drawing shoulder and shoulder girdle could be a problem, but this is observed only in a very small percentage of archers. The nature of the draw (slow stretch) tends to increase the flexibility of the noncontractile tissue of the drawing shoulder and shoulder girdle to a functional range-of-motion for the archer. The draw from its start to the anchor point is a flexibility exercise when held for 20 to 30 seconds at the anchor point.

Strength

A functional definition of strength is the ability of an individual to overcome resistance by the use of internal force developed through muscle contraction. A strength development program for archers is included in this chapter.

In order to elicit the neuromuscular changes in the body needed to produce strength, the following scientifically based guidelines are needed to define the workload:

1. INTENSITY: The weight load should be great enough to limit the number of repetitions to eight for each exercise, i.e., maximum weight load for a maximum of eight repetitions. When strength improves to the point that more than eight repetitions can be performed, add enough weight to return to the eight repetition level. Breathe during the difficult portion of the exercise. This keeps the glottis open in the throat and reduces the probability of herniation and undesired shifts in blood pressure. Maximum weight loads for less than eight repetitions should be avoided.
2. FREQUENCY: Strength workouts should be performed a *minimum* of four days per week in order to obtain best results. Daily workouts may be performed without ill effects, and they are recommended for individuals who are strong and highly motivated as weight trainers. The average workout should be spaced 24 to 36 hours apart.
3. DURATION: The average strength workout should consume approximately one hour. A series of exercises as described later in this chapter should be selected. One series of weight training exercises is called a "set." Three sets would constitute a strength workout following the intensity guideline outlined above. *Always perform the exercises slowly through the complete range of motion.*

If these strength guidelines are followed, the archer will acquire strength. It usually takes from four to six weeks for the initial strength changes to occur.

The term "neuromuscular changes" was used above for good reason. The most significant anatomic and physiologic changes to increase strength will be as a result of *specific adaptations* of central nervous system structures to the *imposed demands* of strength training outlined above. You become stronger by making the interrelationships between the muscular and central nervous systems more efficient. The most important changes for increasing strength levels occur in the central nervous system.

Muscular Endurance

Muscle endurance is the ability of a muscle group to perform repeated contractions against relatively light resistance. Muscle endurance is needed when a performer must repeat joint motions numerous times during competition. The shooting procedure involving the drawing arm segment in target archery is an example of muscle groups needing muscle endurance.

In order to elicit the physiologic changes in the body to increase muscle endurance, the following workload guidelines must be followed:

1. INTENSITY: The weight load to produce muscle endurance should be established to allow the performer to complete a *minimum of twenty repetitions*. More repetitions may be performed at each station as time allows. The physiologic changes associated with this level of intensity will enhance aerobic metabolism for energy production.
2. FREQUENCY: Muscle endurance workouts should be performed a *minimum* of four days per week. Daily workouts may be performed without ill effects. Individuals produce excellent results working six or seven days per week, alternating strength and muscle endurance workouts. That is functional, and boredom is reduced by not performing the same activity on a daily basis.
3. DURATION: The average muscle endurance workout should consume approximately one hour. Three sets of exercises constitute one workout. The maximum number of repetitions per exercise station per set may need to be adjusted periodically as a time consideration. *Perform all exercises slowly through the complete range-of-motion.*

An individual who starts a conditioning program must be patient. The changes of physiologic function may not manifest themselves for weeks, and it is easy to become frustrated. You must remember, for example, that muscular endurance changes involve sophisticated modifications of cells and organelles within cells responsible for aerobic respiration. Using the guidelines above, you will increase your muscular endurance in due time. Persistence will pay off.

Specific recommendations regarding strength and/or muscle endurance exercises for the various muscle groups used by archers are presented in detail in this chapter. Priorities will be established for strength and muscle endurance intensities during workouts.

Cardiovascular Endurance

The principal conditioning difference between target archers, field archers, and bow hunters is in the extent of cardiovascular endurance required to execute the skill. Generally, the target archer does not need to develop more than an average or functional level of cardiovascular endurance. The nature of the sport does not place maximal oxygen consumption demands on the archer. It is recommended, however, that the serious archer perform enough aerobic exercise on a regular basis to maintain a good level of cardiovascular fitness. (See table 8.1.)

Field archers and bow hunters, on the other hand, should analyze the demands placed on them in the field. As an example, if a hunt takes the bow hunter into the field to walk for extended time periods, in cold or hot environments, over hills or into high altitudes, and with the possibility of packing out heavy game (e.g., elk), considerable thought should be given to maintain or develop cardiovascular endurance to meet these increased demands without difficulty when they are confronted on the hunt. Why is this important? It is a tragic fact that a few hunters, usually age thirty-five and beyond, die of myocardial infarctions in the field because they were not capable of handling the added exercise stress in a cold environment in hilly terrain, as experienced during the deer and elk seasons. It pays to be prepared cardiovascularly!

There are other, less traumatic, problems which have been observed more frequently in cardiovascularly unfit bow hunters. Much money is spent on tackle preparing for the hunt. Time is devoted to developing shooting skill and to tune the tackle for the hunt. For example, some people spend large amounts of money traveling to high mountain country for elk or other game. After spending all the money, time, and effort, some bow hunters are not capable of meeting the physiologic challenge of the hunt on foot through rugged terrain at high altitude in the cold. If they pack in, their hunting partners often have to pack them out! That is not an uncommon scenario, and it is very illogical for any bow hunter. *The full preparation of the archer should include concurrent development of shooting skill and cardiovascular conditioning. Cardiovascular endurance is the ability of the circulatory and respiratory systems to supply and transport oxygen and other fuels efficiently during sustained exercise.* How much exercise is needed to produce positive changes in cardiorespiratory efficiency in an individual with a "normal" cardiovascular system? An archer who wishes to increase his or her cardiovascular endurance should first be evaluated by a physician to determine the status of the circulatory and respiratory systems. The scientifically based guidelines below should help the interested bow hunters, field archers, and target archers maintain or develop their cardiovascular fitness.

1. INTENSITY: To improve your cardiorespiratory capacity, intensity of exercise is measured according to two criteria: (1) Heart rate during exercise sufficient enough to produce positive training effects. That level of exercise intensity is known as your *threshold heart rate* or *THR*—See table 8.1 for THR levels according to age and general condition status. (2) *Energy expenditure* during conditioning workouts *beyond 2000 kilocalories per week* (Kcal/wk). Men should expend 3000 to 3500 kilocalories per week, and women should be at the 2000 to 2500 level.

Table 8.1 Threshold Heart Rate Intensity Levels for Cardiovascular Endurance Development

Age Group	Max HR*	Morning Resting Heart Rate Above 75 BPM	Morning Resting Heart Rate 55–75 BPM	Morning Resting Heart Rate Below 55 BPM
15–19	200	114 (120) 126	143 (150) 158	152 (160) 168
20–24	195	111 (117) 123	139 (146) 154	148 (156) 164
25–29	190	108 (114) 120	135 (142) 150	144 (152) 160
30–34	185	105 (111) 117	131 (138) 143	140 (148) 156
35–39	180	102 (108) 114	128 (135) 143	136 (144) 152
40–44	175	99 (105) 111	124 (131) 139	132 (140) 148
45–49	170	96 (102) 108	120 (127) 135	128 (136) 144
50–54	165	93 (99) 105	116 (123) 131	124 (132) 140
55–59	160	90 (96) 102	113 (120) 128	120 (128) 136
60–64	155	87 (93) 99	109 (116) 124	116 (124) 132
65–69	150	84 (90) 96	105 (112) 120	112 (120) 128
70–74	145	81 (87) 93	101 (109) 116	108 (116) 124

*The variability for maximum heart rate is ± 10 BPM.
Note: *This table should read as follows:* A 22-year-old person has a maximum heart rate of 195 BPM ± 10 BPM. If this individual's resting heart rate is 62 BPM, the threshold heart rate (THR) *during exercise* should average 139–154 BPM. The *target number* for THR would be 146 BPM for this person during aerobic activities to produce cardiovascular training effects.

How do you determine what your exercising or threshold heart rate should be? Use table 8.1. The maximum and resting heart rates play a key role in terms of establishing your THR. The heart rate needs to be monitored in the morning while you are lying in bed. This will give you your *resting heart rate*. Take a one-minute reading by gently palpating your radial artery at the wrist. Such a reading is noted in *beats per minute* (BPM). If you are in average cardiovascular condition, your resting heart rate will be between 55 to 75 BPM. Better conditioned people usually will have more efficient cardiac function and slower heart rates, i.e., exercise-induced bradycardia. If, as an example, you are nineteen years of age with a resting heart rate of 46 BPM, table 8.1 will inform you that your heart rate intensity (THR) during exercise should be kept between 152 and 168 BPM. Your target number is 160 BPM.

How do you monitor THR intensity during an aerobic workout? First, you need to know your THR range in BPM during exercise. Second, the midpoint in that range should be kept in mind specifically; this is your exercise target number to monitor as you work out. Third, for individuals beginning an aerobic workout program, it is recommended that the heart rate be monitored every 10 to 15 minutes during exercise. In order to do this and obtain meaningful heart rates, you must stop exercising. *As soon as you stop your aerobic activity, determine your heart rate by palpating the radial artery at the wrist.* Within 5 to 10 seconds of stopping, take a 10-second heart rate count. Multiply that number by six for BPM. If this reading is accomplished in this time frame, it will be very close to your exercising heart rate. A longer delay in monitoring the heart rate following cessation of exercise decreases the accuracy of assuming that the reading reflects the heart rate during exercise. Ideally, a heart rate correctly monitored will be on your target number or within your THR range. (There are electronic devices on the market that will measure your exercising heart rate.)

During the aerobic workout, one attempts to keep the exercising heart rate in BPM in the THR range and fairly close to the target number. As an example, a 52-year-old runner with a resting heart rate of 42 BPM would have an exercise target number of 132 BPM. This means that the *10-second heart rate reading* during exercise should be 22 beats. If this reading were lower, it would indicate that the exercise intensity was below the THR range (e.g., 20 beats/10 second count). This person would need to speed up his or her pace slightly while exercising. Conversely, if the 10-second heart rate reading during exercise were counted at 25 beats (150 BPM), this individual should slow the running pace. That intensity would be 10 BPM above his THR range.

It is important to stay within your THR range during aerobic work. Actually, you should find this range to be relatively comfortable. Breathing should not be labored per se, and you should be able to talk with a companion while moving at a pace to produce your THR.

There is a dangerous myth about exercise which states, "no pain, no gain." The exercise intensity at your threshold heart rate will not produce pain or distress. Exercise does not have to be painful in order to produce positive results. In fact, from physiologic, psychologic, and medical points-of-view, extreme stress exercise is contraindicated and counterproductive.

You can use any form of exercise as long as it is intense enough to keep you in your THR range. Most commonly these are jogging, running, swimming, cycling, and court sports. Can walking be an aerobic activity? Absolutely! If a brisk walk at 3 to 4 miles per hour pace moves you into your THR, you should not be running. Find an activity or activities that you enjoy doing that will keep your THR for the required duration and stick with it!

The other dimension of intensity of exercise is the level of energy expenditure. This is measured in kilocalories. The kilocalorie is used metabolically as the amount of heat required to raise the temperature of one liter of water one degree centigrade. The so-called "large Calorie" is used for measuring energy intake (food) and expenditure (exercise/muscular activities). Minimum and desired energy expenditure levels in Kcal/week to maintain and develop health-related fitness were noted above for men and women.

How can you monitor your Kcal/week? Exercise physiologists have done metabolic measurements on everything from archery to sexual intercourse! So, energy expenditure values are available for most activities humans pursue. The following is the procedure to determine *energy expenditure for target archery practice:*

1. Change your body weight in pounds to kilograms by multiplying the pounds by *0.454.*
2. Multiplying your weight in kilograms by a factor of *0.065* will give you the Kcal/min you use during target archery.

Target archery for a 147 pounder (66.74 Kg) for an hour would result in an energy expenditure of 260 kilocalories (4.34 Kcal/min). He or she most likely would not reach THR intensity, so one can readily see that integration of aerobic activities with archery practice is needed to reach a respectable level of health-related fitness. This is where running, cycling, swimming, or walking can be utilized.

Table 8.2 provides energy expenditure factors to be used in the calculation of Kcal/min for running, swimming, walking, and cycling.

Table 8.2   Energy Expenditure Factors for Determining Kcal/min

Horizontal Running	Factor
11 min 30 sec per mile	0.135
9 min per mile	0.193
8 min per mile	0.208
7 min per mile	0.228
6 min per mile	0.252
5 min 30 sec per mile	0.289
Swimming	
Back stroke	0.169
Breast stroke	0.162
Crawl stroke	0.156
Walking: 3–4 MPH	
Firm surface	0.080
Fields and hillsides	0.082
Grass	0.081
Cycling	
5.5 miles per hour	0.064
9.4 miles per hour	0.100
Racing	0.169

Note: This table should be used as follows: convert your weight in pounds to kilograms by multiplying by 0.454. Multiply your weight in kilograms by the factor to determine your energy expenditure in kilocalories per minute. *Example:* A 147 pounder (66.74 Kg) utilizes 13.88 Kcal/min while running at an 8-min-per-mile pace:
1. 147 pounds × 0.454 = 66.74 Kg
2. 66.74 Kg × 0.208 = 13.88 Kcal/min

If our 147 pounder ran an 8-minute pace per mile for 40 minutes per day at THR intensity four days per week, he or she would expend 2220 kilocalories. Add three hours per week of target archery practice to that at 260 kilocalories per hour, the total would be a very good level of intensity at 3000 Kcal/week. Such a regimen would be desired because it combines cardiovascular conditioning with shooting.

2. FREQUENCY: In order to produce the modifications in the blood chemistry, the blood vascular transport system, and elsewhere, cardiovascular or aerobic workouts at threshold heart rate intensity should be performed a minimum of four days per week. Ideally, workouts should be spaced about thirty-six hours apart. Daily aerobic activity is recommended for individuals who have established good cardiorespiratory endurance with resting heart rates in the morning below 55 beats per minute.

3. DURATION: Thirty minutes of cardiovascular exercise at your threshold heart rate is considered to be the minimum duration for a workout. Durations of 30 to 60 minutes per workout are adequate. If an individual is exercising on a frequency of six to seven days per week, it is a good idea to alternate such components as duration times and activities. For example, an hour bicycle ride on Monday could be followed by a 30-minute jog on Tuesday. *Activities chosen should be of interest and challenge the archer.* That is an extremely important criterion, because long-term continuity of exercise is a must in terms of health-related fitness maintenance and development.

As indicated above, some bow hunters may have a greater need in terms of the physiologic demands of their sport to develop cardiovascular endurance than do target archers. However, in terms of health as well as performance related fitness, cardiovascular endurance is the most important fitness parameter.

Exercises for Stance Stability

All archers need adequate strength in their *antigravity muscles* to maintain a stable, nonmoving stance while shooting. A set of six exercises is recommended. Strength development should be the priority fitness factor for these exercises; therefore, the intensity, frequency, and duration guidelines outlined for strength should be followed when possible while performing these exercises. The figures serve as examples to demonstrate one method to exercise the muscle groups. It is recognized that there are other good exercises using weight machines and free weights to exercise the same muscle groups.

When resistance loads cannot be found to meet the intensity criterion for strength development, muscle endurance exercise intensity should be performed. Some strength gain will be made, which will enhance stance stability. Figures 8.5 through 8.13 show exercises (with the exception of fig. 8.8) that may be performed with or without machines to add strength weight loads. It must be remembered that free weights or weight machines are not always necessary for muscle endurance development. The weight of the body working against and with gravity can be used for muscle endurance gains for some exercises.

Note: For all exercises pictured and/or described in the remainder of this chapter, they should be performed *slowly* both moving against resistance and moving with the gravitational field. Breathing should be done as normal as possible, and the breath should not be held.

Figure 8.5
Heel raise exercise—starting position.

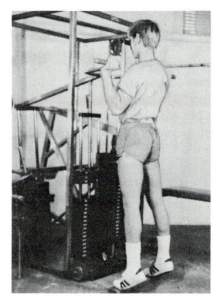

Figure 8.6
Heel raise exercise—finish position. This exercise works the calf or triceps surae muscles.

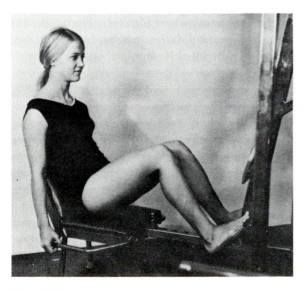

Figure 8.7
The knee extension exercise for the anterior thigh or quadriceps femoris muscles.

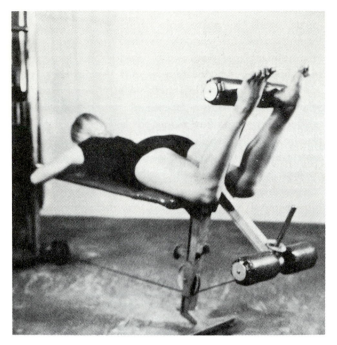

Figure 8.8
The knee flexion exercise for posterior thigh or "hamstring" muscles. These muscles flex the knee as shown and help extend the hip joints.

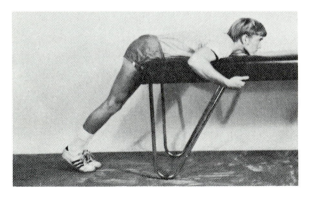

Figure 8.9
Double hip extension exercise—starting position.

Figure 8.10
Double hip extension exercise—finish position. This exercise works the large buttocks muscle, the gluteus maximus.

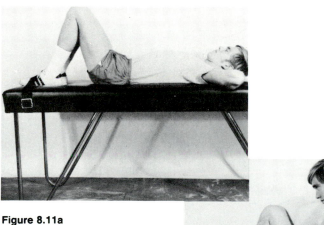

Figure 8.11a
The flexed knee and hip sit-up exercise—starting position.

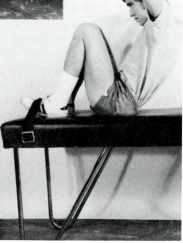

Figure 8.11b
The flexed knee and hip sit-up exercise— finish position. This execise works the stomach or abdominal muscles.

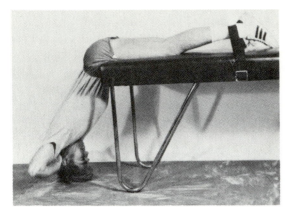

Figure 8.12
The back raise exercise—starting position.

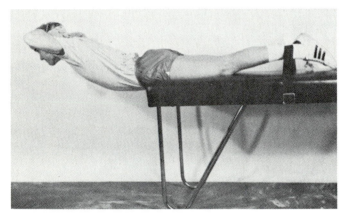

Figure 8.13
The back raise exercise—finish position. This exercise works the deep back muscle group, erector spinae.

Exercises for the Bow Arm

Steadiness of the bow arm is one of the most critical aspects of shooting. The major muscles most involved to produce this stability are located at the shoulder and elbow joints. As a result, the archer needs considerable strength in the deltoid muscle of the shoulder as well as in the triceps and biceps brachii muscles which surround the elbow joint. The strength development guidelines need to be followed for the bow arm exercises.

Figures 8.14 and 8.15 are examples of exercises primarily designed to work the large deltoid muscle over the shoulder. This muscle must be strong enough to support the mass weight of the bow without deviations during every shot in a target or field archery tournament and during a hunt.

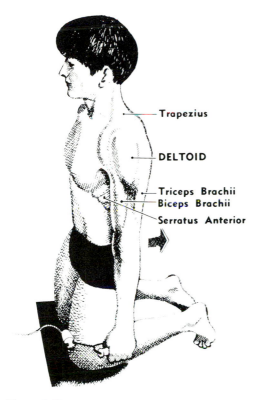

Trapezius

DELTOID

Triceps Brachii
Biceps Brachii

Serratus Anterior

Figure 8.14
A bow arm weight-training exercise using an Exer-Genie Exerciser pulley device. The arm is moved from the side into the shooting position (ABDUCTED) by the shoulder or deltoid muscle.

Figure 8.14 illustrates a resistance exercise using a pulley device. The deltoid muscle is the muscle most involved as the arm is raised or abducted from the body in the same manner as moving the bow into the final shooting position. This exercise also works the important serratus anterior and trapezius muscles. As the arm is moved through its upward range-of-motion (abducted) against resistance, the scapula is upwardly rotated by lower fibers of the serratus anterior and upper and lower portions of the trapezius.

Figure 8.15 shows a traditional weight-training exercise, the overhead press. This is also a good method to develop strength in the bow arm musculature. This exercise involves the large shoulder musculature, some back muscles, plus your triceps brachii muscle which extends the elbow. Keeping the bow arm elbow fully extended at all times is critical while shooting. This requires considerable strength in the triceps brachii muscle.

The bench press as shown in figure 8.16 is another weight-training exercise designed to strengthen the triceps brachii on the posterior side of your elbow. Also, this exercise strengthens the deltoid as well as the large pectoralis major muscle on your chest. Work by the deltoid and triceps brachii during the bench press makes it a good exercise for the bow arm unit. As in the previous two exercises, crucial shoulder girdle musculature is also conditioned.

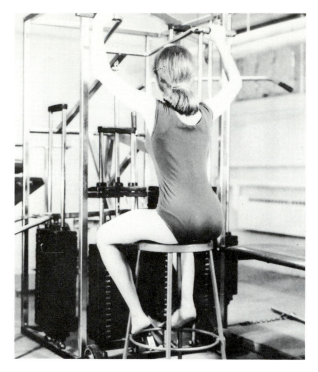

Figure 8.15
The overhead press exercise is a good bow arm exercise because it strengthens the deltoid muscle at the shoulder and the triceps brachii at the elbow.

Figure 8.16
The bench press exercise contributes strength to the bow arm unit by working the elbow extensor muscle, the triceps brachii, plus the deltoid and pectoralis major muscles.

Figure 8.17
The biceps brachii curl exercise adds anterior stabilizing strength to the extended elbow of the bow arm unit, and it adds strength to the drawing arm.

The elbow of the bow arm segment is held in the stable and extended position by all of the muscles surrounding the elbow joint. Therefore, the archer should strengthen not only the muscle on the back of the elbow, the triceps brachii, which extends the elbow, but also the biceps brachii on the front of the elbow. The biceps curl exercise as shown in figure 8.17 is designed to develop strength in all of the muscles located on the anterior or front of your upper arm and elbow, and it should be used on both elbows to enhance efficiency in the bow arm and drawing arm.

Exercises for the Drawing Arm

As noted previously, the main force for the drawing arm does not come from the arm muscles per se. The draw force is derived from strong shoulder and shoulder girdle muscles. Some of these are shown in figure 8.18. They include the *deltoid, infraspinatus, teres minor, trapezius,* and *rhomboid* muscles. (The latter are not seen in figure 8.18 because they lie beneath your trapezius muscle). These are the "back muscles" which your archery instructor or coach wants you to concentrate on during target archery practice as you draw through your clicker. Since these muscles literally provide the force to overcome the bow weight during the draw, they must be strengthened to be functional. The stronger these muscles

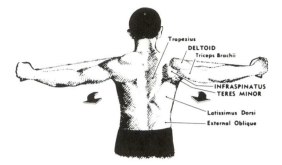

Figure 8.18
The drawing arm exercise using a pulley device that isolates the critical muscles used to exert the force to overcome the bow weight.

Figure 8.19
The drawing arm exercise using dumbbells for resistance. It is important to move the arms from the floor through the complete range-of-motion.

are, the easier it is for you to handle your bow weight. Also, with added strength in these muscles, the archer may be able to increase bow weight. Higher arrow velocities and flatter trajectories can lead to better accuracy and higher scores.

Figure 8.18 shows a drawing arm resistance exercise as it can be performed with a pulley device. It is important for the archer to move the arms through the complete range-of-motion as indicated by the direction of the arrows. One should feel the shoulder blades move toward your spine (scapular adduction) as the arms are moved backward (horizontal abduction) as shown in figure 8.18.

The same exercise is shown in figure 8.19 using dumbbells for resistance. The starting position is with the hands near the floor. It is very important to move the hands and arms as far as possible to the finish position shown in figure 8.19.

As a matter of scientific principle in regard to the development of strength and muscle endurance and also to insure adequate flexibility for the archer in the shoulder and shoulder girdle areas, resistance exercise to work the opposite side muscle groups is recommended. An exercise to work the chest and shoulder

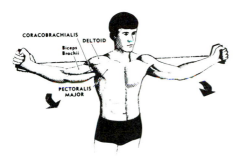

Figure 8.20
Shoulder horizontal adduction exercise to complement the drawing arm exercise using a pulley device.

Figure 8.21
Shoulder horizontal adduction exercise using dumbbells to complement the drawing arm exercise. It is important to move the arms through the complete range-of-motion from below the bench to touching the dumbbells above your head.

is depicted for use with a wall pulley and dumbbells in figures 8.20 and 8.21 respectively. The arms are brought forward (horizontally adducted) by the contracting muscles on the front of the shoulder and chest. This stretches those "back muscles" that were involved while performing the exercise shown in figures 8.18 and 8.19. Strengthening front and back muscles will make the archer's draw easier to handle and prevent loss of shoulder range-of-motion (flexibility).

The Overload Draw Exercise

The archer can and should consider the bow to be a weight training device. The exercises previously described in this chapter can develop general strength and muscle endurance in muscle groups used by the archer. These may be at greater intensity levels than available in most bows. That application of the "Overload Principle" is necessary. However, a very specific muscle endurance overload can be provided to the archer by exercising with a bow that has a bow weight in excess of the normal bow used in competition or while hunting. This practice has the potential to develop strength and muscle endurance in muscle groups through the precise ranges-of-motion and specific joint angles utilized in drawing and holding the bow during a contest or hunt.

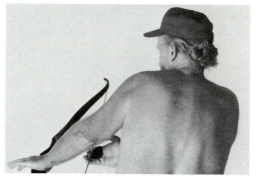

Figure 8.22(a)
The overload draw exercise—starting
position. (Bow courtesy Black Widow
Bow Company, H. C. R. #1, Box 357–
1, Highlandville Missouri 65669)

Figure 8.22(b)
The overload draw exercise—back
musculature—starting position.

As an added component of the conditioning process for archers, it is recommended that *overload drawing* be included within each set of muscle endurance exercises. A bow a few pounds over the normal bow weight can be used, and a *minimum* of 20 draws should be made per exercise set. That would mean that the archer would complete a *minimum* of 60 Overload Draws during a workout. (FITA Round shooters may want to complete 144 consecutive draws periodically just as a drill.)

The bow should be drawn to the anchor point as shown in figures 8.22, 8.23, and 8.24, and held statically long enough to simulate the release and follow-through phases. The bowstring must not be released. The string should be eased back to the starting position, and the next draw would be initiated.

This is more than a weight training exercise. While doing overload drawing, the archer should concentrate on all shooting fundamentals. Each fundamental, body position, and joint angle should be thought through carefully. It is recommended that the position of a body part or segment be given specific attention during each set of overload draws, e.g., the bow hand position at the pivot point during the first set, anchor point on the second set, and string finger position on the third set. Different skill areas could be thought out on different practice days.

Figure 8.23(a)
The overload draw exercise—mid-position.

Figure 8.23(b)
The overload draw exercise—back musculature—mid-position.

It is further recommended that concentration areas be an outgrowth of target practice. If some fundamental skill area is a problem during practice, you should give it critical thought during overload draw work. Overload drawing should be done following practice on a target or field range.

Overload drawing is shown in figures 8.22, 8.23, and 8.24. It is recommended that most of these draws be smooth and continuous from the starting position to anchor. However, an occasional static hold at mid-position for 6 to 8 seconds—the position shown in figure 8.23—could facilitate some strength gain. Also, the hold while at the anchor point, figure 8.24, should be for at least 6 to 8 seconds. The reader should refer to figures 8.4 and 8.18 while observing the changes in the superficial back and shoulder muscles of the archer in figures 8.22, 8.23, and 8.24. Several changes occur in the bow arm and drawing arm musculature. Some of these can be observed by comparing and contrasting the alterations in the external appearance of the back and shoulder muscles of the archer in figures 8.22 and 8.24.

It was noted earlier in this chapter that total energy expenditure is important to consider in terms of Kcal/week of exercise. If you perform the types of weight training exercises described herein for archers, table 8.3 can be used to help you determine Kcal/min for weight training.

Figure 8.24(a)
The overload draw exercise—anchor
position.

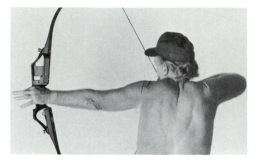

Figure 8.24(b)
The overload draw exercise—back
musculature—anchor position.

Table 8.3   Energy Expenditure Factors for Determining Kcal/min Values for Weight Training

Types of Equipment Used	Factor
Hydra-Fitness	0.132
Universal	0.116
Nautilus	0.092
Free Weights	0.086

Note: This table should be used as follows: Convert your weight in pounds to kilograms by multiplying by
0.454. Multiply your weight in kilograms by the appropriate factor to determine your energy expenditure in
kilocalories per minute. *Example:* A 166 pounder (75.36 Kg) would use 6.48 Kcal/min doing free weight
exercise:
1. 166 pounds $\times$ 0.454 = 75.36 Kg
2. 75.36 Kg $\times$ 0.086 = 6.48 Kcal/min

Summary

When the skill factor between competitors is equal, a conditioned target archer
or field archer can increase his or her probability of outscoring an archer with
average levels of muscle endurance, strength, and cardiovascular endurance. The
serious bow hunter in good condition, who must go after game in wilderness or
rugged terrain will thus facilitate that task, assure his or her own survival, and
increase the likelihood of making the kill and carrying out the meat.

The following thirteen systematic activities are recommended as *one set* of
exercises for archers. *Three sets should be performed to constitute a daily workout.* The guidelines for strength or muscle endurance should be followed re-

garding intensity, frequency, and duration, depending upon the outcomes desired by the archer: (A variety of free weights, weight machines, pulley devices, and the resistance provided by gravity and the body itself may be used to perform these exercises.)

Stance

1. Heel raise (figs. 8.5 and 8.6)
2. Knee extension (fig. 8.7)
3. Knee flexion (fig. 8.8)
4. Hip extension (figs. 8.9 and 8.10)
5. Sit-up (fig. 8.11)
6. Back raise (figs. 8.12 and 8.13)

Bow Arm

7. Shoulder abduction (fig. 8.14)
8. Overhead press (fig. 8.15)
9. Bench press (fig. 8.16)
10. Biceps curl (fig. 8.17)—use for draw arm also

Draw Arm

11. Horizontal abduction (fig. 8.19)
12. Horizontal adduction (fig. 8.21)
13. Overload drawing (figs. 8.22 through 8.24)

When three sets of these exercises are completed at the intensity desired, it is recommended that the archer conclude the workout with a minimum of 30 minutes of cardiovascular endurance exercise (running, cycling, etc.) at the threshold heart rate level of intensity.

It would require approximately 45 minutes to complete the weight-training program. Let us assume that our 147-pound (66.74 Kg) archer did this four times per week with free weights. That would be an energy expenditure of 1032 Kcal/week. If he or she jogged at THR intensity at an 8-minute-per-mile pace for 30 minutes four times per week, 1666 kilocalories would be expended. The total expenditure for these activities would be 2698 Kcal/week. Add two hours of archery practice to that per week, and the grand total would be a respectable 3218 Kcal/week. *Result:* a better archer with a good level of health-related fitness!

Increasing the level of strength, muscle endurance, and cardiovascular endurance produces important physiologic and anatomic changes in the archer. It is of utmost importance that the archer continue target practice concurrently with these developmental changes in the body. That procedure will ensure that changes in accuracy are also positive. If the archer conditions without shooting on a regular basis, it may take time to adapt the skill fundamentals to the bodily changes. For the most positive results, the archer should condition and shoot concurrently and frequently.

Review Questions

1. Why is cardiovascular endurance so important to the bow hunter?
2. When participating in an aerobic workout, how should you monitor your heart rate, at what intervals should you check it, and what is your target level?
3. Describe shooting mechanics by integrating the techniques of shooting (Chapter 4) with the musculature that provide the forces for each of the following: (1) stance; (2) bow arm; (3) drawing arm; and (4) release and follow-through.
4. Compare and contrast the differences in the expected anatomic changes between strength development and conditioning for muscular endurance.
5. Discuss the intensity criteria an archer should use in establishing his or her cardiovascular conditioning program.
6. It takes 3500 kilocalories of energy expenditure to rid one's self of one pound of stored, excess fat. How long would it take for you to get rid of one pound of your fat by using target archery practice as your only exercise?
7. Review the energy expenditure values. What activities can you use and for what duration to expend 2000 to 3000 Kcal/week?
8. Disuss the specificity of training concept related to the overload draw exercise.
9. Write out a complete fitness program for yourself involving developmental activities for strength, muscle endurance, cardiovascular endurance, and skill. What are the frequencies for the activities? Have you adhered to the intensity criteria? What is the daily duration level for the activities chosen? What is the total energy expenditure per week in kilocalories?
10. Under what conditions does the archer most readily realize the importance of the strength and endurance of the antigravity muscle groups?
11. Which muscle groups provide the principal force for the drawing arm?

Archery in Literature and Art

9

Since the bow and arrow have played such an important part in the survival of the human race for centuries, it is not surprising to find that writers and artists have included archers and archery in their creative endeavors. The student of archery is encouraged to stimulate his or her intellectual curiosity by searching for literary and artistic works in which the writers and artists have included archery or archers.

The purpose of this chapter is to briefly alert the student of archery to the fact that there is a strong relationship between the subject of archery and the literature and art produced throughout the ages. Intellectually, it is always useful to look for relationships where one may not initially believe a relationship exists. *There is a strong relationship between archery and the humanities.* The study of that relationship can be fascinating for the individual who is intellectually curious, because the topic quite literally encompasses virtually all societies and cultures throughout the history of the world. Several references are listed in this chapter and in the bibliography to stimulate the interest of those who wish to pursue the topic further.

Literature

There is considerable mythology surrounding the constellation Sagittarius. Sagittarius is a large southern constellation which the Greeks called a centaur. The centaur was supposed to be shooting an arrow. The term "sagittarius" actually means the *archer*. Sagittarius is located south of Aquila, and is partly in the Milky Way. It is east of Antares, one of the central stars in the constellation known as Scorpio. Sagittarius can be seen during the months of August and September in the United States. Figure 9.1 shows a schematic diagram of Sagittarius.

The various stars within Sagittarius form parts of the archer and his bow and arrow. Rukbat is the archer's knee; Arkab is the archer's tendon; Ascella is the archer's armpit or axillary region; Media is the midpoint of the bow; and Al Nasl is the arrow point. As the reader will note in figure 9.1, it took a vivid imagination to visualize an archer amidst the celestial configuration.

Greek mythological literature called the centaur of Sagittarius Chiron. Chiron was the famous son of Philyra and Saturn. Ovid noted that when Chiron was slain by Hercules with a poisoned arrow, Jupiter, the Father of the Gods, placed

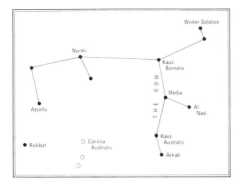

Figure 9.1
The Southern constellation known as Sagittarius, The Archer.

Chiron among the constellations. Ovid wrote: "Midst Golden Stars he stands refulgent now and thrusts the Scorpian with his bended bow." The reference is to the relationship between Al Nasl and Antares.

In mythological literature Apollo was the God of Archery, among other things. He was credited with numerous extraordinary feats with the bow and arrow. One of the most famous of these mythologic events was said to have taken place on Mount Parnassus. A great python was raiding families who lived in the area. The python smashed homes and ate human beings as if there was no end. Apollo decided to put a stop to all of that, and took his bow and arrows in pursuit of the python. He ultimately found the python and invited him to fight. As is the case in most myths, good triumphed over evil. Apollo fought the python for four hours and finally killed him with an accurately placed arrow.

Shortly following the battle with the python, Apollo encountered Eros, or Cupid. He insulted Eros by telling him that a boy should not play with a man's weapons. The reference, of course, was to the bow and arrows carried by Eros. This act by Apollo enraged Eros. He decided to get even with Apollo. This he did by shooting Apollo with a golden arrow of love. Shortly thereafter, Apollo fell in love with Daphne. Daphne was the daughter of Peneun, the River God. Eros promptly shot Daphne with a lead arrow of hate. Daphne's feeling for Apollo was one of disgust. Ultimately, she turned herself into a laurel tree. Apollo, in love with Daphne to the end, showed his undying love by hanging his bow and quiver on her limbs.

Eros with his bow and arrows had many adventures in mythological literature. The term "eros" is rather interesting. It serves as the root word for the term "erotic" which coincides with the purpose of the existence of Eros. The term "eros" also gave rise to the word "arrows."

One of the greatest mythological archers was Hercules, or Herakles. Hercules is better known for his feats of strength, but he was also responsible for many remarkable accomplishments with the bow and arrow. For example, he was primarily responsible for the conquest of Troy due to his prowess with the bow and arrow. Hercules killed Paris with one of his arrows during the Trojan War. Earlier, it will be remembered that Paris had shot Achilles with a poisoned arrow.

Figure 9.2
The Education of Achilles by Chiron. (From E. G. Heath, *The Grey Goose Wing*)

That was described as a remarkable archery shot, because Achilles' heel area was the only vulnerable area of his body. Anatomists refer to the tendon from the *gastrocnemius* and *soleus* muscles to the calcaneus bone as "the Achilles tendon." An artist's portrayal of Achilles is shown in figure 9.2.

In the *Iliad* and *Odyssey,* Homer, the eighth century B.C. Greek poet, wrote about numerous feats by archers. In the *Odyssey,* Homer described ten years of adventures by Odysseus following the Trojan War. Figure 9.3 is an artist's depiction of the business he took care of when he finally arrived home and found his wife with some friendly folk from the neighborhood! A review of many contemporary homicides indicates that the principal change in the scenario depicted in figure 9.3 is the weapon used to commit the crime. Human nature has not changed much over the centuries.

There is another minor constellation known as Sagitta the Arrow. This constellation is located in the Milky Way just north of the constellation known as the Eagle. In comparing and discussing Sagittarius and Sagitta, Aratos wrote, "There further shot another arrow but this with a bow. Towards it the Bird more northward flies." The references are to Sagittarius and the Eagle. Erathosthenes considered Sagitta to be the shaft with which Apollo exterminated the Cyclops. It was also referred to as one of Cupid's arrows in mythological literature.

As we move forward historically, other characters bordering on the mythological emerged in the literature. Robin Hood fits into this category. There is no strong evidence to support the fact that such a person actually lived. However it is possible. As his legend grew, the truth about his feats with the bow and arrow

Figure 9.3
Odysseus, on returning from his many wanderings slays the suitors of Penelope, his wife. The use of a thumb release can be assumed due to the position of his bowstring hand—fifth century B.C. (From E. G. Heath, *The Grey Goose Wing*)

could have been distorted. This is a common characteristic of mythology, i.e., one is apt to find historically substantiated subject matter combined with feats and episodes which are purely mythological in nature.

There is a legendary report of a wand shoot between Robin Hood and Clifton. According to the tale, Clifton shot his arrow first and hit the two-inch wand at 100 yards. Before Clifton's arrow stopped oscillating, Robin Hood released his arrow and completely split the shaft of Clifton's vibrating arrow. The mathematical probability of the occurrence of such an event is fantastic. Even with modern tackle, it is highly improbable that such a feat could occur. The best contemporary trick shot archers usually make their shots at distances of ten to twenty yards. Some movie stunt men do not rely on skill alone for closeup shots of arrows penetrating a human body. To do this the arrow is mounted on wire and guided directly to its mark where it penetrates a large pad strategically placed under the stunt man's clothing. Such procedures by contemporary professional archers make the story of Robin Hood's wand shot appear even more fantastic.

This type of wand shooting is referred to periodically in English literature. A formal Wand Round for competitive purposes evolved as a result. The Wand Round consists of shooting 36 arrows at a piece of balsa wood two inches in width projecting six feet upward from the ground. The scoring is simple, but achieving a score is extremely difficult! Any arrow embedded in the wand counts as a hit. Also, a witnessed rebound from the wand counts as a hit. The challenge of wand shooting lies in the distances involved. Men shoot at the two-inch wand from 100 yards, intermediate boys from 80 yards, and women as well as intermediate girls shoot at the wand from 60 yards. This is an extremely difficult task. The reader may want to try to duplicate the alleged feat of Robin Hood.

Figure 9.4
An eighteenth-century engraving of Robin Hood by Thomas Bewick. (From E. G. Heath, *The Grey Goose Wing*)

There is a grave in England supposedly occupied by Robin Hood. A portion of the epitaph reads, ". . . No archer was like him so good; his wildness named him Robin Hood." (His real name was supposed to be Robert, Earl of Huntington.) It is rather interesting that the vernacular term for someone who lives an obstreperous life outside the law is "hood."

Robin Hood stories have fascinated people for years. As a result, the character and his associates have been portrayed by numerous artists. An eighteenth century engraving is shown in figure 9.4 as one example.

Johann Friedrich von Schiller, the nineteenth century dramatist, wrote a famous drama about the legendary archer, Wilhelm Tell. (Gioacchino Rossini wrote the opera, *William Tell,* about the exploits of the same archer.) The tale centered around a Swiss crossbowman who defied a new regime. The archer was able to demonstrate his skill by shooting through an apple sitting on his son's head. A shot like Tell's in real life would have been remarkable, because the father had to shoot at his son in a stress situation with poorly constructed archery tackle. The student of archery and literature may want to try to duplicate some of the legendary archery feats found within the literature. This is recommended, especially to check on their validity. In the case of the shot by Wilhelm Tell, however, it would be wise for obvious reasons to use an apple sitting on a balloon.

James Fenimore Cooper wrote many portrayals of the American Indian. There are many factual events in Cooper's books regarding how the Indian used and made bows and arrows. Cooper researched his material very carefully, and he also wrote at a time when the Indian had not been completely conquered. Some of Cooper's books are *The Pioneers, The Last of the Mohicans, The Pathfinder, The Deerslayer,* and *The Prairie.*

Henry Wadsworth Longfellow's famous poem, *Song of Hiawatha,* is a good example of factual material being combined with feats bordering on the legendary. Longfellow, however, gave an accurate account of how some Indians made bows and arrows. Iagoo made a bow for Hiawatha from ash. The arrows were made of oak. Flint was used for the point, and the bowstring was of dried deerskin. These materials were actually used by Indians to make archery tackle. (See Chapter 6.)

Longfellow described Hiawatha as capable of breaking world records in such events as the 100- and 200-meter dashes. According to the poet, Hiawatha was so fast that he could shoot an arrow on a horizontal trajectory and outrun the arrow. That is fast, even with the poor and inefficient tackle of an Indian! If any archery student can duplicate this feat, he or she should report to the nearest track coach immediately.

Longfellow also mentioned that Hiawatha could shoot ten arrows vertically so fast that the last arrow would be flying skyward before the first arrow had fallen. This would be virtually impossible with the tackle described in the poem.

It is recommended that the archery student look for archery references and accomplishments in literature and analyze them their feasibility. As a start the reader is referred to the following partial list:

1. Aeschylus. *Agamemnon.*
2. Arnold, Elliot. *Blood Brother.*
3. Clemens, Samuel. *A Connecticut Yankee in King Arthur's Court.*
4. Defoe, Daniel. *The Adventures of Robinson Crusoe.*
5. Gillespy, Frances. *Laymon's Brut: A Comparative Study in Narrative Art.*
6. Homer. *The Illiad* and *The Odyssey.*
7. Lucian. *Dialogues of the Gods.*
8. Millar, George. *A Cross Bowman's Story.*
9. Morley, Christopher. *The Arrow.*
10. Ovid. *The Metamorphoses.*
11. Shakespeare. *Macbeth.*
12. ———. *Pericles.*
13. Stevenson, Robert Louis. *The Black Arrow.*
14. Swift, Jonathan. *Gulliver's Travels.*
15. Thucydides. *The History of The Peloponnesian War.*

There are several good references listed in the Bibliography concerning the study of archery as it relates to the humanities.

Art

There are thousands of sculptures and drawings involving archery in private collections, museums, and art museums throughout the world. Some of these, like the Bayeux Tapestry, are very famous, while others are obscure. Among the earliest art forms of mankind, cave drawings, bow hunters are depicted in pursuit of game. The student interested in art is invited to look for sculptures or carvings and drawings involving archery.

Several examples of artists' depictions of archers or the use of archery have been used throughout this book. The reader should scrutinize these as shown in Chapters 1, 2, 4 and this chapter. They show various artists' concepts of archery feats, tackle, and events. It is useful to critically analyze each of these for: (1) artistic quality and merit, (2) tackle design for the era, as compared with contemporary tackle, (3) aesthetic impact, and (4) the artist's concept of shooting fundamentals.

Richard Pardons Robin Hood—1184—A.D.—Briggs: Beale.

Sennacherib (Assyria). (Courtesy of H. Armstrong Roberts. Printed by permission.)

Cupid with bow—Chas. Lemiore (Louvre). (Courtesy of H. Armstrong Roberts. Printed by Permission.)

Diana—Goddess of Wild Things.

Battle of Marathon—Briggs: Beale.

Roman war elephant.

Buffalo hunt with wolfskin mask—Catlin #13.

Review Questions

1. Who was the God of Archery in mythological literature and how did he happen to be shot with a golden arrow of love?
2. Which constellation supposedly depicts a centaur shooting a bow and arrow? When can this constellation be observed in the United States?
3. Cite examples of literature, music, and art in which archery or archers are prominent.
4. Traditional liberal arts and study of the humanities involve pursuit of such areas as literature, philosophy, and art. Reflect on your studies in these areas and determine how authors and artists integrated archery into their themes.
5. What characters in mythological literature had direct relationships with archery in some form?
6. What is a wand shoot?
7. Was the classic arrow shot depicted by Schiller and Rossini in literature and opera accomplished with a longbow or crossbow?
8. When you visit museums and art galleries, make note of the quantity and quality of paintings, sculptures, and drawings where the artists used archery in one of its forms.
9. From what Greek term is the word "arrows" derived?
10. Feats ascribed to archers appearing in literature are sometimes beyond the capabilities of the modern archer shooting with the finest equipment. How do some trick shot archers and movie stunt actors simulate extraordinary feats?

The Language of Archery

10

Archery, like any sport or specialized area, has a vocabulary all its own, with many terms defined in a unique manner. This is necessary so archers can communicate with each other very succinctly and precisely.

The following list of terms are commonly used in the archery sports:

Addressing the Target
The archer's stance straddling the shooting line prior to shooting the arrow.

Aim
The placement of a sight pin on the center of the target; if a sight is not used, placement of the tip of the arrow on a specific point while shooting at a target over a given distance.

AMO
Archery Manufacturer's Organization.

Anchor Point
The placement of the archer's bowstring hand on the chin or face with the bow at full draw.

Archer's Paradox
The aerodynamically stabilizing condition of the arrow after it deflects around the bow handle at release.

Arm Guard
A leather protective device for the radioulnar (forearm) and wrist areas of the bow arm.

Arrow Plate
The piece to which the arrow rest is attached.

Arrow Rest
A device mounted just above the arrow shelf on the bow to maintain arrow position from nocking until the arrow has cleared the bow at release.

Arrow Shelf
The lowermost area of the sight window on the bow.

Arrowsmith
An individual who specializes in making arrows and arrowheads.

Back
The side of the bow limb away from the archer when the bow is in the draw position.

Barb
Part of the point on a fishing arrow point used to hold the fish; one of the hairlike branches growing from the shaft of a feather.

Bare Bow

A method of shooting which does not include using a bowsight.

Belly

A synonym for the face of the bow or the side of the bow nearest the string.

Blunt

A flattened arrow point usually made of rubber or metal and designed to kill small game upon impact.

Bolt

The projectile shot from a crossbow.

Bow Arm

The arm which the archer prefers to use for holding the bow during shooting.

Bow Bracer

A device designed to insure safety for the archer during the process of bracing or stringing the bow.

Bow Hand

The hand which the archer prefers to use for holding or supporting the bow during shooting.

Bowman

An archer.

Bowsight

An adjustable device attached to the bow which facilitates the aiming process for the archer.

Bow Square

A device used to measure string and nocking heights accurately.

Bowstrap

A leather strap which enables the archer to maintain contact with the bow without actually gripping the handle.

Bow Tip Protector

A cap that fits over the tip of the lower limb of the bow to protect it from damage produced by contact with the ground or floor.

Bow Window

The center shot or sight window area of the bow handle immediately above the grip which aids the archer during the aiming process.

Bowyer

An individual who specializes in making bows.

Brace Height

The bow manufacturer's recommended distance from the pivot point of the bow to the bow string. Replaces the older term "fistmele."

Bracing

The process of stringing the bow in preparation for shooting, by placing the bowstring loops into position in the notches of the bow.

Broadhead

A multiple-edged and razor-sharp arrow point utilized in bow hunting.

Brush Button
A silencer device, usually rubber, placed on each end of the bowstring to reduce string noise following release during bow hunting.

Bull's Eye
The center of the target or that part of the target face with the highest scoring value.

Butt
The term used for target backing when the target face is mounted on a straw or hay bale.

Butt Hook
A curved metal, plastic, or wood hook attached to the butt end of a crossbow stock as an aid in steady aiming.

Cant
Tilting the bow left or right by lateral or medial rotation of the shoulder joint of the bow arm.

Cast
The velocity which the bow can impart to the arrow, and the horizontal distance which the arrow can traverse.

Centerline
The relationship of the bow string to the bow limbs which, when viewed from the face side, should divide the limbs evenly.

Center Shot Bow
A bow designed to allow the arrow rest to be placed in the center of the upper limb instead of being placed at the extreme lateral side of the bow.

Channel Groove
A grooved section down the length of a crossbow barrel which allows the cockfeather to move along the barrel when shot.

Clicker
A small metal device mounted on the sight window in front of the arrow rest which indicates full draw has been attained by snapping off of the arrow point with an audible click.

Clout
An NAA round shot over relatively long distances at a 15 meter (diameter) target drawn on the surface of the ground.

Collapse
An undesired spinal rotation by the archer prior to arrow release, causing the bow arm to move backward while the drawing arm moves forward.

Composite Bow
A bow manufactured by utilizing two or more types of materials such as wood and fiberglass.

Compound Bow
A bow invented by H. W. Allen designed with an eccentric pulley system to maximize pull weight poundage at mid-draw and minimize stacking at full draw.

Creeping

An undesired forward motion of the bowstring from the anchor point immediately prior to release.

Crest

The colored identification bands on the arrow immediately inferior to the fletching.

Crossbow

A tool for shooting bolts. It consists of a short bow mounted crosswise near the end of a wood, metal, or plastic stock.

Cushion Pressure Point

A plastic or leather device which will absorb some of the shock of the arrow as it passes after release.

Dead Release

Extension of the interphalangeal joints of the fingers gripping the bowstring due to the kinetic energy of the bowstring instead of muscular force.

Draw

The process of moving the bowstring with nocked arrow from brace height to the archer's anchor point on the face.

Draw Weight

See "Weight."

Drift

The lateral displacement of an arrow from its normal trajectory due to crosswind velocity.

End

A set number of arrows which are shot before going to the target to score and retrieve them; the number may be three, five, or six in target archery.

Eye

The loop at the end of the bowstring which fits into the notch of the bow during bracing.

Face

The side of the bow limb closest to the archer when the bow is in the draw position—replaces the term "belly."

Field Captain

The person in charge of an archery tournament.

Field Point

A point used in field archery which is as heavy as a broadhead.

Finger Sling

A small piece of leather with loops at each end designed to fit around the archer's thumb and index or middle finger during shooting. It helps prevent the bow from falling to the ground after release.

Finger Tab

A leather device worn to prevent blistering on the anterior surface of the three drawing fingers.

FITA

Federation Internationale DeTir a L'Arc—The organization responsible for conducting world championship contests in archery.

Fletcher

An arrow maker.

Fletching

The stabilizing feathers or plastic vanes attached to an arrow between the nock and crest.

Flight Shooting

An archery event in which the object is to attain the greatest distance possible for the arrow or bolt.

Flinching

An undesired and sudden motion of the bow arm (usually horizontal abduction of the bow shoulder) at release.

Flu-Flu

An arrow with large or spiraled fletching designed to increase the drag coefficient in order to diminish flight distance.

Follow-Through

The act of holding the release position until the arrow has struck the target.

Foot Markers

Devices used by archers to mark the placement of the feet as the target is addressed in target archery.

Freestyle

A method of shooting where the archer uses a bowsight to aim.

Freeze

The inability to release the arrow while at full draw.

Gap Shooting

An aiming technique whereby the archer estimates the distance (gap) between a selected point and the target. Release is made when the gap no longer exists.

Goat's Foot

A cocking-assist device used with crossbows to lever the string back to its cocked position.

Gold

The center of the target used in target archery.

Grip

The center portion of the bow where the hand exerts pressure during the draw. (Grip is often used interchangeably with the term "handle.")

Grouping

The arrangement of the end of arrows on the target face after they have been shot.

Handle

The middle portion of the bow.

Handle Riser

The area just below and above the bow grip.

Hanging Arrow

An arrow which does not penetrate the target mat, but dangles across the target face.

Hen-Feathers

The two feathers on either side of the index feather. Traditionally, these feathers are not as flamboyant as the index feather.

Hit

An arrow which embeds itself within one of the scoring areas on the target face.

Holding

The act of maintaining the bow and arrow in a stable position at full draw prior to release.

Index Feather

The feather at right angle to the slit in the nock of the arrow and usually different in color from the remaining feathers. This term replaces the older term, "cock feather."

Jig

A device used for making and repairing fletching and bowstrings.

Keeper

A piece of material used to hold the bowstring to the nock when the bow is not braced.

Kiss Button

A contact point on the bowstring for the archer's lips to touch to insure consistency and accuracy of the anchor point.

Lady Paramount

The woman in charge of an archery tournament.

Laminated Bow

A bow constructed of several layers of different materials glued together.

Limbs

The energy-storing parts of the bow located above and below the riser.

Long Bow

A bow with no built-in curvatures to increase leverage.

Loop

The ends of the bowstring made to attach securely into the bow notches when braced.

Loose

The act of releasing or shooting the arrow.

Mass Weight

The actual or physical weight of the bow in pounds.

Mat

The firmly constructed area of the target upon which the target face is mounted.

NAA

National Archery Association of the United States.

NFAA

National Field Archery Association of the United States.

Nock

The plastic device on the end of the arrow opposite the point, made with a groove for holding the arrow to the bowstring when placed in position for shooting.

Nocking

The technique of placing the arrow on the bowstring in preparation for shooting.

Nock Locator

The stops on the serving of the bowstring which mark the exact nocking point for the arrow.

Nose

The solid metal portion at the front of the crossbow which retains the prod.

Oblique Stance

A foot position whereby the toe of the foot nearest the target is placed on a line to the target and then rotated laterally forty-five degrees. The heel of the foot farthest from the target is placed in line with the center of the target.

Open Stance

A foot position whereby the line to the target is from the instep of the foot farthest from the target while the leg nearest the target has been extended at the hip to form at least a toe-heel relationship with the foot online to the target.

Overbowed

The act of drawing a bow which has a weight out of proportion to the archer's strength.

Overdraw

Drawing the arrow beyond the face of the bow or drawing the bow to its point of maximum stress on the limbs.

Overstrung

The use of a bowstring too short for the bow, a condition which results in an excessive brace height and inefficiency in shooting.

PAA

Professional Archer's Association.

Palm Rest

A device which extends below the mid-portion for a crossbow stock and placed in the shooter's non-trigger hand.

Peeking

Undesired motion of the archer's head at the time of release in an attempt to follow the arrow trajectory into the target.

Perfect End

A situation when all arrows shot are grouped tightly into the highest scoring area on the target face.

Petticoat
The outermost perimeter of the target face outside the scoring area.

Pile
A term used as a synonym for the arrow point.

Pinch
The undesired act of squeezing the arrow nock too tightly during the draw, causing the arrow to move off the arrow rest.

Pivot Point
The part of the bow grip farthest from the string when the bow is braced.

Plucking
Undesired lateral motion of the string hand and arm away from the bowstring at the time of release.

Point-Blank Range
The distance at which the archer may utilize the center of the target as an aiming point.

Point-of-aim
An antiquated technique of aiming, whereby the archer used a mark unattached to the bow and usually placed on the ground as an alignment point.

Pressure Point
The place on the arrow plate against which the arrow lies and exerts pressure when the arrow is released; it can be cushioned or spring loaded.

Prism Sight
A sophisticated aiming device utilizing refraction principles to gain a clear view of the target.

Prod
The bow section of the crossbow.

Pull
The process of disengaging embedded arrows from the target.

Pushing
The undesired process of moving the bow parallel to the earth at the time of release and follow-through.

Quiver
Any device designed to hold arrows not actually being shot.

Range
(1) A specified distance to be shot during a round or while hunting; (2) an area designated for target or field archery.

Rebound
An arrow which does not penetrate the target face or mat but bounces off the target.

Recurved Bow
A bow manufactured so the ends of the limbs deflect toward the back of the bow to increase leverage when the bow is braced.

Reflexed Bow
A bow with straight limbs where the backs form an obtuse angle at the conjunction of the handle riser and grip.

Release
The act of putting the arrow into flight due to a release of the pressure on the bowstring by either the fingers or the release device.

Round
The term used to designate the number of arrows to be shot at specific distances at specified target faces or targets.

Roving
An archery game of shooting at natural targets in woods and fields.

Scatter
Arrows distributed unevenly over a large portion of the target face and/or ground.

Scoring Area
The concentric circles on the target face worth prescribed point values.

Serving
The protective thread wrapped around the bowstring where the arrow is nocked.

Shaft
The body of the arrow upon which the nock, fletching, and point are mounted, and the crest is painted.

Shooting Glove
A three-fingered protective device utilized by some archers for the bowstring-gripping fingers, in lieu of a finger tab.

Shooting Line
The line straddled by archers during shooting which indicates a specific distance from the target in target archery.

Sight Bar
The piece of the bowsight to which the sight block is attached.

Sight pin
The part of the bowsight placed on the center of the intended target during aiming.

Sight Window
The area of the bow cut away to allow the arrow rest to be mounted in the center of the bow.

Skirt
The outer cloth on a target face which holds the face on the mat; sometimes called the petticoat.

Snake
Embedding of an arrow under grass and horizontal to the ground, making the arrow extremely difficult to locate.

Spine

The measured deflection in inches of an arrow shaft when it is depressed by a two-pound weight at its center.

Stabilizer

A weighted device added to the handle-riser areas of the bow and designed to reduce torque and absorb shock upon release.

Stacking

A disproportionate increase in bow weight during the last few inches of the draw.

Stirrup

A cocking device which allows the shooter to hold the crossbow in a stationary position while using both hands to cock the bowstring.

String Fingers

The fingers used to hold the nocked arrow in place on the bowstring.

String Height

See "Brace height."

String Notch

The grooves at the distal end of the bow limbs, designed to hold the bowstring when the bow is braced.

String Peep

An oval insert into the strands of the bow string at eye level, used as a rear-mounted aiming device by the archer.

Tackle

All equipment used by an archer.

Target Captain

The inidividual at each target designated to determine and call the score of each arrow and pull each arrow from the target.

Target Face

The scoring area of a target.

Target Mat

The backing of the target which the arrows penetrate.

Tassel

A piece of material used to clean arrows.

Timber

A verbal warning given in field archery that an arrow is being released.

Tip

The ends of the bow limbs.

Torque

An undesirable twisting of the bow and/or bowstring during any part of the shooting process.

Toxopholite

An individual interested in archery as a performer and/or from an academic point of view.

Trajectory
The parabolic flight pattern of an arrow following release.

Tuning
An adjustment of the arrow rest, pressure point, string height, and nocking height to improve arrow flight; includes determination of correct spine.

Underbowed
The act of drawing a bow with a weight too light to enable the archer to accomplish the shooting objective.

Understrung
A bow with a bowstring too long which results in an improper brace height and reduced efficiency.

Unit
A 14-target course in field archery including all official shots.

Vane
A term used most commonly when fletching is made of plastic or rubber instead of feathers.

Wand
A historic type of target; a piece of balsa wood two inches in width embedded in the ground and projecting six feet upward from it.

Weight
The bow manufacturer's determined number of pounds required to draw each bow's string a given distance.

Windage
The left-right adjustment of the bowsight or the pin on the bowsight.

Wrist Sling
A device which fits around the bow and the archer's wrist designed to prevent the bow from falling to the ground as the arrow is released.

Yarn Tassel
A tuft of yarn used by archers to clean arrows.

Yaw
Unstable or erratic motion of the arrow during its flight path or trajectory toward the target.

Selected Bibliography

Archery Magazine. Route 2, Box 514, Redlands, California 92373.

ASCHAM, ROGER. *Toxophilus.* London: A. Murray and Son, 1545.

AUSTIN, NORMAN. *Archery at the Dark of the Moon.* Berkeley: University of California Press, 1975.

BAIER, PATRICIA, and others. *The National Archery Association's Instructor's Manual.* Colorado Springs: National Archery Association of the United States, 1982.

BARRETT, JEAN A. *Archery.* New York: Scott, Foresman and Company, 1980.

BEAR, FRED. *The Archer's Bible.* Garden City, New York: Doubleday and Company, Incorporated, 1980.

————. *World of Archery.* Garden City, New York: Doubleday and Company, Incorporated, 1979.

Bow and Arrow Magazine. P.O. Box HH, Capistrano Beach, California 92624.

Bowfishing Magazine. P.O. Box 2005, Wausau, Wisconsin 54402–2005.

Bowhunter. 3808 South Calhoun Street, Fort Wayne, Indiana 46807.

Bowhunting World Magazine. P.O. Box 611, Wayzata, Minnesota 55391.

BROWN, KEN. *The Ken Brown Guide to Bowfishing.* Hugo, Oklahoma: Ken Brown Publications, 1980.

BURKE, EDMUND H. *Archery Handbook.* New York: Arco Publishing Co., Inc., 1965.

————. *The History of Archery.* New York: William Morrow & Co., 1957.

BUTLER, DAVID F. *The New Archery.* New York: A. S. Barnes & Co., 1968.

CAMPBELL, DONALD W. *Archery.* Englewood Cliffs, N.J.: Prentice-Hall, Inc., 1971.

COMBS, ROGER (Ed.). *Crossbows.* Northbrook, Illinois: DBI Books, 1987.

Crossbow Shooting International Magazine. 9 Manor Street, Tettenhall, Wolverhampton, WV6 8RA England.

DRISCOLL, MARGARET L., ed. *Selected Archery Articles.* Washington, D.C.: American Association for Health, Physical Education, and Recreation, 1971.

ELMER, ROBERT P. *American Archery.* Ronks, Pa.: National Archery Association of the United States, 1917.

ELMER, ROBERT P. *Archery.* Philadelphia: Penn Publishing Co., 1926.

ELMER, ROBERT P., and FARIS, NABIH A. *Arab Archery.* Princeton, N.J.: Princeton University Press, 1945.

FOLEY, VERNARD; PALMER, GEORGE, and SOEDEL, WERNER. "The Crossbow." *Scientific American* 252 (January, 1985):104–110.

FORD, HORACE A. *Archery: Its Theory and Practice.* London: J. Buchanan, 1856.

GANNON, ROBERT. *The Complete Book of Archery.* New York: Coward-McCann, Inc., 1964.

GILLELAN, G. HOWARD. *The Complete Book of the Bow and Arrow.* Harrisburg, Pa.: The Stackpole Co., 1977.

GROGAN, HIRAM J. *Modern Bow Hunting.* Harrisburg, Pa.: The Stackpole Co., 1958.

HAUGEN, ARNOLD O., and METCALF, HARLAN. *Field Archery and Bowhunting.* New York: Ronald Press Co., 1963.

HEATH, E. G., ed. *Anecdotes of Archery.* London: The Tabard Press Ltd., 1970.

HEATH, E. G. *The Grey Goose Wing.* Reading, Berkshire, England: Osprey Publishing Ltd., 1971.

————. *A History of Target Archery.* South Brunswick: A. S. Barnes, 1974.

HENDERSON, AL. *On Target for Understanding Target Archery.* Mequon, Wisconsin: Target Communications Corporation, 1983.

HERRIGEL, EUGEN. *Zen in the Art of Archery.* New York: Pantheon Books, 1953.

HERTER, GEORGE L., and HOFMEISTER, RUSSELL. *Professional & Amateur Archery Tournament and Hunting Instructions and Encyclopedia.* Waseca, Minn.: Herter's Inc., 1963.

HICKMAN, C. N.; NAGLER, F.; and KLOPSTEG, PAUL E. *Archery: The Technical Side.* Redlands, Calif.: National Field Archery Assoc. of the U.S., 1947.

HILL, HOWARD. *Hunting the Hard Way.* Chicago: Follet Publishing Co., 1953.

HONDA, SHIG; LAMMERS, MARJORY E.; and NEWSON, RALPH W. *Archery.* Boston: Allyn and Bacon, 1975.

KELLY, GENE. "Memorial Lands: A Bowmaker's Legacy." *Missouri Conservationist* 48 (December, 1987): 28–29.

KLANN, MARGARET L. *Target Archery.* Reading: Pa.: Addison-Wesley Publishing Co., 1970.

KLOPSTEG, P. E. "Physics of Bows and Arrows." *American Journal of Physics* 11(August, 1943):175–92.

LOGAN, GENE A., and McKINNEY, WAYNE C. *Anatomic Kinesiology.* Dubuque: Wm. C. Brown Publishers, 1982.

LONGMAN, C. J., and WALROND, H. *Archery.* New York: Frederick Ungar Publishing Co., 1894.

LOVE, ALBERT J. *Field Archery Technique.* Corpus Christi, Tex.: Dotson Printing Co., 1956.

MARKHAM, GERVASE. *The Art of Archerie.* London: Arms and Armour Press, 1968.

North American Bowhunter Magazine. P.O. Box 5487, Tucson, Arizona 85703.

NORTHRIP, JOHN W., LOGAN, GENE A., and McKINNEY, WAYNE C. *Analysis of Sport Motion: Anatomic and Biomechanic Perspectives.* Dubuque: Wm. C. Brown Publishers, 1983.

POPE, SAXTON. *Yahi Archery.* Berkeley: University of California Press, 1918.

———. *Hunting with Bow and Arrow.* New York: G. P. Putnam's Sons, 1947.

———. *The Adventurous Bowman.* New York: G. P. Putnam's Sons, 1926.

PSZCZOLA, LORRAINE. *Archery.* Philadelphia: W. B. Saunders Co., 1983.

RHODE, ROBERT J. *Archery Champions.* Norristown, Pa.: The Archer's Publishing Co., 1961.

SCHAAR, JOHN. *Modern Archery Ballistics.* Tempe: Grand Slam Archery, Inc., 1986.

SCHUMM, MARYANNE M. *Clarence N. Hickman: The Father of Scientific Archery.* Minisink Hills, Pennsylvania: Maples Press, Inc., 1983.

SHORE, PAUL T. "Ramboat, Part I, The Ultimate Bowfishing Machine." *Bowfishing* 1(Fall/Winter, 1986):8–12.

———. "Ramboat, Part II, The Ultimate Bowfishing Machine." *Bowfishing* 1(Winter/Spring, 1987):4–6.

STERLING, SARA. *Robin Hood and His Merry Men.* Philadelphia: George W. Jacobs and Co., 1921.

The Professional Bowhunter Magazine. P.O. Box 5275, Charlotte, North Carolina 28225.

The U.S. Archer. 7315 North San Anna Drive, Tucson, Arizona 85704.

THOMPSON, MAURICE. *The Witchery of Archery.* New York: Charles Scribner's Sons, 1878.

THOMPSON, MAURICE and THOMPSON, WILL H. *How to Train in Archery.* New York: E. I. Horsman, 1879.

WALKER, DOROTHY. *Instructor Manual for Basic Archery.* Jefferson City, Missouri: Missouri Department of Conservation, 1981.

Official Wildlife Agencies in the United States and Canada

Information regarding current bow hunting and/or bow fishing rules, regulations, and seasons may be obtained by contacting the appropriate wildlife agencies. Their addresses and phone numbers are listed below for the reader's convenience:

United States

Alabama Department of
  Conservation and Natural
  Resources
64 North Union Street
Montgomery, AL 36130
(205) 261–3468

Alaska Department of Fish and
  Game
Box 3–2000
Juneau, AK 99802
(907) 465–4190

Arizona Game and Fish
  Department
2222 West Greenway Road
Phoenix, AZ 85023
(602) 942–3000

Arkansas Game and Fish
  Commission
#2 Natural Resources Drive
Little Rock, AR 72205
(501) 223–6300

California Department of Fish and
  Game
1416 Ninth Street
Sacramento, CA 95814
(916) 324–8347

Colorado Division of Wildlife
Department of Natural Resources
6060 Broadway
Denver, CO 80216
(303) 297–1192

Connecticut Department of
  Environmental Protection
Franklin Wildlife Management
  Area
RR1, Box 241
North Franklin, CT 06254
(203) 642–7239

Delware Division of Fish and
  Wildlife
P.O. Box 1401
Dover, DE 19903
(302) 736–5297

District of Columbia Metropolitan
  Police
300 Indiana Avenue NW
Washington, DC 20001

Florida Game and Freshwater Fish
  Commission
620 South Meridan Street
Tallahassee, FL 32399–1600
(904) 488–4676

Georgia Department of Natural
  Resources
Floyd Towers East, SE
205 Butler St., Suite 1362
Atlanta, GA 30334
(404) 656–3523

Hawaii Division of Forestry and
Wildlife
1151 Punchbowl Street
Honolulu, HI 96813
(808) 548–2861

Idaho Department of Fish and
Game
P.O. Box 25
600 South Walnut
Boise, ID 83707
(208) 334–3746

Illinois Division of Fish and Wildlife
Resources
P.O. Box 286
Monmouth, IL 61462
(309) 374–2492

Indiana Division of Fish and
Wildlife
607 State Office Building
Indianapolis, IN 46204
(317) 232–4080

Iowa Department of Natural
Resources
Wallace State Office Building
Des Moines, IA 50319
(515) 281–6154

Kansas Department of Wildlife and
Parks
Box 54A, RR2
Pratt, KS 67124
(316) 672–5911

Wildlife
#1 Game Farm Road
Frankfort, KY 40601
(502) 564–4406

Louisiana Department of Wildlife
and Fisheries
P.O. Box 4004
Monroe, LA 71211
(318) 343–4044

Maine Department of Inland
Fisheries and Wildlife
284 State Street
Augusta, ME 04333
(207) 289–2871

Maryland Forest, Park and Wildlife
Service
P.O. Box 68
Wye Mills, MD 21679
(301) 827–8612

Massachusetts Division of Fisheries
and Wildlife
100 Cambridge Street
Boston, MA 02202
(617) 727–3151

Michigan Department of Natural
Resources
P.O. Box 30028
Lansing, MI 48909
(517) 373–1263

Minnesota Department of Natural
Resources
Box 7, 500 Lafayette Road
St. Paul, MN 55146
(612) 296–3344

Mississippi Department of Wildlife
Conservation
P.O. Box 451
Jackson, MS 39205
(601) 961–5300

Missouri Department of
Conservation
P.O. Box 180
Jefferson City, MO 65102
(314) 751–4115

Montana Department of Fish,
Wildlife, and Parks
1420 East 6th Avenue
Helena, MT 59620
(406) 444–2535

Nebraska Game and Parks
  Commission
P.O. Box 30370
Lincoln, NE 68503
(402) 464–0641

Nevada Department of Wildlife
P.O. Box 10678
Reno, NV 89520
(702) 789–0500

New Hampshire Fish and Game
  Department
34 Bridge Street
Concord, NH 03301
(603) 271–2462

New Jersey Division of Fish, Game
  and Wildlife
CN 400
Trenton, NJ 08625
(609) 292–2965

New Mexico Department of Game
  and Fish
State Capitol
Santa Fe, NM 87503
(505) 827–7885

New York Department of
  Environmental Conservation
Wildlife Resources Center
Delmar, NY 12054
(518) 439–0098

North Carolina Wildlife Resources
  Commission
512 North Salisbury Street
Raleigh, NC 27611
(919) 733–7291

North Dakota Game and Fish
  Department
100 North Bismarck Expressway
Bismarck, ND 58501
(701) 221–6300

Ohio Division of Wildlife
Fountain Square
Columbus, OH 43224
(614) 265–6305

Oklahoma Department of Wildlife
  Conservation
1801 North Lincoln
P.O. Box 53465
Oklahoma City, OK 73152
(405) 521–2739

Oregon Department of Fish and
  Wildlife
P.O. Box 59
Portland, OR 97207
(503) 229–5403

Pennsylvania Game Commission
P.O. Box 1567
Harrisburg, PA 17105–1567
(717) 787–5529

Rhode Island Department of
  Environmental Management
Division of Fish and Wildlife
Government Center
Wakefield, RI 02879
(401) 789–0281

South Carolina Wildlife and Marine
  Resources Department
P.O. Box 167
Columbia, SC 29202
(803) 734–3888

South Dakota Department of Game,
  Fish, and Parks
445 East Capitol
Pierre, SD 57501
(605) 773–3485

Tennessee Wildlife Resources
  Agency
P.O. Box 40747
Nashville, TN 37204
(615) 360–0500

Texas Parks and Wildlife
  Department
4200 Smith School Road
Austin, TX 78744
(512) 389–4800

Utah Division of Wildlife Resources
1596 W. N. Temple
Salt Lake City, UT 84116
(801) 533–9333

Vermont Fish and Wildlife
Department
103 S. Main St.
Waterbury, VT 05676
(802) 244–7331

Virginia Commission of Game and
Inland Fisheries
P.O. Box 11104
Richmond, VA 23230–1104
(804) 367–1000

Washington Department of Game
600 North Capitol Way
Olympia, WA 95804
(206) 753–5700

West Virginia Department of
Natural Resources
1800 Washington Street
Charleston, WV 25305
(304) 348–2771

Wisconsin Department of Natural
Resources
P.O. Box 7921
Madison, WI 53707
(608) 266–2621

Wyoming Game and Fish
Department
5400 Bishop Boulevard
Cheyenne, WY 82002
(307) 777–7735

Canada

Alberta Forestry, Lands and
Wildlife
Fish and Wildlife Division
Main Floor, Information Center
Bramalea Bldg.
9920 108 Street
Edmonton, AB T5K 2G6
(403) 427–3590

British Columbia Wildlife Branch
780 Blanshard
Victoria, BC V8V 1X5
(604) 387–9737

Manitoba Department of Natural
Resources
1495 Saint James Street
Winnipeg, MB R3H OW9
(204) 945–6784

New Brunswick Fish and Wildlife
Branch
P.O. Box 6000
Fredericton, NB E3B 5H1
(506) 453–2440

Newfoundland Department of
Development and Tourism
P.O. Box 2006, Suite 502
Herald Tower
Corner Brook, NF A2H 6J8
(709) 637–2280

Northwest Territory Renewable
Resources
Government of NWT
Box 2668
Yellowknife, NWT X1A 2P9
(403) 873–7181

Nova Scotia Wildlife Division
Box 516
Kentville, NS B4N 3X3
(902) 678–8921

Ontario Wildlife Branch
Room 4640, 99 Wellesley W.
Toronto, ON M7A 1W3
(416) 965–4252

Quebec Department of Recreation,
Hunting and Fishing
P.O. Box 22000
150 East Saint Cyrille
Quebec City, PQ J1K 7X2
(418) 643–2464

Saskatchewan Department of Parks and Renewable Resources
Wildlife Branch
3211 Albert Street
Regina, SK S4S 5W6
(306) 787–9071

Yukon Department of Renewable Resources
Box 2703
Whitehorse, YK Y1A 2C6
(403) 667–5237

Archery Organizations

There are a wide variety of archery organizations that function to meet the needs and interests of all aspects of archery. The reader is encouraged to contact organizations in which he or she has an interest. Information regarding the purposes, functions, and programs offered will be sent to you.

American Archery Council
604 Forest Avenue
Park Rapids, MN 54670

Archery Manufacturer's
  Organization
200 Castlewood Road
North Palm Beach, FL 33408
(305) 842–4100

Bowhunters Who Care
Box 476
Columbus, NE 68601

Crossbow Archery Development
  Association
Frost Street
Wolverhampton WV4 6UD
England

Federation Internationale de tir a' l'
  Arc
FITA
Via Cerva 30
20122 Milano, Italy

International Armburst Union
(International Crossbow Shooting
  Association)
Schosslirain 9
CH-6006 Luzern
Switzerland

International Bowhunting
  Association
2 S 668 Raddant Road
Batavia, IL 60510

International Field Archery
  Association
604 Forest Avenue
Park Rapids, MN 56470
(218) 732–4436

NAA Flight Shooting Committee
2782 McClelland Street
Salt Lake City, UT 84106

National Archery Association
1750 East Boulder Street
Colorado Springs, CO 80909–5778
(303) 578–4576

National Field Archery Association
Route 2, Box 514
31407 Outer Interstate 10
Redlands, CA 92373
(714) 794–2133

National Handicapped Sports and
  Recreation Association
Capitol Hill Station
P.O. Box 18664
Denver, CO 80218
(303) 733–9349

National Wheelchair Athletic
  Association
3617 Betty Drive
Suite S
Colorado Springs, CO 80907
(719) 597–8330

National Wheelchair Athletic
  Association
Archery Section
Courage Center
3915 Golden Valley Road
Golden Valley, MN 55422

NFAA Bowfisher Program
Route 2, Box 514
Redlands, CA 92373
(714) 794–2133

Pope and Young Club (Game
  Records)
6471 Richard Avenue
Placerville, CA 95667
(916) 621–1133

Professional Archer's Association
7315 North San Anna Drive
Tucson, AZ 85704
(602) 742–5846

Senior Olympics (Archery)
11516 Natural Bridge
Bridgeton, MO 63044
(314) 731–1600

The National Crossbow Hunter's
  Association
8740 West 86th Avenue
Arvada, CO 80005

The National Crossbowmen of the
  United States
203 Washington Grove Lane
Washington Grove, MD 20880
(301) 926–0492

The Society for Creative
  Anachronisms (Crossbow)
Office of the Registry
P.O. Box 360743
Milpitas, CA 95035–0743

United States Armburst Association
  (Crossbow)
P.O. Box 261
Cape May Court House, NJ 08210

U.S. Match–Crossbow Shooting
  Association
P.O. Box 261, Winding Way
Cape May Court House, NJ 08210

World Bowhunting Association
604 Forest Avenue
Park Rapids, MN 56470
(218) 732–3879

Index

Stance, 53–56, 65, 71, 151, 152
    Closed, 54, 55
    Even, 53, 54
    Oblique, 53–55
    Open, 53–55
Sterling, Sara, 200
Stevenson, Jan, 163, 164
Stevenson, Robert Lewis, 182
Strength guidelines, 156, 157
Stress reduction, 7
String height, 53, 76
String silencer, 117
String slaps, 62
Sullentrop, Lance, 146
Swift, Jonathon, 182

Tackle
    Care, 45, 46
    Defined, 23
    Fishing, 134–39
    Hunting, 101–19
    Matched, 23, 24, 26, 36, 76, 109
    Target archery, 23–46
Target archery, 1, 2, 4–8, 21, 23–46, 49–77,
    80–84
Target faces, 72, 73
Targets, three dimensional, 120, 121
Tell, Wilhelm, 102, 181
Thompson, Maurice, 200
Thompson, Will H., 200
Threshold heart rate (THR), 158–60, 162,
    175

Thucydides, 182
Torque, 39, 58
Toxopholite, 3, 4
Toxophilus, 19
Trojan War, 178, 179
Trombetta, Alex, 73

U.S. Archer, The, 2, 79, 86, 87, 92, 93, 200
U.S. Match-Crossbow Shooting Association,
    208
Unit, field archery, 50, 95, 96
United States Armburst Association
    (Crossbow), 208

Vanes, 29, 108, 109
Varmint calling, 123, 124
Vietnam War, 13, 20

Waders, 139
Walker, Dorothy, 200
Walrond, H., 200
Wand Round, 180
Wars of the Roses, 18
West, Jim, 140, 141
Wildlife agencies, 201–6
Wilson, Bob, x
Wilson, Jack, x
Wilson, Norman, x
World Bowhunting Association, 208
World War I, 20
World War II, 13, 20

Young, Art, 103

Zen Buddhists, 11, 12